LA CUCINA ITALIANA

THE COMPLETE
ITALIAN COOKBOOK

LA CUCINA ITALIANA

THE COMPLETE ITALIAN COOKBOOK

Crescent Books
New York

This book was devised and produced by
Multimedia Publications (UK) Ltd

Editor in Chief: Jeff Groman
Editor: Valerie Passmore
Design: Terry Allen
Production: Zivia Desai
Copyright © Multimedia Publications
(UK) Ltd 1987
Original recipes and pictures copyright
©NEPI La Cucina Italiana
Via Mascheroni, 1-20123 Milan

1987 edition first published in the United
States by Crescent Books, distributed by
Crown Publishers, Inc.

ISBN 0 517 61037 X

Typeset by Sole Cast '85 Ltd
Origination by La Cucina Italiana, Editrice
Quadrarum SpA, Via Della Posta 10, Milan
Printed in Italy by New Interlitho SpA, Milan

CONTENTS

INTRODUCTION

Italian food and wines are second only to French in Europe, with Italian cooking generally simpler and more robust than French. Depending on excellent raw materials, it uses less butter, cream, wine and garlic than its neighbor's and treats vegetables with notably more respect, often serving them as a separate course.

Some outstanding features of Italian food are the superb cured, smoked or raw hams; salamis; veal; pasta; pizza; and sweets: nougat, macaroons, zabaglione and especially ice cream are all Italian confections.

Pasta, made with flour bound with eggs, oil or both, possibly colored with spinach or beetroot, comes in all shapes and sizes, many regional specialities. Eaten hot or cold, with a classic sauce or one improvised from seafood, meat, cheeses, herbs, vegetables or oil, pasta is infinitely versatile. Fresh pasta is easily home made: a simple pasta machine will give you a more uniform result, but you can roll and cut pasta dough (about four eggs to a pound of flour) with standard kitchen equipment and the result is far superior to the manufactured product.

Pizza, once a hearty, all-in-one Nepolitan snack has become an international fast food and now appears in flavor combinations the Nepolitans never dreamed of!

Real Italian ice cream is a delight far removed from its commercially produced namesake: a soft confection of pure fruit juice, sugar, cream and eggs – and fairly simple and well worthwhile to make at home.

The climate range, neighbors, tradition and geography have developed marked regional variations in Italian cooking. In the north butter is more widely used for cooking, in the south olive oil; rice, grown in the north, is eaten there as a staple alongside pasta; coastal regions abound in seafood; the delicious cakes and pastries of the north, and its game, have perhaps a Germanic accent. Apart from these general characteristics there are a wealth of individual regional dishes, pastas, cheeses and drinks throughout Italy.

The Italian way of constructing a meal is to start with an *antipasto* ("before the pasta"); then a soup or pasta, but not both; followed possibly by a vegetable course; then the *piatto di mezzo* ("middle dish") of fish, meat or poultry, often accompanied by a salad, rarely a non-salad vegetable. Desserts range from simple fresh fruit in season to elaborate *torte*. Cheese tends to be eaten as an *antipasto*, as a snack or as an ingredient of some other dish.

Italy is the world's largest wine producer and her population is high in the world's wine-drinking league with 120 bottles per person per year, and the home of the internationally known Martini and Cinzano also produces scores of other *aperitivi* and *digestivi*.

An increasing number of the very many Italian wines are becoming available outside Italy: whites such as Orvieto, Soave, Verdicchio and Frascati and reds such as Valpolicella, Bardolino and Barolo are only a few of the excellent wines to join Chianti exports from Italy.

Essential store cupboard ingredients for Italian cooking are olive oil, lighter for cooking and heavier for salads, and oregano, basil, sage and rosemary, preferably fresh. Simple pasta machines are inexpensive and easy to use, and a really large saucepan for cooking pasta, one that allows ten pints of water for every pound of pasta, is vital. Otherwise, the recipes in this book can mostly be achieved with standard kitchen equipment. Some call for specialist ingredients, available from the increasing number of Italian food shops, but don't be daunted if you can't find the precise ingredients: substitute a similar cheese, fish or meat.

La Cucina Italiana is the title of Italy's leading cookery and home interest magazine. Every month its pages display a marvelous selection of seasonal recipes and menus, some traditional, some newly invented and tested. All the recipes and photographs in this books are reproduced by kind permission of the magazine and accurately reflect the wide scope and the careful balance of traditional and modern which the magazine's consultant panel has always insisted upon. In the pages which follow there are recipes and ideas to suit cooks of all temperaments, from the modest to the ambitious, and all occasions, from the family picnic to the gala supper.

Baked rabbit with vegetables (bottom, see recipe page 198)

ANTIPASTI

Meaning literally "before the pasta", antipasti can be a
selection of the superb salami, hams and cured meats of
Italy. Possibly accompanied by olives, hard-boiled eggs,
anchovies or melon, these call for little more than a flair
for presentation in serving. Or antipasti can be more
elaborate dishes, substantial snacks in themselves.

Cheese Dome
Cupola di Formaggio

To serve 6

¼ lb Philadelphia cream cheese

¼ lb Stracchino cheese

¼ lb Robiolina cheese

2oz soft Gorgonzola cheese

½ cup grated Parmesan cheese

½ cup very fresh whipping cream

4 slices white bread

Preparation time: about 40 minutes

Remove the cheeses from the refrigerator at least 2 hours before preparation. Finely dice the cheeses and place them all, including the grated Parmesan, in a bowl. Beat and mix to form a smooth, creamy mixture.

Whip the cream and carefully fold into the cheese mixture. Add a pinch of salt and plenty of pepper. Mix well and then place the mixture in the center of a large, round plate. Mold into a dome shape and, using a fork, decorate it with vertical lines.

Cut the slices of bread diagonally into 8 triangles and either toast them or fry them gently in butter until golden brown. Arrange some of the toast or *croûtons* around the cheese dome and serve the rest separately. Garnish as desired and serve.

Ham Rolls
Involtini di Prosciutto

To serve 4

1 small carrot

1 tender rib celery

¼ lb Emmental cheese

2 tbsp mayonnaise

1 tsp mustard

8 fairly thick slices lean ham

a little gelatin dissolved in warm water

1 slice any mild-flavored cheese

2 stuffed olives

Preparation time: about 40 minutes

Trim and wash the carrot and celery and slice the celery thinly. Cut the carrot and Emmental cheese into thin strips. Place the carrot, celery and Emmental cheese in a bowl and stir in the mayonnaise and mustard. Taste and add salt if necessary.

Spread the slices of ham out on a surface, trimming off any fat. Place a tablespoon of the prepared filling on each slice and fold the ham up into rolls, carefully enclosing the filling. Arrange the rolls on a plate and brush them with a little cool liquid gelatin, making sure that it does not drip. Place in the refrigerator. When the first coating of gelatin has set, remove the rolls from the refrigerator and brush them with another coat of gelatin. Replace in the refrigerator.

Cut the slice of cheese into 8 triangles and the olives into 8 slices.

Decorate each roll with a triangle of cheese and a slice of olive. Garnish as desired and serve.

Augustan Tomatoes
Pomodori Augustei

To serve 6

1 egg

3 very large tomatoes

1 carrot

1 potato

1 slice white bread

5 tsp butter

¼ lb canned shrimp

2 tbsp mayonnaise

1 tbsp mustard

1 tbsp tomato ketchup

a few young celery leaves

Preparation and cooking time: about 40 minutes

Hard-boil the egg, cool it under running water and shell it. Wash and dry the tomatoes and cut them in half with a sharp knife. Discard the seeds and sprinkle the insides with salt. Place the tomatoes upside-down on paper towels and leave to stand.

Trim, wash and dice the carrot and place in a saucepan. Cover with water, add a little salt and bring to the boil. Peel and dice the potato and add it to the carrot once the water has been boiling for 5 minutes. When the vegetables are tender, drain and dry them on paper towels.

Finely dice the bread and fry it gently in the butter. Finely chop the drained shrimp and mix them with the mayonnaise, mustard and tomato ketchup. Blend carefully and then stir in the cooked vegetables and diced bread.

Wipe the insides of the tomatoes with paper towels and stand them on a work surface. Stuff them with the prepared filling. Finely crumble the hard-boiled egg yolk and sprinkle it on to the tomatoes. Arrange on a plate, garnish with a few young leaves of celery and serve.

Cheese dome (top), **Augustan tomatoes** (center) and **ham rolls**

Lobster and Avocado

Aragosto e Avocado

To serve 4

¼lb boiled lobster meat

2 perfectly ripe avocados

Worcestershire sauce

2 tsp mustard

juice of ½ lemon

4 tbsp olive oil

4 crisp lettuce leaves

Preparation time: about 40 minutes

Dice the lobster into ½-inch cubes and put them in a bowl. Cut the avocados in half lengthwise and remove the pits. Peel and slice them lengthwise and then cut into irregular-shaped pieces a little larger than the lobster cubes. Mix the two together carefully.

Prepare the dressing immediately: Put a pinch of salt in a bowl and add a dash of Worcestershire sauce, the mustard and the strained lemon juice. Mix with a fork until the salt has completely dissolved. Then mix in the olive oil and continue stirring vigorously for a few minutes until the dressing emulsifies. Then pour it over the lobster and avocado mixture, mix very carefully and leave for a few minutes. Place a lettuce leaf in each of 4 glass goblets and put some of the mixture in each goblet.

■ ANTIPASTI ■ ANTIPASTI ■

Lobster and Melon

Aragosto sul Melone

To serve 4

1 medium-sized sweet winter melon

½lb boiled lobster meat

¼ cup best Port wine

⅜ cup ready-made mayonnaise

tomato ketchup for accompaniment (optional)

Preparation time: about 40 minutes

Cut the melon in half and remove the pits and fibers. Scoop out the flesh in little balls and place these in a bowl. Cut the lobster into 12 medallions (not too thick) and dice the rest. Mix the cubes of lobster with the melon balls, pour in the port and mix carefully. Cover the bowl with plastic wrap and refrigerate for about 10 minutes.

Arrange the melon and lobster mixture in 4 chilled goblets and place 3 medallions of lobster on top of each. Pipe a swirl of mayonnaise in the center of each one. Serve accompanied by ketchup, allowing everyone to help themselves.

■ ANTIPASTI ■ ANTIPASTI ■

Lobster Tarts

Tartellette all'Aragosta

To serve 6

1 cup flour

¼ tsp dried yeast

¼ cup butter

1 egg yolk

¼ medium celeriac, peeled

½ cup fairly thick mayonnaise

1 tsp mustard

Worcestershire sauce

12 small medallions boiled lobster, weighing about ¼ lb in all

Preparation and cooking time: about 1 hour

Preheat the oven to 375°F. Sieve the flour on to a pastry-board and add a pinch of salt and the dried yeast. Mix, and make a well in the center. Soften the butter and cut it into pieces. Put these, the egg yolk and 2 tablespoons of cold water into the well and mix quickly to a smooth dough.

Lightly flour the pastry-board and roll out the dough to a thickness of ⅛ inch. Using a serrated 5-inch round cookie cutter, cut out 6 rounds. Put these into buttered cup-shaped molds and prick the bases with a fork. Bake for about 15 minutes until the pastry cases are golden brown. Remove from the oven and leave to cool in the molds.

Meanwhile, shred the celeriac and mix immediately with half the mayonnaise, 1 teaspoon of mustard and a dash of Worcestershire sauce. When the pastry cases are cold, remove them from the molds and place a little of the celeriac mixture in the bottom of each one. Lay two medallions of lobster on top, then pipe swirls of mayonnaise and garnish with a few lettuce leaves.

■ ANTIPASTI ■ ANTIPASTI ■

Gourmet Asparagus

Asparagi di Bassano alla Buongustaia

To serve 4

2½lb fresh asparagus

a few parsley leaves

8 tbsp butter

4 egg yolks

Preparation and cooking time: about 45 minutes

Wash and trim the asparagus and tie in a bundle with kitchen twine. Stand the bundle upright in a saucepan of salted boiling water (the water should come about halfway up the asparagus). Simmer over a moderate heat for about 15 minutes, or a little longer if the asparagus are very thick.

Drain thoroughly, discard the kitchen twine and spread the asparagus out to dry on paper towels. Arrange in warmed asparagus dishes and garnish with a few leaves of parsley.

Melt the butter, season with salt and pepper and pour into a well in the asparagus in each dish. Place 1 egg yolk in the center of each well containing the melted butter. Serve immediately. Each diner should blend the butter and egg yolk to form a delicate sauce and use it as a dip for the asparagus.

Lobster and avocado (top left), *lobster and melon* (right) and *lobster tarts*

Savory Canapés
Tartine Dolcipiccanti

To serve 4

3 tbsp butter, cut into small pieces

¼ lb soft Gorgonzola cheese

1 tsp lemon juice

1 tbsp chopped parsley

4 slices white bread

1 red pimiento

1 tender lettuce leaf, cut into strips

Preparation time: about 30 minutes.

Beat the butter with a pinch of salt and pepper until creamy. Add the sieved and mashed Gorgonzola cheese and a teaspoon of lemon juice. Stir vigorously for a few minutes and then blend in the chopped parsley. Check and adjust the seasoning according to taste.

Spread the mixture on the slices of bread. Cut each slice in half diagonally to form 2 triangles and arrange on a plate. Cut the pimiento into 8 small strips and use to decorate the canapés. Garnish the center of the plate with the strips of lettuce and serve immediately.

Lettuce "Cigars"
"Sigari" di Lattuga

To make 24 "cigars"

1 fresh Boston lettuce

⅝ cup fresh Ricotta cheese

2oz Gorgonzola cheese

1 tbsp juniper-flavored *grappa* or brandy

dried tarragon

Preparation time: about 25 minutes

Pull out the tender leaves of the heart of the lettuce and wash and dry them gently. Using a sharp knife, remove the central stalks and divide each leaf in half.

Drain and mash the Ricotta and place it in a bowl. Finely dice the Gorgonzola cheese and beat it with the Ricotta to form a smooth, creamy mixture. Stir in the juniper-flavored *grappa*, a pinch of salt and pepper and a generous pinch of dried ground tarragon.

Blend thoroughly and then place a teaspoon of the mixture on each piece of lettuce. Fold up to form cigar-shaped rolls, making sure that the filling does not ooze out.

Arrange the "cigars" around the edge of a plate and garnish the center as desired. This dish makes an excellent light appetizer or can be served with aperitifs.

Lettuce cigars (above); savory canapés (left)

Tasty Toast Appetizer

Fette Biscottate "Golose"

To serve 4

6oz canned tuna in oil

1½ tbsp capers in vinegar

4 anchovy fillets in oil

½ cup thick mayonnaise

8 toasted bread slices

1oz pimiento

a little fresh parsley

Preparation time: about 15 minutes

Drain the tuna fish, capers and anchovies. Roughly chop the capers and anchovies, mash the tuna and place everything in a bowl. Add the mayonnaise and stir well until all the ingredients are blended. Spread the mixture thickly over the toasted slices.

Drain, then chop the pimiento very finely, reducing it almost to a pulp, and place 1 teaspoon on each slice. Garnish with fresh parsley, arrange the slices on a tray and serve at once.

Little Savory Pastries

"Crescentine" di Grasso

To serve 6-8

1 sprig fresh rosemary

1 slice mortadella sausage, finely chopped

2oz salami, finely chopped

1 egg

¼ cup grated Parmesan cheese

ground nutmeg

1½ cups flour

½ tsp baking powder

1 tbsp butter

⅜ cup cold stock (or use bouillon cube)

1 egg white, lightly beaten

oil for frying

Preparation and cooking time: about 1 hour

Chop the rosemary leaves finely and bind with the mortadella, salami, egg and grated Parmesan cheese. Season with a pinch of ground nutmeg and a little pepper.

Sift the flour, baking powder and a pinch of salt on to a board and make a well in the center. Cut the butter into small pieces and rub into the flour. Add the stock a little at a time and mix to form a soft pastry dough.

Roll the pastry out and cut it into 2½-3 inch rectangles with a serrated cookie cutter. Brush the edges of the rectangles with the beaten egg white. Place a little of the prepared stuffing mixture in the center of half of the rectangles and then cover with the remaining pieces of pastry. Press the edges together and seal carefully.

Heat plenty of oil in a large skillet and fry the parcels until golden brown on both sides. Drain and dry on paper towels. Place in a large dish and serve immediately.

Little savory pastries

Cauliflower à la Grecque
Cavolfiore del Pireo

To serve 4-6

⅜ cup olive oil

juice of 2 large lemons

2 bay leaves

2 garlic cloves

3-4 black peppercorns

1½lb cauliflower

Preparation and cooking time: about 1 hour plus chilling

Bring to the boil a large saucepan containing 2¾ cups of cold water, add the olive oil, the strained lemon juice, 2 bay leaves, 2 large halved garlic cloves, 3-4 black peppercorns and salt.

Meanwhile, wash the cauliflower and separate it into flowerets, without breaking them. Cook in boiling water, with the pan covered and over a low heat, for about 12 minutes, keeping them covered by the liquid.

Remove the pan from the heat and, keeping it covered, let the flowerets cool. Only at this point remove the garlic and pepper (leave the bay leaves) then pour the preparation into a salad bowl. Cover it with plastic wrap and keep it in the refrigerator for at least 1½ hours before serving. This appetizer, kept in its liquid and tightly covered, keeps well in the refrigerator for up to a week.

Avocado Appetizer
Antipasto di Avocado

To serve 6

¼lb shrimp

½ cup white wine

1 bay leaf

parsley

peppercorns

a little mayonnaise

Worcestershire sauce

mustard

3 avocados

1 large lemon

Belgian endive

Preparation and cooking time: about 40 minutes

Heat ¾ cup of water and the white wine in a saucepan, add the bay leaf, 3 sprigs of parsley, 2 black peppercorns and salt. Simmer for a few seconds, then turn down the heat and pour the shrimp into the shallow boiling liquid, cover and boil for a couple of minutes. Remove them with a slotted spoon, drain well and leave to cool. Then put them in a bowl with a little mayonnaise, a generous dash of Worcestershire sauce and two teaspoons of mustard.

Cut the avocados in two and remove the seed. Using a teaspoon, scrape out some of the flesh and add it to the shrimp. Finally, stir in a few drops of lemon juice. Place the mixture in the hollowed-out avocados and arrange on a serving dish. Decorate with mayonnaise. Place ½ slice of lemon between each avocado with some chopped endive. In the center, place half a lemon decorated with mayonnaise. Serve at once.

Cauliflower à la Grecque

Piquant Peppers

Peperoni Aromatici

To serve 6-8

8 small yellow bell peppers, weighing about 2lb in all

⅓ cup capers

4 large anchovy fillets in oil

½ garlic clove

a handful of parsley

Tabasco sauce

Worcestershire sauce

1 tbsp mustard

5 tbsp olive oil

Preparation and cooking time: about 50 minutes plus at least 2 hours' chilling

Gently broil the bell peppers and remove the scorched skin. Halve them, discarding the stalks and seeds, and open out "flat". Arrange in a single layer on a large plate.

Thoroughly drain the capers and chop coarsely, together with the anchovy fillets, half a garlic clove and a small handful of parsley. Sprinkle the mixture over the bell peppers.

Prepare the dressing: Mix together a pinch of salt, 2-3 drops of Tabasco and a dash of Worcestershire sauce. Blend in a tablespoon of mustard, stirring with a fork. When the salt has completely dissolved, add 5 tablespoons of olive oil and blend to a smooth sauce.

Pour the prepared dressing over the bell peppers, cover with plastic wrap and leave to stand in a cool place for at least 2 hours. This dish improves if left to stand and is best eaten a day after preparation.

Salmon and Crab Rolls

Involtini di Salmone al Granchio

To serve 6

¼-½ lb smoked salmon

¼-½ lb canned crab meat

Worcestershire sauce

¼ cup mayonnaise

1 tbsp mustard

Tabasco sauce

a little gelatin dissolved in ⅜ cup warm water

celery leaves for garnish

1 pimiento for garnish

2 slices lemon for garnish

Preparation time: about 40 minutes

Divide the smoked salmon into 18 slices and spread them out on a large sheet of aluminum foil. Drain and squeeze the crab well, then put it in a bowl and remove any filaments or bits of cartilage. Flavor with a generous dash of Worcestershire sauce, the mayonnaise, mustard and 2 or 3 drops of Tabasco. Stir thoroughly, then place some of the mixture on one edge of each slice of salmon and roll the salmon up tightly.

Arrange the rolls neatly on a serving dish and brush them all two or three times with the gelatin, refrigerating between applications to help the gelatin to set. Garnish the dish with the celery leaves, pimiento and lemon slices. Cover the dish with plastic wrap and keep it in the refrigerator until it is time to serve it.

Stuffed grapefruit (top) *and* **salmon and crab rolls**

Stuffed Grapefruit

Pompelmi Ripieni

To serve 6

3 medium-sized grapefruit

2 kiwi fruit

1½oz Emmental cheese

2 thick slices ham

½ cup mayonnaise

Worcestershire sauce

2 tbsp mustard

Preparation time: about 40 minutes

Using a short, sharp knife, cut the grapefruit into halves. Separate them, scoop out the pulp and put it in a bowl, taking care not to include any pith. Peel the kiwi fruit, halve them lengthwise and slice thinly. Cut the Emmental cheese into matchsticks and the ham into short strips. Pour off the juice that has run out of the grapefruit and mix the flesh with the kiwi fruit, cheese and ham. Put the mayonnaise in a bowl, flavor it with a dash of Worcestershire sauce and the mustard and stir into the prepared mixture. Fill the grapefruit halves with the mixture and serve at once.

∎ ANTIPASTI ∎ ANTIPASTI ∎

Salmon Canapés

Tartine Salmonate

To make 16 canapés

¼lb smoked salmon

2oz fresh Mascarpone cheese

1 tbsp Framboise liqueur

2 tbsp cream

1 tbsp tomato ketchup

Worcestershire sauce

8 slices white bread

a few olives in brine

a few chicory leaves

Preparation time: about 20 minutes

Process the salmon in a blender and place in a bowl. Mix in the Mascarpone cheese and the Framboise liqueur. Stir in the cream and tomato ketchup. Season with a few drops of Worcestershire sauce.

Spread a heaping tablespoon of the mixture on each slice of bread, spreading it right to the edges. Cut the slices of bread in half diagonally to form triangles.

Slice a few olives lengthwise and use to garnish the canapés, together with a few leaves of chicory if desired. The canapés may be served as an appetizer or as an accompaniment to apéritifs.

∎ ANTIPASTI ∎ ANTIPASTI ∎

Egg with Tuna Fish and Peas

Uova al Tonno e Piselli

To serve 4

¼lb frozen young peas

1 small onion

olive oil

about 6oz canned tuna fish

4 eggs

Preparation and cooking time: about 25 minutes

Boil the peas, still frozen, in salted water for 5 minutes, then drain them. Peel and finely slice the onion, then fry in 2 tablespoons of olive oil on a low heat until transparent. Add the peas and leave. Drain the tuna fish of oil and mash it coarsely. Add it to the peas and leave over the heat for 7-8 minutes.

Meanwhile heat 2 tablespoons of olive oil in a large skillet and break in the eggs, which should be at room temperature, taking care not to break the yolks. Add a little salt and pepper, and turn the heat down low. Cook until the whites are opaque. Remove the eggs one at a time with a flexible spatula and drain off any excess oil.

Place each egg on a warmed plate and surround with the tuna fish and pea mixture. Serve at once.

Chef's Roulades

Involtini dello Chef

To make 20 roulades

a handful of fresh parsley

1 cup very fresh Robiola cheese (or mild soft cheese)

Worcestershire sauce

20 very thin slices fillet of beef, weighing about ½lb in all

olive oil

fresh rosemary

Preparation and cooking time: about 30 minutes

Preheat the oven to 475°F. Finely chop the parsley and put in a bowl with the Robiola cheese, a little salt, a little freshly ground black pepper and a dash of Worcestershire sauce. Mix carefully to form a smooth paste. Lay out the slices of beef on a large tray and put a little of the cheese mixture in the center of each one. Fold the meat over to make a little parcel so that the stuffing is sealed in. Sprinkle with salt and pepper.

Brush an ovenproof dish with olive oil and arrange the roulades on it then pour a little olive oil over them. Place a few rosemary leaves on each one and put in the oven (or under the broiler) for no

longer than 1 minute to cook the meat without melting the cheese. Serve immediately.

Royal Aspic
Aspic Regale

To serve 12

1 small onion

1 clove

3 large carrots

1 small stalk celery

1 garlic clove

2-3 sprigs fresh parsley

¾-1 lb chicken on the bone

2½ cups prepared aspic gelatin
1 tbsp gelatin, soaked, added to an additional 1¾ cups prepared aspic gelatin

4 eggs

¾-1 lb potatoes

about ½lb zucchini

¼-½ lb cooked French beans

2oz canned tuna in oil

2 tbsp capers

2 anchovy fillets in oil

½ cup mayonnaise

1 tsp lemon juice

1 large red pimiento

½lb ham, diced

Worcestershire sauce

1 tbsp tomato ketchup

oil

Preparation and cooking time: about 1½ hours plus at least 4 hours' refrigeration

Bring to the boil a saucepan containing 3¼ cups of water, the onion (halved and pierced with a clove), ¼ cup diced carrot, the celery, a lightly crushed garlic clove and the parsley, salt it and add the chicken. Half-cover the pan and simmer for about 40 minutes.

Meanwhile, prepare the aspic. Hard-boil the eggs, cool under running water and shell.

Peel and dice the potatoes and cook them in salted boiling water for about 12 minutes. Drain and leave to dry on paper towels, reserving the water. Cut the zucchini into ⅛-inch slices and cook in the potato water for about 10 minutes. Drain and spread out on a plate. Slice the remaining carrot and, using the same water again, cook it for about 15 minutes. Drain and dry.

Cut the French beans into ¾-inch lengths. Bone and skin the chicken and cut the meat into thin strips. Place in a bowl and leave to cool.

Meanwhile, finely chop the tuna, capers and anchovy fillets and place them in a bowl. Stir in the mayonnaise and lemon juice and use the mixture to dress the chicken. Add 3-4 tablespoons of the cooled aspic.

Brush the inside of a 3-pint semispherical mold with the aspic gelatin coating it 3-4 times and setting it in the refrigerator after each coating.

Slice the hard-boiled eggs. Using a cookie cutter, cut 6 tear-drop shapes out of the pimiento. Line the mold with some of the slices of egg, slices of carrot and zucchini, cubes of potato and tear-drops of pimiento. Fill the mold with layers of the remaining vegetables, the chicken mixture and the rest of the slices of egg, pouring a little aspic on top of each layer. By the time all the ingredients and aspic have been used up, the mold should be almost full. Tap the mold gently and then refrigerate for at least 4 hours or until the aspic has set completely.

Meanwhile, add the soaked gelatin to the 1¾ additional cups of aspic while it is still hot and stir until the gelatin has dissolved completely. Liquidize. Pour the mixture into a blender and add the diced ham, a dash of Worcestershire sauce and the tomato ketchup. Pour the mixture into a 9½-inch round shallow container which has been greased with a little oil. Refrigerate for a couple of hours to set. Turn out on to a large plate.

Submerge the mold containing the aspic in hot water for a few seconds, dry it and then turn the aspic out on to the center of the ham. Garnish as desired and serve.

Little Chicken Pastries
Piccoli Calzoni Ripieni di Pollo

To make 24 pastries

2 slices white bread soaked in milk

¼lb chicken breast, trimmed

fresh chives

a little fresh parsley

4-5 sprigs fresh chervil

¼ cup grated Parmesan cheese

1 egg

nutmeg

1 lb bread dough

a little flour

oil for frying

Preparation and cooking time: about 45 minutes

Squeeze out the milk from the bread and, together with the chicken, put it through a meat grinder, using the finest disk, two or three times. Collect the ground chicken and bread in a bowl. Finely chop 6-8 chives together with 2-3 large sprigs of parsley and 4-5 sprigs of chervil. Add the herbs to the chicken mixture. Add the Parmesan, the egg, salt, pepper and a little grated nutmeg. Mix thoroughly.

Roll out the bread dough, a little at a time, on a lightly floured pastry-board to about 1-inch thickness. Using a cookie cutter, cut out rounds, 5 inches in diameter. Place a little of the chicken mixture on one side of each round then fold it in half and seal by pinching the two edges together. As the pastries are ready, line them up on a tray covered with a lightly floured cloth.

Heat a deep skillet with plenty of oil. When the oil is hot, but not smoking, put in the pastries, a few at a time, and cook until they are golden brown. Drain them as you lift them from the oil and lay them on a plate covered with absorbent paper towels. Put them in a basket lined with a cloth. Garnish with fresh chervil leaves and serve at once.

Smoked salmon with tuna fish (top); *sturgeon cornets* (center); *little chicken pastries* (bottom)

Tuna mousse

Sturgeon Cornets
"Cornetti" di Storione

To serve 4

1 egg

a little fresh parsley

1 anchovy fillet in oil

2 green olives, pitted

1 tbsp mayonnaise

8 very thin slices smoked sturgeon

toasted wholemeal bread

Preparation and cooking time: about 30 minutes

Hard-boil the egg then cool under cold running water. Shell and finely chop it then put in a bowl. Finely chop a little parsley together with the drained anchovy fillet and the olives and add to the egg. Add the mayonnaise and mix to a smooth paste. Taste and adjust the seasoning, then spread the mixture on one side of each fish slice. Roll the slice into a funnel shape, sealing in the filling. When all the "cornets" are ready, fan them out on a round serving dish and garnish to taste. Serve with slices of warm toasted wholemeal bread.

Smoked Salmon with Tuna Fish
Salmone Tonnata

To serve 6

10 capers

10 dill pickles

¼ lb canned tuna fish in oil

2 tbsp mayonnaise

¼ tsp mustard

6 large slices smoked salmon

2 slices wholemeal bread

anchovy paste

a little white wine vinegar

Worcestershire sauce

lettuce leaves for garnish

Preparation and cooking time: about 40 minutes

Drain the capers and dill pickles thoroughly and chop them finely, together with the well-drained tuna fish. Add 1 tablespoon of mayonnaise and the mustard and mix thoroughly. Spread this on the salmon slices, taking care not to go over the edges. Using the blade of a knife, roll up the salmon into 6 roulades and put them in the least cold part of the refrigerator for a few minutes.

Meanwhile, toast the bread and cut each slice into 3 fingers. Squeeze about 1¼ inches of anchovy paste into a bowl

and add 2 drops of vinegar and a dash of Worcestershire sauce. Incorporate 1 tablespoon of mayonnaise. Spread on one side only of the toast fingers. Press a smoked salmon roulade firmly on to each piece of toast. Arrange on a serving dish and garnish with fresh lettuce leaves.

■ ANTIPASTI ■ ANTIPASTI ■

Tuna Mousse
Anello di Tonno

To serve 6

1 package gelatin

about ¾ lb canned tuna in oil

5 tsp butter

1 tbsp flour

½ cup milk

juice of ½ lemon

oil

1 cup mayonnaise

3 tbsp whipping cream

1 tbsp tomato ketchup

Worcestershire sauce

Preparation and cooking time: about 30 minutes plus chilling

Prepare the aspic according to the instructions on the package, using ½ cup of water. Leave to cool. Drain the tuna and mash it finely in a bowl.

Melt the butter in a small saucepan and blend in a tablespoon of flour. Gradually add the milk and bring almost to the boil, stirring constantly. The sauce should be thick and smooth. Remove from the heat, season with a little salt and blend with the mashed tuna. Add the lemon juice and stir well.

Add the prepared aspic and stir vigorously. Pour the mixture into a 2 pint ring mold which has been lightly oiled. Place in the freezer for 40 minutes.

Prepare the sauce: Pour the mayonnaise into a bowl and blend in the cream, tomato ketchup and a few drops of Worcestershire sauce. Test and adjust the seasoning according to taste.

Turn the tuna mousse out on to a round plate and coat it with the prepared sauce. Garnish as desired and serve.

Three-flavored Pie
Torta ai Tre Gusti

To serve 8

½ lb puff pastry

¼ cup butter

¼lb endive, boiled and drained

¼lb spinach, boiled and drained

1 medium onion

1 tbsp olive oil

½ bouillon cube

¾ cup very fresh Ricotta cheese

1 thick slice ham, finely chopped

3 eggs

3 tbsp grated Parmesan cheese

nutmeg

1 tbsp breadcrumbs

Preparation and cooking time: about 1 hour plus any defrosting time

Defrost the pastry if using frozen. Butter a 10-inch pie dish. Finely chop the endive and spinach and put in a bowl. Then finely chop the onion and sauté in 2 tablespoons of butter and the olive oil, taking care not to let it brown. Crumble in the bouillon cube and keep the pan over the heat until it has dissolved. Then combine the onion with the endive and spinach, mixing thoroughly. Rub the Ricotta through a sieve, letting it fall on to the mixture in the bowl. Then add the ham. Beat the 3 eggs with a pinch of salt and a little freshly ground pepper, the Parmesan cheese and a little grated nutmeg. Pour this into the bowl with the other ingredients. Stir vigorously after the addition of each new ingredient until smooth. Taste and adjust the seasoning.

Preheat the oven to 375°F. Roll out the pastry on a lightly floured pastry-board to a thickness of about ⅛ inch then line the pie dish and trim the edges. Prick the pastry with a fork and sprinkle with breadcrumbs. Spread the filling mixture evenly in the dish, then bang the dish lightly on the table to eliminate air bubbles. Decorate the top with the pastry offcuts and bake for about 30 minutes in the bottom of the oven. Serve piping hot.

Spicy Eggs
Uova Piccante

To serve 4-6

6 very fresh eggs

6oz canned tuna in oil

handful of parsley

2 tbsp capers in oil

1 pickled gherkin

4 anchovy fillets in oil

⅜ cup thick mayonnaise

1 tbsp mustard

Worcestershire sauce

6 stuffed olives

1 head chicory

white wine vinegar

olive oil

Preparation and cooking time: about 40 minutes

Hard-boil the eggs and cool thoroughly under running water. Shell and halve the eggs lengthwise. Remove the yolks and rub them through a sieve into a bowl. Drain the oil from the tuna and put the fish through a vegetable mill with a medium disk, letting it fall on to the egg yolks. Finely chop the parsley with the capers, gherkin and anchovy fillets and add the mixture to the other ingredients. Mix with the mayonnaise, mustard and a generous dash of Worcestershire sauce to a smooth paste. Taste and adjust the seasoning.

Put the mixture into a pastry bag with a round serrated nozzle and fill the 12 egg halves. Arrange on a serving dish. Cut the olives in half and press them into the filling. Place the chicory leaves in the center of the dish, seasoned simply with salt, pepper, vinegar and olive oil. Serve at once.

Savoy Cabbage with Smoked Salmon
Antipasto Pazzerello

To serve 4

2 leaves tender savoy cabbage

¼ lb smoked salmon

2½oz Fiorello cheese

juice of ½ lemon

1 tbsp tomato ketchup

1 tbsp mustard

Worcestershire sauce

a little stock (or use bouillon cube)

Preparation time: about 30 minutes

Cut the salmon and cabbage into long strips. Prepare the dressing: Pour the Fiorello cheese into a bowl and whisk until slightly stiff. Add the lemon juice, the tomato ketchup and the mustard. Blend carefully and season with a pinch of salt and pepper and a generous splash of Worcestershire sauce. Stir in 2 tablespoons of stock and blend until smooth and creamy.

Arrange the strips of salmon and cabbage on a serving dish and dress with the sauce at the table. This is an unusual combination of ingredients, but the result is delicious and the dressing enhances the flavor of both the cabbage and the salmon.

Three-flavored pie (top) and *spicy eggs*

Tuna Delight
Delizia di Tonno

To serve 6

1 envelope gelatin (to make 2¼ cups)

1 tbsp lemon juice

1 egg

12oz canned tuna

1½ tbsp capers

4 anchovy fillets in oil

Worcestershire sauce

a little oil

a few leaves chicory

1 red bell pepper, cut into strips

Preparation and cooking time: about 1 hour

Dissolve the gelatin in 1¾ cups of warm water and add a tablespoon of lemon juice. Hard-boil the egg, shell and chop it and blend with the well-drained tuna, the drained capers, the anchovy fillets, a dash of Worcestershire sauce and the gelatin. Blend gently for a couple of minutes.

Oil a 3 cup fluted mold and pour in the tuna mixture. Place the mold in the freezer and allow the mixture to set. Turn out, slice it and arrange on a large plate. Garnish with strips of red bell pepper and sprigs of chicory. Serve.

Tuna delight

Egg Surprise
Sorpresa d'Uova

To serve 4

butter

olive oil

1 small onion, finely sliced

flour

1 cup good meat stock

tomato paste

4 eggs

1 thick slice ham

Preparation and cooking time: about 35 minutes

Heat a knob of butter and a tablespoon of olive oil in a small saucepan and lightly fry the onion until transparent. Sprinkle with flour and add the boiling stock in which half a teaspoon of tomato paste has been dissolved. Bring to the boil, stirring constantly. Lower the heat and simmer for 3-4 minutes. Purée and return to the pan. Check and adjust the seasoning to taste.

Hard-boil the eggs, cool under cold running water, shell them and cut them in half lengthwise. Arrange on a plate, curved side up, and coat with the prepared sauce. Garnish each piece of egg with a diamond of ham and serve warm.

Melon with Shrimp
Melone e Gamberetti

To serve 6

⅜ cup dry white wine

1 small bay leaf

2-3 whole black peppercorns

2-3 sprigs fresh parsley

1 small onion, halved

¾lb fresh shrimp

1 medium-sized melon

2 tender lettuce leaves

⅝ cup thick mayonnaise

2 tbsp mustard

2 tbsp tomato ketchup

1 tbsp whipping cream

Worcestershire sauce

1 tsp brandy

Preparation and cooking time: about 1 hour

Bring to the boil a saucepan containing 2¼ cups of water, a little salt, the white wine, bay leaf, peppercorns, parsley and onion and simmer for at least 5 minutes. Add the shrimp, cook for about 4 minutes and then remove them from the pan with a slotted spoon, discarding the other ingredients. When the shrimp have cooled, peel them and place them in a bowl.

Cut the melon in half using a sharp, pointed knife. Discard the seeds. Scoop out the flesh, cut into ½-inch cubes and place in a bowl. Put a lettuce leaf in the bottom of each empty melon rind.

Prepare the dressing: blend the mayonnaise with the mustard, tomato ketchup, cream, a dash of Worcestershire sauce and the brandy. Test and adjust the seasoning according to taste.

Mix the shrimp and melon cubes and dress with the prepared sauce. Divide the mixture between the 2 halves of melon and serve immediately.

Melon with shrimp (right)

Shrimp Pie
Sfogliata di Gamberetti

½lb puff pastry

butter

1 tbsp breadcrumbs

6 slices very fresh white bread

⅜ cup milk

¾lb shrimp, unpeeled

4 tbsp olive oil

1 garlic clove

2-3 tbsp dry white wine

1 small onion

a handful of parsley

2 eggs

Preparation and cooking time: about 1¼ hours plus any thawing time

Preheat the oven to 375°F. Defrost the pastry if using frozen. Line a buttered 10 × 4 inch pie dish with the pastry and prick with a fork. Sprinkle with the breadcrumbs. Arrange the slices of bread on a plate and soak for at least 15 minutes in the milk. Peel the shrimp and sauté them in a skillet with 1 tablespoon of olive oil and ½ garlic clove. Season with salt and pepper. Pour in 2 or 3 tablespoons of wine and wait until this has evaporated before removing the shrimp from the heat and leaving to cool.

Finely chop the onion with a small handful of parsley and fry in 3 tablespoons of olive oil and a little salt. Put these ingredients in a bowl. Break in the eggs and beat well. Add the bread soaked in milk and break up into small pieces. Beat well until smooth. Finally, add the shrimp and season with a little salt and pepper.

Pour the mixture into the pie dish and level it. Bang the dish lightly to remove any air bubbles. Bake in the lower part of the oven for about 35 minutes. Remove the pie from the oven and turn out on to a serving dish or wooden board and serve at once, cutting it at table.

Shrimp pie

Christmas Pâté
"Delizia" delle Feste

To serve 6-8

¼ lb chicken livers

½ lb pork loin

1 medium leek, white part only

⅜ cup butter

1 tbsp olive oil

4 tbsp dry Marsala wine

½ bouillon cube

¼ lb raw ham

1 tsp white truffle paste

1 tbsp pine-nuts

1 small black truffle

a little gelatin dissolved in water

toasted bread for accompaniment

Preparation and cooking time: about 1¼ hours

Remove any traces of gall from the chicken livers then carefully wash and drain them. Cut the pork loin into small slices. Finely slice the leek and fry in 3 tablespoons of the butter and 1 tablespoon of olive oil, taking care not to let it brown. Then add the chicken livers and the pork, turn up the heat and allow to brown a little. Pour in the Marsala and crumble in the bouillon cube, stirring continuously with a wooden spoon.

When the Marsala has been completely absorbed, remove the skillet from the heat and pour the contents into a blender. Add the chopped raw ham with the white truffle paste and the remaining butter cut into slivers. Blend on minimum speed for a minute and then on maximum for a couple of minutes. Sieve through a fine mesh into a bowl and leave to cool, stirring from time to time.

Mix again, vigorously, with a wooden spoon to make the pâté light and fluffy. Heap into 2 earthenware pâté dishes and garnish one with the pine-nuts and the other with slices of black truffle. Finally, brush the surface with the gelatin. As soon as it sets, cover the dishes with plastic wrap and refrigerate. Serve with toast.

Artichoke and Shrimp Salad

Insalata di Carciofi e Gamberetti

To serve 4

4 small artichokes

2 juicy lemons

5 tbsp olive oil

1 tbsp white wine vinegar

½lb fresh shrimp, unpeeled

Preparation and cooking time: about 1 hour

Trim the artichokes, removing the tough outer leaves, the tips and the stalks. (You can save the latter for a soup or risotto.) Cut the artichokes in half, remove the chokes and immerse them in cold water to which a little lemon juice has been added. Heat a saucepan containing 3½ cups of water and add salt as soon as it begins to boil. Put in 1 teaspoon of lemon juice and 1 tablespoon of olive oil. Cut the artichoke halves into fairly thin slices and put them into the boiling water for 3 minutes. Remove with a slotted spoon. Drain and leave them to dry on a sloping dish.

Wash out the saucepan and fill it with another 2¼ cups of water. When it boils, add a little salt and 1 tablespoon of vinegar. Boil the shrimp for 3 minutes then drain, peel and leave them to cool. Then mix the shrimp with the artichokes in a bowl and make a dressing with a pinch of salt, a little fresh ground pepper, 1 tablespoon of strained lemon juice and 4 tablespoons of olive oil. Mix and serve garnished with scalloped half-slices of lemon.

Artichoke and shrimp salad (top); *Christmas pâté* (left)

SOUPS

Italian soups can be light meals in themselves, including pasta, rice, eggs, meat, fish and vegetables, or less substantial versions served as an alternative to the pasta course. Fish soups, a speciality of the Adriatic coast, and variations on minestrone, the rich vegetable soup with dried beans or pasta, are among the soups featured here.

Clam and Angler-Fish Soup

Zuppa di Vongole e Pescatrice

To serve 4-6

¾lb "tail" of angler-fish, skin and bones removed

1 medium onion

1 large garlic clove

3 tbsp butter

3 tbsp olive oil

⅜ cup dry white wine

2 small tomatoes, peeled and puréed

2 fresh basil leaves

oregano

1 tbsp cornstarch

3½ pints fish stock

6oz frozen clams

3 slices white bread

Preparation and cooking time: about 1¼ hours

Dice the fish. Slice the onions very finely and cut the garlic clove in half. Fry the onion and garlic in 5 teaspoons of the butter and 3 tablespoons of olive oil until transparent. Add the diced fish and fry gently. Sprinkle with the white wine and allow the wine to evaporate before adding the puréed tomatoes. Season with 2 leaves of fresh basil, a pinch of oregano and plenty of pepper.

Dissolve a tablespoon of cornstarch in the fish stock and add to the pan with the rest of the stock. Stir well and bring to the boil. Lower the heat and simmer gently for about 20 minutes. Then blend the mixture until smooth. Stir in the frozen clams, replace the pan on the heat and bring back to the boil. Simmer for a further 10 minutes. Test and adjust the seasoning. Dice the bread and toss gently in the remaining butter until golden. Serve hot with the soup.

Mussel Soup
Zuppa di Cozze

To serve 4

50 large mussels

2 small garlic cloves

¼ cup olive oil

¾lb ripe tomatoes

2 fresh basil leaves

a few parsley sprigs

slices of toasted home-made bread

Preparation and cooking time: about 1 hour

Wash the mussels thoroughly under cold running water, and scrape them clean with a small knife. As they are ready, put them in a large skillet or saucepan over a moderate heat. As the shells open, remove them from the pan and extract the mussels, throwing away the shells. Divide the mussels among 4 individual bowls. Cover each bowl with a piece of wet wax paper and keep them hot by placing them in a low oven with the door open.

Strain the liquid from the mussels through a clean cloth. Remove the central green shoot from the garlic and put in a garlic crusher. Collect the crushed garlic in a skillet with the olive oil and fry gently for a few seconds. Put the tomatoes, washed and cut into pieces, through a food processor using the medium disk, and add to the garlic in the skillet.

Stir and add the basil leaves, salt and pepper. Simmer for about 10 minutes then stir in the liquid from the mussels and a sprig of parsley, coarsely chopped. Remove the basil leaves and continue simmering for 3-4 minutes. Check the seasoning and divide the sauce among the 4 bowls of mussels. Garnish each bowl with a sprig of parsley and serve with slices of toasted home-made bread.

Quick Minestrone
Minestrone Rapido con i Ditaloni

To serve 4-6

1 small onion

1 garlic clove

7 tbsp olive oil

½ celery heart

3 small carrots

1 medium zucchini

1 small turnip

2 small potatoes

1 cup frozen peas

¾ cup canned red kidney beans

½ cup peeled, puréed tomatoes

5⅝ cups stock (or use bouillon cube)

½ cup fluted ditaloni pasta

3 tbsp grated Parmesan cheese

Preparation and cooking time: 1¼ hours

Finely chop the onion with the garlic and fry in 4 tablespoons of olive oil in a large saucepan, taking care not to let the vegetables brown. Meanwhile, clean and dice the celery, carrot, zucchini, turnip and potatoes into ¾-inch cubes. Add to the onions and leave for a few moments. Add the peas, the beans with their liquid and the tomatoes. Stir with a wooden spoon and simmer for about 10 minutes.

Boil the stock and pour this in. Stir, and simmer for about 45 minutes over a moderate heat with the pan covered. Stir 2 or 3 times during cooking. Then add the pasta and stir. Simmer until the pasta is cooked *al dente* and remove from the heat. Add a little freshly ground pepper, 3 tablespoons of olive oil and the grated Parmesan cheese. Serve at once.

Quick minestrone (above); minestrone with semolina (below)

Minestrone with Semolina
Minestrone di Verdure con Semolino

To serve 4

½ small onion

1 large garlic clove

2 slices bacon, diced

5 tsp butter

olive oil

3 cups frozen mixed vegetables

1 tbsp tomato paste

2 bouillon cubes

1½ tbsp semolina

grated Parmesan cheese

Preparation and cooking time: about 1 hour

Finely chop the onion and garlic and fry gently in a saucepan with the bacon, butter and 2 tablespoons of olive oil until transparent and then add the mixed vegetables. Cover the pan and cook for a few minutes on a low heat.

Stir in the tomato paste and pour on 3½ pints of boiling water. Season with the crumbled bouillon cubes, cover the pan and cook for 30 minutes. Slowly add the semolina, stirring constantly. Cook for a further 10 minutes and serve with grated Parmesan cheese, black pepper and olive oil.

Leek, Pea and Asparagus Soup

Passato di Porri, Piselli e Asparagi

To serve 4-6

¾-1 lb fresh asparagus

2 small leeks, white part only

2 tbsp butter

2 tbsp olive oil

1¼ cups fresh shelled peas

2 small potatoes, peeled and cut into large cubes

1 garlic clove, halved

3½ pints good meat stock

croûtons

Preparation and cooking time: about 1¼ hours

Wash, peel and tail the asparagus and chop it into small pieces. Wash and thinly slice the leeks and lightly fry them in the butter and olive oil. Add the asparagus, peas, potatoes and garlic and fry gently.

Gradually stir in the boiling stock. Bring to the boil and then lower the heat, cover the pan and simmer gently for about 40 minutes.

Process the soup in a blender and pour it back into the saucepan. Reheat, check and adjust the seasoning according to taste. Serve with the *croûtons*.

Minestrone with Pesto

Minestrone al Pesto

To serve 4

1 small onion

2 garlic cloves

2 tbsp butter

1¼lb frozen mixed vegetables

3 bouillon cubes

1 large potato

15 fresh basil leaves

1 tbsp pine-nuts

5 tbsp grated Parmesan cheese

7 tbsp olive oil

a little chopped parsley

Preparation and cooking time: about 1 hour

Finely chop the onion with a garlic clove, then soften them in a pan in 2 tablespoons of melted butter and 2 tablespoons of oil; make sure they don't brown. Add the frozen vegetables and fry for a few moments, stirring with a wooden spoon. Pour in 4 pints of boiling water and crumble in the bouillon cubes. Peel the potato, chop into 2-3 pieces and add to the *minestrone*; cook covered over a medium heat for about 45 minutes, stirring two or three times.

Meanwhile, place the basil leaves, wiped with a damp cloth, half a large garlic clove, a tablespoon of pine-nuts, a tablespoon of grated Parmesan cheese and a pinch of salt in a mortar. Pound with a wooden pestle, adding, in a trickle, 5 tablespoons of olive oil, until you have obtained a smooth *pesto*.

Remove the pieces of potato from the soup with a slotted spoon and mash them with a fork; return them to the soup. Add the *pesto*, stir, pour the *minestrone* into 4 soup bowls and sprinkle with chopped parsley. Serve with more Parmesan cheese.

Minestrone with pesto (top); *leek, pea and asparagus soup* (left)

Valpelline Soup
Zuppa di Valpelline

To serve 4

¼ cup shortening

about 1 lb cabbage

home-made bread

5oz rindless Fontina cheese

juices from a roast

¼ cup butter

4oz raw ham

about 4½ cups good stock

Preparation and cooking time: about 2 hours

Preheat the oven to 325°F. Heat the blade of a sharp knife and finely chop the shortening on a chopping board. Melt it in a large skillet over a low heat. Trim the cabbage, removing the outer leaves and the thick ribs. Wash the rest, drain well and fry in the fat until tender and slightly browned.

Meanwhile, slice the bread and toast, either in the oven or under the broiler. Cut the Fontina cheese into very thin slices. Prepare to serve the soup in 4 individual dishes (preferably earthenware). Place a slice of toast in each one and pour over a little of the juices from the roast. Then make a layer of cabbage and sprinkle with freshly ground pepper. Then make a layer of raw ham followed by a layer of Fontina. Cover with another layer of bread and continue alternating the ingredients until they are all used up. Finish with a layer of Fontina and add slivers of butter. Pour enough stock into each bowl to cover the layers of bread. Place in the oven for about 1 hour until the surface is golden brown. Serve piping hot straight from the oven.

Farmhouse Soup with Egg
Zuppa Contadina all'Uovo

To serve 4

2 bouillon cubes

⅜ cup butter

4 slices white bread

4 very fresh eggs

⅜ cup grated Parmesan cheese

Preparation and cooking time: about 20 minutes

Heat about 4½ cups of water in a saucepan, dissolve the bouillon cubes and bring to the boil. Melt half the butter in a large skillet and fry the 4 slices of bread, lightly browning them on both sides. Then place them on a baking tray or plate and keep them hot.

As soon as the stock begins to boil, reheat the skillet in which the bread was fried and melt the remaining butter. When it is bubbling hot, break in the eggs, which have been kept at room temperature until this point, very carefully, so as not to break the yolks, and fry. Do not let the whites become brown and dry. Cook until the yolks are done on the outside but still almost raw inside.

Place a slice of fried bread in each soup plate and sprinkle with a teaspoon of grated Parmesan cheese. Remove the eggs from the skillet and drain off as much fat as possible. Place an egg on each square of toast and then, using a ladle, pour in the soup very carefully at the side of the plate so as not to break the egg.

Cabbage and Cheese Soup
Zuppa di Verza e Fontina

To serve 4-6

2-3 slices bacon

¼ cup butter

savoy cabbage heart, ribs removed

4 pints meat stock

small loaf French bread

6 oz Fontina cheese

Preparation and cooking time: about 1¾ hours

Pound the bacon and fry it gently in 2 tablespoons of the butter. Add the cabbage and sauté it slowly, then add 1 cup of the stock, put a lid on and leave it on a moderate heat for about 40 minutes or until tender.

Preheat the oven to 375°F. Cut the bread into slices about ¾ inch thick, melt the rest of the butter and let the bread soak it up, then toast the slices in the oven. Increase the oven temperature to 400°F.

Slice the Fontina thinly. In a wide soup dish arrange layers of toast, cabbage and cheese, finishing with the cheese. Bring the remaining stock to the boil and pour it over the other ingredients. Cook for 15 minutes in the oven, then serve.

Right: **Valpelline soup**

Farmhouse soup with egg

Pasta and Kidney Bean Soup

Pasta e Fagioli

To serve 6

⅝ cup kidney beans

a bunch of fresh parsley

2 large garlic cloves

1 medium onion

1 piece celery heart

4 sage leaves

1 small bay leaf

2 large peeled potatoes

1 medium peeled tomato

2 bouillon cubes

½ cup maltagliati pasta

3 tbsp olive oil

3 tbsp grated Parmesan cheese

Preparation and cooking time: 2½ hours plus overnight soaking

Soak the beans overnight in cold water. The following day, finely chop a handful of parsley together with the garlic, onion and celery. Make a cheesecloth bag for the sage and bay leaf. Place all these ingredients in a saucepan. Drain the beans and add to the rest of the ingredients. Add the potatoes and put the tomato through a food processor using the finest disk before adding it.

Pour in 4½ pints of cold water and crumble in the bouillon cubes. Bring to the boil, turn the heat down to the minimum, cover and simmer for about 2 hours, stirring from time to time. Then remove the potatoes and put them through the food processor, using the medium disk, with a third of the beans and return the purée to the saucepan. Stir, bring to the boil and then add the pasta and cook in the uncovered pan, stirring from time to time. Remove the dish from the heat, incorporate the olive oil, the Parmesan cheese and a little freshly ground pepper. Sprinkle each portion with chopped parsley and serve immediately.

Hake-flavored Pasta Soup

Minestra del Marinaio

To serve 4

2 small ripe tomatoes

a bunch of fresh parsley

1 garlic clove

olive oil

1 fresh hake weighing about 1lb

1lb small pasta shells (conchigliette)

Preparation and cooking time: about 40 minutes

Wash the tomatoes and blanch them for a few minutes in lightly salted boiling water. Skin them, cut in half and remove the seeds, then chop coarsely (they should remain in pieces). Rinse and dry the parsley and coarsely chop this too. Peel the garlic, remove the green shoot and slice finely.

Heat a large saucepan containing the tomatoes, half the parsley, the garlic, a tablespoon of olive oil and about 4 pints of water. Season with a pinch of salt and a little freshly ground pepper. Bring to the boil and simmer for about 10 minutes. Meanwhile clean and rinse the fish. Remove the tail and fins and clean the hake. Wash thoroughly then add to the boiling liquid.

Cook for about 10 minutes then very carefully remove the fish from the soup. Pour in the pasta, cook until it is *al dente* and remove the pan from the heat. Add the remaining parsley, mix and pour into a soup tureen. Serve at once. (The hake is not eaten with the soup. It can be served as a second course dressed with olive oil and strained lemon juice.)

Pasta and kidney bean soup

March Soup
Zuppa Marzolina

To serve 6

1 medium leek

½ celery heart

3 large carrots

1 lb cauliflower

a piece of dried cep mushroom

1 artichoke

¼ cup butter

4 tbsp olive oil

2 tbsp flour

3 cups canned tiny peas

2 bouillon cubes

6 slices French bread

¼ cup grated Parmesan cheese

Preparation and cooking time: about 1¾ hour

Finely slice the leek, dice the celery and carrot and coarsely chop the cauliflower. Crumble the dried mushroom and clean the artichoke, including the stalk. Cut it in half and then into small pieces. Melt 2 tablespoons of butter in a saucepan with 3 tablespoons of the olive oil and gently fry the vegetables, stirring with a wooden spoon. Sift in the flour, stir again and pour in 4 pints of boiling water. Stir again, cover the pan and simmer over minimum heat for about 50 minutes. Then add the peas, including the canning liquid, and crumble in the bouillon cubes. Mix and simmer for another 20 minutes or so, keeping the pan covered.

Meanwhile, heat a large pan with the rest of the butter and a tablespoon of oil. Fry the bread until it is golden brown, then place in the bottom of a soup tureen and sprinkle with the Parmesan cheese. Remove the soup from the heat, taste and add salt if required. Stir in a little freshly ground pepper and a thin trickle of olive oil. Then pour the soup over the bread. Wait for a few minutes before serving.

Cream of Carrot
Crema di Carote

To serve 4

½lb small tender carrots

3 tbsp butter

3 tbsp flour

3 cups milk

1 bouillon cube

2 egg yolks

6 tbsp fresh whipping cream

ground nutmeg

croûtons

Preparation and cooking time: about 1 hour

Scrape and wash the carrots, then cut into ¼ inch cubes. Plunge them into lightly salted boiling water and boil for 5 minutes, then drain and sauté them in 2 tablespoons of butter for a few moments, without browning them.

Meanwhile slowly bring 3 cups of milk to a boil. Melt the remaining butter in a small saucepan, add the flour, stirring with a small whisk to prevent lumps forming, then dilute the mixture with the boiling milk, stirring constantly; salt very lightly and add the crushed bouillon cube. Bring the liquid to the boil, then add the carrot cubes with their butter. Stir and simmer gently for 20 minutes, keeping the pan partly covered.

In a bowl beat the 2 egg yolks with the cream. Remove the soup from the heat, fold in the mixture of egg yolks and cream, taste and add a little ground nutmeg and more salt, if necessary. Accompany this delicate cream soup with bread *croûtons* fried in butter.

March soup

Saffron-flavored Soup

Minestra all'Aroma di Zafferano

To serve 4

1 onion, peeled

¼ cup butter

½ lb potatoes

1 firm medium tomato

1 cup frozen young peas

¼ cup whipping cream

4½ cups good meat stock

1 envelope powdered saffron

½ cup quadrucci pasta

⅓ cup grated Parmesan cheese

a little chopped parsley

Preparation and cooking time: about 1¼ hours

Finely chop the onion and gently fry in 2 tablespoons of butter, melted in a large saucepan. Take care not to let it brown. Peel and wash the potatoes then dice into ½-inch cubes. Wash the tomato, cut it in half and remove the seeds. Dice this too. Add the potato and the tomato to the onion and also the frozen peas. Mix carefully and cook for a few minutes. Pour in the cream, stir, and simmer until the cream has been reduced by two-thirds. Bring the stock to the boil and pour into the pan containing the vegetables. Stir, and cover the saucepan. Turn the heat down low and simmer for about 20 minutes.

Uncover the pan, turn up the heat a little and put in first the saffron and then the pasta; cook until it is *al dente*. Remove the soup from the heat and stir in the rest of the butter, in slivers, and the Parmesan. When they have melted, pour the soup into 4 soup plates, sprinkle with chopped parsley and serve.

Saffron-flavored soup

Cream of Leek

Crema di Porro

To serve 4

5½ cups beef stock

¾lb leeks

5 tbsp butter

¼ cup flour

ground nutmeg

4 slices fresh white bread

olive oil

Parmesan cheese

Preparation and cooking time: about 1¼ hours

Bring the stock slowly to the boil. Wash the leeks thoroughly, drain, then slice them finely. Melt 3 tablespoons of the butter in a large pan without letting it sizzle, add the leeks and leave them to stew over a low heat, covered, for at least 10 minutes. Stir occasionally with a wooden spoon. Next sprinkle the leeks with the sifted flour, stirring to prevent lumps forming. Finally pour in the boiling stock in a trickle, stirring constantly.

Bring to the boil, then lower the heat, cover and cook for about 35 minutes, stirring occasionally. At the end of cooking, taste the soup, adjust the seasoning if necessary, and add the ground nutmeg. Remove from the heat and pour the soup into a tureen, cover and let it rest for a few minutes. Cut the slices of bread into ½-inch cubes and brown them in the remaining butter and 2 tablespoons of olive oil in a skillet. Serve the soup piping hot, with the bread *croûtons* and grated Parmesan cheese.

■ SOUPS ■ SOUPS ■ SOUPS ■

Cold Vegetable Soup

Zuppa Verde, Fredda

To serve 4

½lb beet greens or Swiss chard

½lb spinach

¼lb cucumber

½lb cooked French beans

5 or 6 large basil leaves

5 or 6 celery leaves

1 tbsp Chartreuse

4 cups meat stock, skimmed

fried or toasted *croûtons*

Preparation and cooking time: about 1 hour

Thoroughly wash the beet and spinach leaves under running water then put them in a saucepan with only the water that remains on them. Salt lightly and heat for about 10 minutes, then drain and lay the leaves to dry and cool on a large dish, tilting it to drain off the water, then squeeze them well. Peel the cucumber and cut in half lengthwise. Remove the seeds and parboil the cucumber in salted water for about 5 minutes. Remove with a slotted spoon, drain well and leave to cool.

Put the cucumber, spinach, and beet leaves in a blender together with the French beans. Wipe the basil leaves with a damp cloth and add these and the celery leaves as well as the Chartreuse. Pour in half the cold stock and blend in two batches, first at minimum speed and then at maximum speed, for 2 minutes in all. Pour into a soup tureen and check the seasoning. Serve with *croûtons*.

■ SOUPS ■ SOUPS ■ SOUPS ■

Cream of Vegetable Soup

Crema di Verdure alla Fantesca

To serve 8

2 medium zucchini

1½ cups Brussels sprouts

1 medium onion

few tender Savoy cabbage leaves

1 large carrot

½ celery heart

2 tbsp butter

3 tbsp olive oil

3-4 pieces dried mushroom

4½ pints light stock (or use bouillon cube)

½ tbsp tomato paste

⅓ cup rice

nutmeg

grated Parmesan cheese for garnish

croûtons

Preparation and cooking time: about 1½ hours

Wash and drain all the vegetables well, then slice them finely and soften them in the butter and oil in a large pan. Add the pieces of dried mushroom and pour in the stock (which you have first brought to the boil). Stir, and add half a tablespoon of tomato paste, then bring to the boil again. Add the rice, stir with a wooden spoon and simmer gently, with the pan half-covered, for about 1 hour, stirring occasionally.

Blend the mixture, a little at a time, and collect it in the pan. Adjust the salt to taste, season with a grinding of pepper and one of nutmeg. Serve the soup with grated Parmesan cheese and, if you wish, with bread *croûtons* fried in butter.

Cream of Lettuce and French Bean Soup

Crema di Lattuga e Fagiolini

To serve 6

6 tbsp butter

⅜ cup rice flour

3 pints meat stock (or use bouillon cube)

2 fresh lettuces, washed and separated into leaves

¼lb fresh French beans

2 egg yolks

grated Parmesan cheese

¾ cup whipping cream

croûtons

Preparation and cooking time: about 1½ hours

Melt 4 tablespoons of the butter in a large saucepan and stir in the rice flour. Gradually stir in the boiling stock and bring to the boil, stirring constantly. Add the lettuce leaves, cover the pan and cook over a moderate heat for about 1 hour, stirring frequently.

Meanwhile, top and tail the beans and cook them in salted boiling water for about 15 minutes or until just tender.

Drain the beans thoroughly and chop them coarsely. Mix the egg yolks, the remaining butter, melted, and a tablespoon of grated Parmesan cheese in a bowl and stir in the cream.

Sieve the lettuce soup into a clean saucepan, season with pepper and stir in the beans. Bring to the boil and gradually blend in the egg and cream mixture, stirring constantly with a whisk. Serve with hot *croûtons* and grated Parmesan cheese.

Cream of Potato, Leek and Squash

Crema di Patate, Porro e Zucchina

To serve 4-6

¾lb small potatoes

⅜ cup butter

1 medium-sized leek

1 medium-sized zucchini squash

olive oil

2 bouillon cubes

grated nutmeg

½ cup whipping cream

2 thin slices ham

3oz chicken breast

tender young fennel leaves

Preparation and cooking time: about 1½ hours

Put the peeled potatoes in a saucepan and cover with 3½ pints of cold water. Bring to the boil and cook for a further 30 minutes. Put the potatoes through a food processor with half the water and collect the purée in the saucepan with the rest of it. Add 2 tablespoons of butter which has been softened and cut into small pieces and beat with a small whisk until smooth. Reheat the contents of the saucepan.

Meanwhile, wash the leek and the squash and cut into thin rings. Heat 1½ teaspoons of butter and a tablespoon of olive oil in a skillet and put in the leek and squash. Salt, and fry gently until they are softened, but do not brown. Add these to the potato mixture. Stir, cover and simmer for about 30 minutes.

While the leek and squash are simmering, cut the ham into short thin strips and do likewise with the chicken, cutting slightly thicker pieces. Sauté in the rest of the butter in the skillet in which the leeks and squash were fried. Ten minutes before removing the soup from the heat, crumble in the bouillon cubes and add a little grated nutmeg. Stir in the cream. A couple of minutes before removing from the heat add the sautéed ham and chicken to the soup. Stir, and serve garnished with the young fennel leaves.

Bean Soup with Sweetcorn

Passato di Fagioli con Maïs

To serve 6

2 sprigs fresh sage, chopped

1 minced garlic clove

1 small onion, sliced

2 small carrots, sliced

1 small stalk celery, sliced

¼ cup butter

olive oil for frying

14oz canned navy beans

3 medium potatoes, peeled and cubed

1 bouillon cube

a little ground cinnamon

1 medium peeled tomato, chopped

1 small onion, chopped

3 cups canned yellow corn, drained

a little stock (or use bouillon cube)

¼ cup grated Parmesan cheese

a little chopped fresh parsley

Preparation and cooking time: about 1½ hours

Sauté the sage, garlic, onion, carrots and celery in 2 tablespoons of butter and 2 tablespoons of olive oil until the onion is transparent. Add the beans, together with their juice, and the cubed potatoes. Stir and simmer for a few minutes and then add 6¼ cups of boiling water. Season with the crumbled bouillon cube, a pinch of salt and pepper and a little ground cinnamon. Add the tomato, stir and bring back to the boil. Lower the heat, half-cover the pan and simmer gently for about 45 minutes.

Sauté the onion in the remaining butter and a tablespoon of oil. Add the corn and cook for about 10 minutes, pouring on a little boiling stock.

Process the bean soup in a blender, return it to the pan and bring it back to the boil. Taste and adjust seasoning. Add the onion and corn mixture and cook for a further few minutes.

Remove the pan from the heat and blend in the grated Parmesan cheese and 3 tablespoons of olive oil. Sprinkle with the chopped parsley and serve.

■ SOUPS ■ SOUPS ■ SOUPS ■

Cream of Leek and Watercress Soup

Crema di Porri e Crescione

To serve 4

¾lb leeks

¼lb watercress

---

4 tbsp butter

¼ cup flour

---

2 cups milk

---

1 cup beef stock

¼ cup fresh cream

---

bread *croûtons* fried in butter

Preparation and cooking time: about 1 hour

Wash the leeks and cut them into small rings; rinse the watercress. Boil some salted water in a saucepan and add the watercress; after a couple of minutes add the leeks and let them boil for 2 more minutes. Drain and squeeze the vegetables and chop finely. Rinse out the saucepan, place it over a medium heat and melt 2 tablespoons of the butter. Add the chopped vegetables and sauté for a few minutes, stirring occasionally.

Melt the remaining butter in a saucepan, stir in the flour with a whisk to prevent lumps forming, then add the hot milk, pouring it in a trickle. Stirring constantly, bring the sauce to the boil then mix it into the vegetables. Bring to the boil again then simmer for about 10 minutes. Purée the mixture in a blender. Stir in the hot stock and reheat the soup without bringing it to the boil. Remove from the heat, stir in the cream, adjust the seasoning and serve with hot *croûtons*.

Tapioca and Egg Soup

Pavese di Tapioca

To serve 4

---

6 tbsp butter

---

8 slices white bread, 1 day old

4½ cups good meat stock

½ cup tapioca

---

4 eggs

¼ cup grated Parmesan cheese

---

a little chopped parsley

Preparation and cooking time: 30 minutes

In each of two separate pans melt 2 tablespoons of butter. Fry the bread slices until they are golden brown, then place them in 4 soup plates. Keep them warm in the lighted oven with the door open. Heat the stock in a saucepan and gradually bring to the boil. As soon as it starts boiling, sprinkle in the tapioca and mix with a little whisk. Simmer gently for about 10 minutes, stirring occasionally.

Meanwhile, heat the rest of the butter in a skillet. When it has melted, break the eggs into the pan and fry over a low heat so that the white cooks but does not fry. Cut the eggs out with a 4-inch cookie cutter and place them on top of the bread. Sprinkle the Parmesan cheese over the eggs and pour in the boiling tapioca soup. Garnish with a little parsley and serve.

Tapioca and egg soup

Fish Soup Cooked in the Oven

Zuppa di Pesce, in Forno

To serve 4

4½lb mixed fish (red mullet, skate, dogfish, John Dory, gurnard, hake and dentex)

5-6 sprigs parsley

1 medium-sized onion

2 bay leaves

1 celery heart and a few leaves

2 garlic cloves

1-1¼lb ripe tomatoes

⅜ cup olive oil

½ cup dry white wine

4 slices bread

Preparation and cooking time: about 1½ hours

Gut and wash the fish; leave the smaller ones whole and cut the others in pieces, removing as many of the bones as possible and cutting off the heads. Place the heads in a saucepan with the bones and scraps, cover them with water, salt lightly, add a sprig of parsley, a quarter of the onion cut in slices and a bay leaf. Put the saucepan on the heat and let the stock simmer for about 30 minutes covered.

Preheat the oven to 400°F. In an ovenproof dish with a lid place the rest of the sliced onion, the celery heart and 4-5 finely chopped parsley sprigs, a whole garlic clove, a bay leaf and the tomatoes, chopped and puréed through the food processor using the fine disk. Arrange the fish on top of the vegetables, pour in the oil, salt and pepper lightly and then moisten with the white wine and the fish stock strained carefully through a fine cloth.

Cover the pan and place it in the oven for about 30 minutes. Toast the slices of bread in the oven; when golden brown brush them with a garlic clove and place them in 4 soup plates. Pour over the soup, sprinkle each portion with a few finely chopped celery leaves and a few drops of olive oil, then serve.

Rich Fish Soup

Zuppa di Pesce, Ricca

To serve 6

6½lb mixed fish (scorpion fish, gurnard, mullet, John Dory, skate)

1-1¼lb squid and small octopus

1-1¼lb shrimp and jumbo shrimp

2¼ cups dry white wine

¾ cup olive oil

3 garlic cloves

6 anchovy fillets

1 small piece red chili pepper

2 bunches parsley

6 basil leaves

1-1¼lb ripe tomatoes, chopped and seeded

12 mussels

6 razor-shell clams

oregano

6 slices home-made bread toasted in the oven

Preparation and cooking time: about 2 hours

Gut and wash the fish thoroughly, cut off the heads and fillet the larger ones. Cut the others into regular pieces, wash again and leave to drain. Clean the squid and octopus, removing the heads, the hard beaks and the viscera, then wash several times in plenty of water. Wash the shrimp.

Heat in a large saucepan the white wine, 4½ cups of water and all the fish heads and bones. Salt lightly and simmer on a very low heat for about 1 hour. Meanwhile, in ⅜ cup of oil in a small saucepan brown 3 crushed garlic cloves and dissolve the anchovy fillets. Add the shrimp, salt lightly, pepper and leave to brown for about 10 minutes, turning them often. Pour the mixture into the large saucepan containing the fish heads, add the piece of chili pepper and continue to cook, still over a very low heat.

Wash the parsley and basil and chop

them finely. Heat about ⅜ cup of oil in a very large saucepan; as soon as it is hot add the tomatoes puréed through a food processor, salt lightly and cook until the sauce is thick. Place the squid and octopus in the pan and, after about 20 minutes, add the fish. Cover and cook over quite a high heat without stirring.

Strain the prepared stock through a fine cloth, discarding the heads; if you wish you can keep the shrimp and add the shelled meat to the soup. Pour the stock into the pan containing the fish and cook for another 10 minutes. Five minutes before removing the soup from the heat, add the washed mussels and razor-shell clams and season with the mixture of chopped parsley and basil and a pinch of oregano. Serve the soup with the toasted bread slices.

■ SOUPS ■ SOUPS ■ SOUPS ■

Shellfish Soup

Zuppa di Molluschi

To serve 4

4½lb mixed shellfish (mussels, clams, razor-shell clams, Venus clams)

8 slices home-made bread

about ¾ cup olive oil

3 garlic cloves

a small piece red chili pepper

2 tbsp ready-made tomato sauce

3 cups good fish stock

a few tender celery leaves

Preparation and cooking time: about 40 minutes plus 2 hours' soaking

Scrape the shells of the shellfish, holding them under cold running water, then place them all in a large bowl, cover with cold water and leave them undisturbed for about 2 hours. Then leave them to drain for a while to remove any sand.

Fry the slices of bread on both sides in ⅜ cup oil; while still hot brush them with a large halved garlic clove and arrange them in 4 soup bowls. Heat a large skillet with ⅜ cup of oil, 2 large lightly crushed garlic cloves and the chili pepper: fry lightly until the garlic and pepper have browned, then discard them. Place the shellfish in the pan, cover and keep on

the heat until all the shells have opened. Remove them, one by one, from the pan, detaching one half-shell and placing the other one containing the mussel or clam in a clean saucepan.

Strain through a fine cloth the liquid which the shellfish gave out during cooking and add it to the saucepan. Add 2 tablespoons of ready-made tomato sauce blended with the hot fish stock, shake the saucepan slightly and keep it on the heat for a few moments, then pour the soup over the bread slices. Sprinkle each portion with chopped celery leaves and a few drops of olive oil. Serve immediately.

Shellfish soup (top left), **fish soup with anchovy** (center left, recipe on page 50), **rich fish soup** (top right) and **fish soup cooked in the oven** (bottom right)

Fish Soup with Anchovy
Zuppa "Marechiaro"

To serve 4

4 small striped mullet

4 small scorpion fish

¾-1lb cleaned skate

8 crayfish

12 cleaned baby cuttlefish

4 anchovy fillets

3 garlic cloves

olive oil

1 small onion

1 carrot

a few sprigs parsley

1lb ripe tomatoes

1 bay leaf

white wine

⅔ cup good fish stock

4 slices home-made bread

Preparation and cooking time: about 1½ hours

Clean and scale the mullet and scorpion fish, cut off the fins, then wash and drain them well.

Chop the skate and wash the crayfish and cuttlefish. Slightly crush 2 large garlic cloves and place them in a large saucepan with the anchovy fillets and 6 tablespoons of oil. Fry gently and mash the anchovies. Discard the garlic and add the onion and carrot, finely chopped with a sprig of parsley; soften for a few minutes, then add the cuttlefish and cook for about 10 minutes.

Meanwhile peel and purée the tomatoes and add them to the pan. Season with salt, pepper, and a small bay leaf. Simmer for about 20 minutes with the pan covered, then add the mullet, the scorpion fish and the pieces of skate in a single layer. Moisten with the white wine and pour in the fish stock.

Shake the saucepan gently and cook for 15 minutes, then add the crayfish and keep on the heat for a further 5 minutes.

(illustrated on page 49)

Rice, Potato, and Mushroom Soup
Minestra di Riso, Patate e Funghi

To serve 4-6

1oz dried cep mushroom caps

4 pints light stock

1 onion

1 garlic clove

2 stalks celery

4 tbsp butter

olive oil

¾-1lb potatoes

⅔ cup rice

¼ cup grated Parmesan cheese

ground nutmeg

a little chopped parsley

Preparation and cooking time: about 2 hours including soaking

Soak the dried mushrooms in warm water for about 1 hour. Drain them well and slice thinly. Heat the stock. Finely chop the onion with a garlic clove and the celery. Place the chopped mixture in a saucepan, add 2 tablespoons of the butter and 2 tablespoons of olive oil, then sauté without browning, stirring occasionally.

Peel the potatoes, wash, and cut them into cubes of about ¾ inch, add them to the lightly fried mixture together with the mushroom slices and leave for a few moments, then pour in the hot stock. Stir and slowly bring to the boil, then reduce the heat, cover the pan and leave to simmer for 15 minutes.

Mash a few of the potato cubes, pressing them with a wooden spoon against the side of the pan, then add the rice to the boiling soup, stirring with a wooden spoon. Cook over a rather high heat until the rice is *al dente*. Remove the pan from the heat, stir in the remaining butter with the Parmesan cheese and the ground nutmeg. If you like, sprinkle the soup with chopped parsley.

Chestnut and Mushroom Soup
Zuppa di Castagne e Funghi

To serve 4

1 medium onion

4-5 tbsp olive oil

3 tbsp butter

2 small cep mushrooms, trimmed

2 tbsp *dry* Marsala wine

10 chestnuts, boiled and puréed

5⅝ cups good meat stock

2 tsp cornstarch

½ cup whipping cream

4 thick slices white bread

Preparation and cooking time: about 1 hour

Cut up the onion and process in a blender together with 2-3 tablespoons of olive oil. Put the purée into a saucepan over a low heat. Add 5 teaspoons of butter, cut into small pieces, and fry without letting the onion brown. Meanwhile, clean and wash the mushrooms and cut into small pieces. Add to the onion mixture and fry for a few minutes, stirring all the time. Pour in the Marsala and, as soon as it has evaporated, add the chestnut paste. After 4-5 minutes, gradually pour in the boiling stock and mix with a small whisk. Bring to the boil, stirring occasionally. Lower the heat and simmer.

Put the cornstarch in a bowl with the cream and mix until it has completely dissolved. After 20 minutes, add this to the soup. Bring the soup back to the boil and continue simmering for another 5 minutes. Cut the bread into small squares and fry in the rest of the butter and 2 tablespoons of olive oil. When the soup is ready, taste and adjust the seasoning. Serve with the hot *croûtons*.

Chestnut and mushroom soup

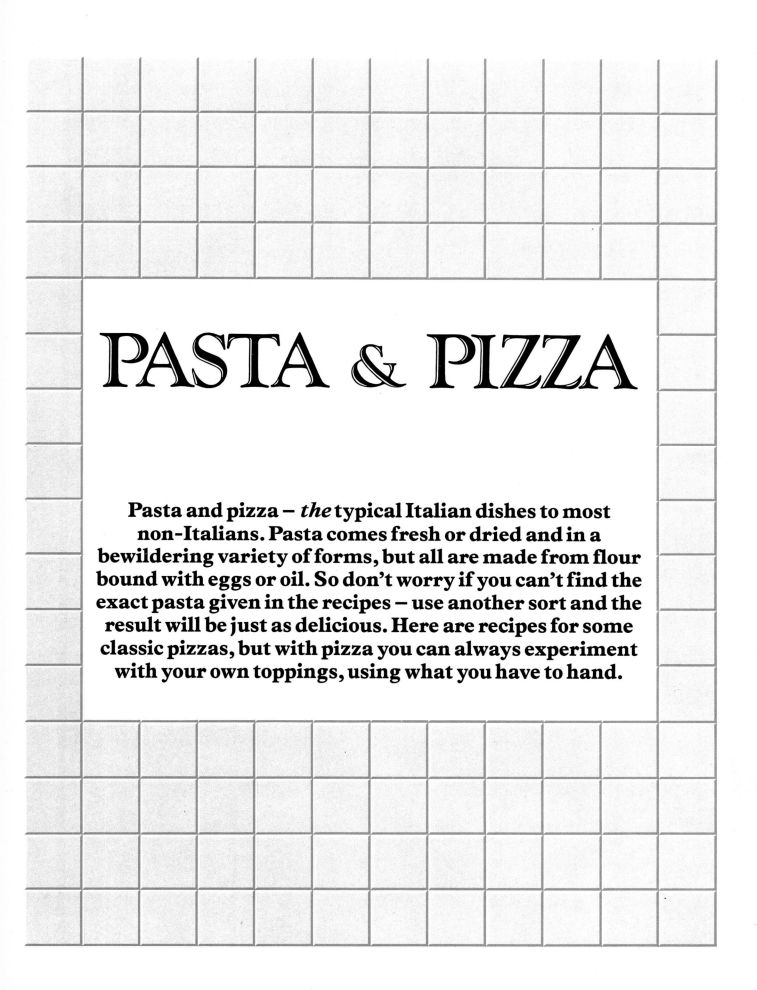

PASTA & PIZZA

Pasta and pizza – *the* typical Italian dishes to most non-Italians. Pasta comes fresh or dried and in a bewildering variety of forms, but all are made from flour bound with eggs or oil. So don't worry if you can't find the exact pasta given in the recipes – use another sort and the result will be just as delicious. Here are recipes for some classic pizzas, but with pizza you can always experiment with your own toppings, using what you have to hand.

Home-made Agnolotti Pasta with Cep Mushroom Sauce

Agnolotti con Sugo di Porcini

To serve 4-5

2 cabbage leaves

2 small onions

¼ cup butter

3 tbsp olive oil

¼ cup sausage meat

¼-½ lb stewed beef, dry

2 slices roast pork

7 tbsp grated Parmesan cheese

nutmeg

5 small eggs

2½ cups flour

½ lb cep mushrooms

1 garlic clove

2-3 sprigs fresh parsley

4 tbsp dry Marsala wine

½ bouillon cube

ground thyme

1 cup milk

3 tbsp whipping cream

1 tsp cornstarch

Preparation and cooking time: about 2 hours

Wash the cabbage leaves thoroughly then cook in boiling salted water for about 15 minutes. Drain, and when the cabbage has cooled, squeeze out all moisture well. Finely slice 1 onion and fry in 5 teaspoons of butter and 1 tablespoon of olive oil. Add the cabbage leaves and crumble the sausage meat before adding that too. Cook for about 10 minutes then put through a meat grinder together with the stewed beef and pork, using the finest disk. Collect the mixture in a bowl and add 4 tablespoons of grated Parmesan cheese, a little salt, pepper and grated nutmeg. Bind with 2 small eggs to a smooth consistency. Taste and adjust the seasoning if necessary.

Prepare the pasta dough from 2¼ cups of flour and the remaining 3 eggs. Knead energetically until smooth. Roll out the dough a little at a time, keeping the rest beneath an upturned earthenware dish. Cut out with a cookie cutter regular rounds, 2 inches in diameter. Place a little of the stuffing on one half of each round, then fold over to make semicircular *agnolotti*, pressing down the edges well to seal in the filling. As they are completed, lay them on a lightly floured cloth on a tray. Roll the pastry offcuts into a ball and put this underneath the earthenware dish. When both the pasta dough and the filling are used up, cover with a clean dish towel and leave in a cool place.

Trim the mushrooms, wash them rapidly under running water and drain carefully. Finely chop the remaining onion together with a garlic clove and a handful of parsley and fry in the remaining butter and 2 tablespoons of olive oil, taking care not to brown them. Finely slice the mushrooms and add to the other ingredients. Cook for 3-4 minutes on a fairly high heat, stirring with a wooden spoon. Pour in the Marsala and crumble in half the bouillon cube. Add a pinch of thyme, stir and, when two-thirds of the Marsala has evaporated, pour in the boiling milk. Dissolve the cornstarch in the cold cream and stir that in too. Mix well and simmer for a further few minutes until the sauce has thickened. Cook the *agnolotti* in salted boiling water and when they are cooked, after a few minutes, remove with a slotted spoon. Pour over the sauce and the remaining Parmesan. Mix carefully and serve.

Pasta with zucchini

Pasta with Zucchini
Pasta con Zucchini

To serve 4

1-1¼lb tender zucchini

1 medium onion

a little parsley

1 large garlic clove

7 tbsp olive oil

½ bouillon cube

¾lb fresh pasta

a little grated Parmesan cheese

Preparation and cooking time: 45 minutes

Clean the zucchini and trim them. Wash and dry well, cut them into rounds about ¼ inch thick. Finely chop the onion, parsley and garlic and fry in 5 tablespoons of olive oil in a skillet, without browning. Then add the zucchini and crumble in the bouillon cube. Add a little freshly ground pepper. Pour in ⅜ cup of boiling water and stir well.

Cover the pan and cook over a moderate heat for about 10 minutes until the zucchini are tender and the liquid has been absorbed. Taste and add salt. Cook the pasta in salted boiling water until it is *al dente*. Drain and stir in 2 tablespoons of olive oil. Mix in the sauce and serve at once with the Parmesan cheese.

■PASTA & PIZZA■PASTA & PIZZA■

Bacon Sauce for Ridged Macaroni
Sugo Affumicato per Mezze Maniche Rigate

1 large onion

2 tbsp olive oil

½lb smoked bacon

2¼ cups canned tomatoes

2½ cups ridged macaroni (mezze maniche rigate)

Chop the onion finely and sweat it in a pan with the olive oil without browning. Cut the bacon into short strips ½ inch wide and add it to the softened onion. Process the chopped tomatoes in a blender and add them, with salt and pepper to taste. Stir, put the lid on and cook for about 20 minutes, then pour over the pasta, cooked until *al dente*.

Tagliatelle with Salmon

Tagliatelle Emiliane al Salmone

To serve 1

1 thick slice red onion

1 garlic clove

2 tbsp butter

2oz canned salmon

1 tsp tomato paste

¼ cup milk

1 tsp cornstarch

¼lb noodles (tagliatelle)

1-2 slices smoked salmon

Preparation and cooking time: about 30 minutes

Finely chop the red onion and garlic together, then melt 5 teaspoons of the butter in a pan without browning. Sauté the chopped mixture without browning, stirring occasionally with a wooden spoon. Next add the canned salmon, first drained and with any skin and bones removed, and break into small pieces with a fork. Add a teaspoon of tomato paste, stir and cook for a few moments. Meanwhile, dissolve a teaspoon of cornstarch in the cold milk, then pour it over the salmon and, stirring constantly, bring to the boil. Season with pepper and remove from the heat.

Heat 2 pints of water in a saucepan and salt it as soon as it starts to boil. Plunge in the pasta and cook until *al dente*. Meanwhile, cut the smoked salmon into short strips. Drain the pasta and pour over the prepared sauce. Garnish with the strips of salmon and with the remaining butter cut in small pieces. Serve at once.

■PASTA & PIZZA■PASTA & PIZZA■

Pasta Twists with Tomato Sauce and Peas

Fusilli "Melchiorre"

To serve 4-5

¼lb leeks, white part only

1 celery stalk

2oz carrot

olive oil

1 garlic clove

1¼lb ripe tomatoes

3-4 basil leaves

granulated sugar

¼lb fresh peas

1 shallot

2 tbsp butter

stock (or use bouillon cube)

¾lb pasta twists

a little parsley

Parmesan cheese or mild Pecorino cheese, grated

Preparation and cooking time: about 1¼ hours

Finely slice the leek, the celery and the carrot. Soften the vegetables in 4 tablespoons of olive oil in a pan with a garlic clove. Remove the garlic once it is browned. Chop the tomatoes in small pieces and add them to the lightly fried vegetables. Stir, flavor with 3-4 leaves of basil, salt, pepper and a pinch of sugar. Stir once more, cover the pan and let the sauce cook for about 25 minutes on a medium heat, stirring occasionally.

Cook the peas in salted boiling water until tender. Meanwhile finely chop the shallot and soften it gently in the butter, without browning. Drain the peas, add them to the shallot and let them absorb the flavor for a few moments, then moisten them with the boiling broth, cover and let simmer until the liquid has been almost entirely absorbed.

Meanwhile cook the pasta in plenty of salted boiling water and, while it cooks, purée the tomato sauce. Taste it and, if necessary, adjust the salt and pepper to taste. Drain the pasta when it is *al dente* and sprinkle it with 2 tablespoons of olive oil. Season it with the tomato sauce and the peas, mixing carefully. Sprinkle with chopped parsley and serve it with the grated cheese.

Tagliatelle with salmon (left); *pasta twists with asparagus sauce* (above right)

Peppery Sauce for Noodles

Salsa Peverada per Tagliatelle

¼lb chicken livers

¼lb calves' liver

1 onion

4-5 sprigs fresh parsley

¼lb smoked bacon

3 tbsp capers

rind of ½ lemon

olive oil

6 anchovy fillets

2 cloves garlic

½ cup red wine

1lb noodles (tagliatelle)

Mince or chop the livers and reserve them. Chop the onion, parsley, bacon, capers and lemon rind together. Heat 3 tablespoons of olive oil and add the chopped anchovies and the garlic. When the garlic is golden, remove and discard it. Add the chopped onion and bacon mixture to the pan. As soon as it is browned, pour in the red wine and add the livers. Cook over a high heat for 5 minutes and season with freshly ground black pepper. Cook and drain the pasta and serve with the sauce.

■PASTA & PIZZA■PASTA & PIZZA■

Pink Sauce for Noodles

Sugo Rosa per Fettucine

1 sprig fresh rosemary

1 large clove garlic

⅔ cup meat gravy, skimmed

⅔ cup cream

1 tbsp tomato ketchup

brandy

6 canned tomatoes

14oz noodles (fettucine)

¼ cup grated Parmesan cheese

¼ cup grated Gruyère cheese

fresh parsley

ground paprika

Chop the rosemary leaves finely with the garlic. Place them in a pan large enough to hold all the pasta, add the gravy and cream and simmer for 5 minutes, stirring frequently. Then add the ketchup, a dash of brandy and the tomatoes, finely chopped. Simmer for about 10 minutes. Cook and drain the pasta, tip it into the sauce, bind with the two cheeses and sprinkle with chopped parsley and a pinch of paprika.

■PASTA & PIZZA■PASTA & PIZZA■

Pasta Twists with Asparagus Sauce

Fusilli con Asparagi

To serve 1

5 tsp butter

5-6 green asparagus tips, boiled and cooled

1 tsp flour

⅜ cup milk

¼ bouillon cube

ground nutmeg

1 cup pasta twists (fusilli)

2 tbsp whipping cream

Preparation and cooking time: about 30 minutes

Melt the butter in a small saucepan, add the asparagus tips and sauté gently, making sure that they do not brown. Sprinkle with a teaspoon of sifted flour, stir and, after a few moments, pour in the hot milk in a trickle. Crumble a quarter of a bouillon cube and add a pinch of nutmeg. Stirring constantly, bring the sauce to the boil, then remove it from the heat and purée it.

Heat 2 pints of water and salt it when it starts to boil. Plunge in the pasta and cook until *al dente*. Place the cream of asparagus on a very low heat in the saucepan and reheat gently. Stirring constantly, mix in the cream. Adjust the seasoning to taste. Drain the pasta, but not too thoroughly, pour over it the creamy asparagus sauce and garnish, if you like, with more asparagus tips tossed in a little butter. Serve at once.

Pasta Tubes with Crab Meat

Rigatoni al Granchio

To serve 1

small shallot

1 small piece celery heart

5 tsp butter

1 tsp olive oil

2oz canned crab meat

2 tbsp sparkling white wine

1 tbsp tomato paste

2-3 tbsp concentrated fish stock

¼ lb large fluted pasta tubes (rigatoni)

Preparation and cooking time: about 30 minutes

Finely chop together the shallot and celery heart and sauté, without browning, in the butter melted in a skillet pan with a teaspoon of olive oil. Meanwhile drain the crab meat, removing any cartilage, and shred finely before adding to the pan. Cook for a few minutes, stirring.

Next, moisten the crab with a sprinkling of sparkling wine and let it evaporate almost completely, keeping the heat low and stirring often. Then add the tomato paste and 2 tablespoons of fish stock. Stir once more and leave the sauce to simmer for 5-7 minutes. If it dries out too much, moisten with another tablespoon of fish stock. Season with salt and white pepper.

Heat 4½ cups of water in a saucepan and salt it when it starts to boil. Plunge in the pasta and cook it until *al dente*. Drain, remove to a heated plate and pour the hot crab sauce over it. Garnish, if you like, with celery leaves. Serve at once.

Green and White Noodles with Bolognese Sauce

Paglia e Fieno con Ragú Pasquale

To serve 6

1 medium onion

1 large garlic clove

½ sprig rosemary

1 small bunch parsley

1 stalk celery

2 small carrots

2 tbsp butter

5 tbsp olive oil

¼lb beef

¼lb lamb

¼lb sausage meat

2 slices bacon

⅜ cup dry white wine

1 tbsp flour

¾lb tomatoes

1 bouillon cube

1 cup frozen young peas

1lb green and white noodles (tagliatelle)

¼ cup grated Parmesan cheese

Preparation and cooking time: about 2 hours

Finely chop the onion with a large garlic clove, the leaves of half a sprig of rosemary and a small bunch of parsley. Dice the celery and carrot. Put these ingredients into a saucepan with the butter and 3 tablespoons of the oil. Soften but do not allow to brown.

Meanwhile, put the beef, lamb and sausage meat through the meat grinder using the medium disk. Dice the bacon. Add to the vegetables in the pan, stir and brown slightly. Then pour the white wine in and allow to evaporate almost completely. Sprinkle in a level tablespoon of flour. Stir well to prevent lumps forming.

Put the tomatoes through a food processor using the medium disk and add immediately after the flour together with a pint of cold water, the crumbled bouillon cube and some freshly ground black pepper. Stir and bring to the boil, then turn the heat down to simmer, cover the pan and cook for about 1½ hours. Stir occasionally and dilute with a little boiling water if neccessary.

Parboil the frozen peas and add them 15 minutes before cooking is completed. Heat at least a gallon of water in a saucepan and add salt as it begins to boil. Plunge in the pasta, and cook until it is *al dente*. Drain and mix in 2 tablespoons of olive oil, then serve with the sauce and the grated Parmesan cheese.

Noodles with Bolognese sauce (left); *pasta tubes with crab meat* (right)

Pasta with Fennel
Pasta al Finocchio

To serve 4

1 small onion

3 tbsp butter

4 tbsp olive oil

1 large fennel bulb

1 tsp flour

¾ cup stock (or use bouillon cube)

1 tbsp fresh cumin leaves, chopped

⅜ cup cream

3 cups pasta rings

2 tbsp grated Pecorino cheese

a little chopped parsley

Preparation and cooking time: about 1 hour

Finely slice the onion and gently fry it in the butter and 2 tablespoons of the olive oil. Trim and slice the fennel almost as finely as the onion and add to the pan. Leave for a few minutes, stirring from time to time. Then stir in the flour and the boiling stock. Put in the cumin leaves, stir, cover and cook over a low heat for about 20 minutes. Dilute with more boiling stock if the sauce becomes too dry.

When the fennel is tender, add the cream, stir, add salt and keep the pan over a low heat for a few more seconds.

Cook the pasta in salted boiling water until it is *al dente*. Drain and stir in 2 tablespoons of olive oil. Pour over the fennel sauce and the Pecorino cheese. Mix and serve at once, sprinkled with a little chopped parsley.

Corsair Sauce for Pasta Quills
Sugo alla Corsara per Penne Rigate

1-1¼lb razor-clams

⅜ cup olive oil

½ cup dry white wine

2 garlic cloves

a small piece chili pepper

4-5 sprigs fresh parsley

a few fresh basil leaves

1 bouillon cube

4 large ripe tomatoes

3½ cups fluted pasta quills (penne)

¾ cup grated Pecorino cheese

Wash the clams well and put them in a skillet with the olive oil, wine and the finely chopped garlic, chili pepper, parsley and basil. Add the bouillon cube, dissolved in ¼ cup of hot water, and simmer for 10 minutes.

Remove the opened clams from their shells, and cut each one into three. Scald the tomatoes, remove the skins and seeds and cut the flesh into strips. Strain the clam liquid into a large pan, add the tomatoes and clams and toss the cooked pasta in it. Sprinkle with the grated Pecorino cheese.

Angler's Sauce for Vermicelli
Sugo alla Pescatora per Vermicelli

2½lb mussels

olive oil

1 onion

1 garlic clove

2 firm, ripe tomatoes

½ tsp anchovy paste

2-3 sprigs fresh parsley

a few fresh basil leaves

¾-1 lb vermicelli

Wash the mussels well, heat them in a covered skillet with a little olive oil and take them out of their shells when they open. Chop the onion and garlic and sweat them in ⅜ cup of olive oil. Scald, peel and de-seed the tomatoes, chop them and add them to the onion with the mussels, anchovy paste, freshly ground pepper and a little salt. Chop the parsley and basil finely. Cook and drain the pasta and serve it with the sauce, sprinkled with the chopped herbs, 3 or 4 tablespoons of olive oil and a final seasoning of black pepper.

Pasta with fennel

Home-made Cannelloni in Cream Sauce
Cannelloni Ripieni in Bianco

To serve 10

1 small onion

1 carrot

1 tender rib celery

1 bay leaf

half a chicken, weighing about 1¼lb

½lb calves' brains

4 chicken livers

1 stale roll

¼lb ham

1½ sticks butter

about 3 tbsp dry Marsala wine

⅔ cup grated Parmesan cheese

6 eggs

3½ cups flour

olive oil

⅞ cup cream

Preparation and cooking time: about 3½ hours

Bring about 4½ cups of water to the boil in a saucepan and add a little salt, half the onion, the carrot, the celery rib, bay leaf and chicken. Cover the pan and cook on a moderate heat for about 1 hour.

Soak the calves' brains in plenty of cold water for about 20 minutes, changing the water 2 or 3 times during soaking. Trim and wash the livers.

Crumble the roll and soften it with some of the cooking liquid from the chicken. Finely chop the fat of the ham and the remaining half onion. Drain the calves' brains, remove the outer membrane and cut into small pieces.

Place the chopped onion and ham fat in a small skillet with a large knob of butter and cook on a very low heat for a few minutes. Add the chicken livers and the calves' brains and cook for a further 10 minutes, occasionally pouring on a little Marsala. Remove from the heat.

Remove the chicken with a slotted spoon and allow it to cool slightly. Strain the stock. Bone the chicken and grind the meat finely in a blender with the calves' brains, chicken livers and ham. Place the mixture in a bowl and stir in 4 tablespoons of grated Parmesan cheese, the drained bread and 3 of the eggs. Season to taste with salt and pepper. The mixture should be fairly soft.

Prepare the pasta: sift 3 cups of flour into a bowl and make a well in the center. Place 3 eggs and a tablespoon of olive oil in the well and hand mix with the flour to form a firm dough, kneading for about 10 minutes. Roll out thinly.

Heat plenty of water in a large saucepan. Coat the rolled-out dough in flour, roll it up and cut it into pieces about 4-inches wide. Unroll the strips and cut them into 4 inch lengths. Once the water has come back to the boil, add salt and a tablespoon of olive oil. Put the squares of pasta in the water one at a time. As soon as the water comes back to the boil, drain the pasta and spread it out on a dish-towel to dry.

Place some of the prepared filling on each square of pasta and then roll them up to form cannelloni. Arrange the cannelloni on a large greased baking tray.

Preheat the oven to 400°F. Melt 4 tablespoons of butter in a saucepan and blend in ½ cup of flour to form a smooth *roux*. Pour in 2½ cups of the strained chicken stock, stirring constantly. Bring to the boil, blend in the cream and season.

Cover the cannelloni with the prepared sauce and dot with about 4 tablespoons of butter, cut into small pieces. Sprinkle with the rest of the grated Parmesan cheese and bake in the oven for about 15 minutes. Serve.

Thin Noodles with Clams
Linguine alle Vongole

To serve 4

1 garlic clove

4 tbsp olive oil

1 small onion, finely chopped

½lb frozen clams

1½ cups clam sauce

1 cup frozen garden peas

1 bouillon cube

¾lb thin noodles (linguine)

Preparation and cooking time: about 20 minutes

Sauté the whole garlic clove in 4 tablespoons of olive oil. Discard the garlic and add the finely chopped onions to the pan. Fry them gently. Place the clams in the pan and allow to defrost on a low heat. Add the clam sauce and the peas. Stir in the crumbled bouillon cube and simmer on a moderate heat.

Cook the pasta until *al dente*, in salted boiling water, drain and pour into a warmed tureen. Dress with the prepared sauce and serve immediately.

Thin noodles with clams

Pasta Shells with Four Cheeses

Lumaconi ai 4 Formaggi

To serve 1

¼ cup Parmesan cheese

1oz Sbrinz cheese

1oz Emmental cheese

1oz Fontina cheese

5 tsp butter

¼ cup milk (not skimmed)

nutmeg

1 egg yolk

1 cup pasta shells (lumaconi)

a little chopped parsley for garnish

Preparation and cooking time: about 30 minutes

Grate the Parmesan and Sbrinz cheeses and cut the Emmental and Fontina cheeses into small cubes and mix these 2 cheeses together well.

In a saucepan melt the butter, without browning; remove the saucepan from the heat and add the 4 cheeses, stirring vigorously with a small wooden spoon. Place the saucepan again over a very low heat (or in a *bain-marie*) and, stirring constantly, melt the cheeses slightly. Then add the warm milk in a trickle, mixing constantly until thoroughly smooth and blended, then season it with a grinding of nutmeg. Off the heat, add a fresh egg yolk. Keep the sauce warm in a *bain-marie*, stirring often.

Cook the pasta in salted boiling water with the pan uncovered, until *al dente*. Drain, pour the cheese "fondue" over it and sprinkle with a pinch of finely chopped parsley. Serve at once before the cheese mixture becomes firm.

Delicate Polenta with Mushrooms

Polenta Delicata ai Funghi

To serve 4

3 cups milk

1 cup corn meal

½ cup semolina

¾-1 lb small mushrooms (preferably ceps)

6 tbsp butter

2½ tsp flour

ground nutmeg

scant 1 cup grated Emmental cheese

2 egg yolks

1 garlic clove

a handful of parsley

2 tbsp olive oil

powdered thyme

Preparation and cooking time: about 1 hour

Place on the heat a large saucepan with 2¼ cups of water and 2½ cups of the milk and slowly bring to the boil. Mix the corn meal with the semolina. As soon as the liquids start to boil add the salt and, after a few moments, sprinkle in the mixed corn meal and semolina gradually. At the beginning stir with a small whisk, then with a wooden spoon. Cook the polenta over a medium heat for about 40 minutes, stirring frequently.

In the meantime, clean the mushrooms, trim the stems and wipe the mushrooms with a damp cloth, then cut them into thin slices. In a small saucepan melt 2 tablespoons of the butter, add the flour and stir with a wooden spoon to prevent lumps forming. Moisten with ½ cup of boiling milk poured in a trickle and, stirring constantly, bring the sauce to the boil.

Remove from the heat, season with salt and ground nutmeg, then stir in the Emmental cheese and 2 egg yolks, stirring vigorously after each addition. Keep the sauce warm in a *bain-marie*, stirring it once in a while.

Finely chop a garlic clove together with a handful of parsley; soften the mixture in 5 teaspoons of butter and 2 tablespoons of oil, without browning. Add the mushrooms and leave for not more than 5 minutes, seasoning with salt and pepper and a pinch of thyme.

Remove the polenta from the heat and fold in the remaining butter softened and cut in small pieces, then pour it on to a round serving board and make a hollow in the center; pour in the cheese sauce, spread over the mushroom slices and sprinkle with a little chopped parsley. Serve at once.

Pasta Twists with Pork Ragout

Fusilli con Ragú du Lonza

To serve 4

½ small onion

5 tsp butter

1-2 tbsp olive oil

½ lb pork loin

⅜ cup dry white wine

1 bouillon cube

½ envelope saffron

3 cups pasta twists (fusilli)

1 tsp cornstarch

⅜ cup milk

15 capers in vinegar

Worcestershire sauce

Preparation and cooking time: about 40 minutes

Chop the onion and soften it in the butter and 1 tablespoon of oil. Cut the meat into small cubes and brown them quickly in the pan, then moisten with the white wine, let it evaporate, then season with the crumbled bouillon cube. Boil a gallon of water, salt it, then sprinkle in the saffron and, after a few moments, plunge in the pasta and cook until *al dente*.

Dissolve the cornstarch in the cold milk and add to the ragout together with the well-drained capers. Season with a dash of Worcestershire sauce, stir and remove from the heat. Drain the pasta, place it in a warmed bowl and pour over it a few drops of oil and then the ragout sauce. Serve at once.

You can use other types of short pasta for this dish such as penne, rigatoni, sedani, farfalle and so on. The Worcestershire sauce is important and, should you not have any, substitute a bit of anchovy paste and a little white pepper.

■PASTA & PIZZA■PASTA & PIZZA■

Creamy Fluted Macaroni

Penne "due Torri"

To serve 4

1 slice mortadella sausage

1 thick slice ham

1 small onion, thinly sliced

1 garlic clove

2 tbsp butter

2 tbsp olive oil

⅜ cup dry white wine

1 tsp cornstarch

2¼ cups light stock (or use bouillon cube)

Worcestershire sauce

3 cups fluted macaroni

⅜ cup light cream

2 tbsp grated Parmesan cheese

2 tbsp chopped fresh parsley

Preparation and cooking time: about 40 minutes

Cut the mortadella and ham into ¼-inch cubes. Gently fry the onion and a crushed garlic clove in the butter and olive oil until transparent. Add the cubes of mortadella and ham and cook for a few minutes. Pour on the wine and allow it to evaporate almost completely. Dissolve the cornstarch in 3 tablespoons of cold water and add it to the pan, together with the boiling stock and a splash of Worcestershire sauce. Stir and simmer gently until the liquid has reduced by two-thirds to form a creamy sauce.

Cook the pasta until *al dente* in salted boiling water, drain it and stir it into the prepared sauce. Blend in the cream. Remove the pan from the heat and stir in the grated Parmesan cheese and chopped parsley. Serve immediately.

Pasta with Turnip Greens

Fettuccia Riccia con Cime di Rapa

To serve 4

2¼lb turnip greens

¼lb onions

2 large garlic cloves

olive oil

¾-1lb peeled tomatoes

4-5 sprigs fresh coriander

sugar

¾lb scalloped wide pasta noodles (fettuccia)

grated Pecorino cheese

Preparation and cooking time: about 1 hour

Boil a large saucepanful of salted water. Clean and wash the turnip greens and put them in the boiling water for 5-6 minutes. Meanwhile finely chop the onion and 1 garlic clove together and fry in 5 tablespoons of olive oil in a small saucepan. Purée the tomatoes and add to the onion. Season with salt and pepper and add the fresh coriander and a pinch of sugar. Stir and gradually bring to the boil. Turn the heat down low and simmer for about 20 minutes, stirring from time to time.

Remove the turnip greens from the water with a slotted spoon and drain well. Sauté them in a large skillet in 3 tablespoons of olive oil with 1 lightly crushed garlic clove. Add enough water to the saucepan in which the turnip greens were boiled to make at least 6 pints and bring to the boil. Pour in the pasta and cook until it is *al dente*. Drain and put the pasta in the pan with the turnip greens; add the tomato sauce. Sauté for a few minutes then serve with grated Pecorino cheese.

Devilled Sauce for Pasta Dumplings

Sugo alla Diavola per Malloreddus

4 Italian poaching sausages

½ cup dry white wine

1 cup frozen peas

2 sprigs fresh rosemary

1 small piece hot chili pepper

¼ cup butter

2 tbsp vinegar

¾lb pasta dumplings (gnocchi)

½ cup grated Parmesan cheese

½ cup grated Pecorino cheese

Wash the sausages, place in a small pan with ⅝ cup of water and the wine, cover and cook for about 20 minutes. Skin and dice them and return them to the pan with the same liquid, add the frozen peas, season with salt and pepper and cook for about 15 minutes, stirring occasionally.

Finely chop the rosemary leaves. Melt the butter in a large pan, gently fry the rosemary then add the vinegar and the sausages and peas with their liquid. Toss the cooked gnocchi in this sauce, adding the ground chili pepper and the two cheeses.

Mushroom Sauce for Fine Noodles

Sugo ai Funghi per Capellini

2 garlic cloves

½lb mushrooms

3 tbsp olive oil

2-3 sprigs fresh parsley

½ cup dry white wine

½ cup light cream

1 tsp cornstarch

3 egg yolks

1 bouillon cube

6 tbsp butter

¾lb fine noodles (capellini)

½ cup grated Parmesan cheese

Fry the crushed garlic and the finely sliced mushrooms together in the olive oil, then add the chopped parsley and a little salt. Put the mixture into a blender with the wine, cream, cornstarch, egg yolks, bouillon cube and half the butter, melted. Blend into a smooth sauce then return it to the pan and simmer for 5 minutes. Serve the fine noodles with this sauce, the rest of the butter in knobs and the grated Parmesan cheese.

Creamy fluted macaroni (far left);
pasta twists with pork ragout (above)

Pasta and Chick Peas
Pasta e Ceci

To serve 6

¼lb dried chick peas

¼lb onions

1 large garlic clove

1 small carrot

1 stalk celery

8 fresh sorrel leaves

½ sprig of rosemary

¼lb peeled tomatoes

2 large potatoes, together weighing about ¾lb

olive oil

2 bouillon cubes

¼lb pasta

4 tbsp grated Parmesan cheese

Preparation and cooking time: 2½ hours plus overnight soaking

Soak the chick peas overnight in cold water. The following day, finely chop the onion with the garlic, carrot and celery together with the sorrel and rosemary leaves. Drain the chick peas and put in a saucepan with all the other ingredients. Chop the tomatoes finely and add these, along with the whole peeled potatoes. Pour in 4½ pints of cold water and 3 tablespoons of olive oil. Crumble in the bouillon cubes and bring to the boil. Then turn the heat down, cover the pan and simmer for about 2 hours, stirring from time to time.

Remove the potatoes with a slotted spoon and purée them with about a third of the chick peas, returning the purée to the saucepan. Bring back to the boil and pour in the pasta. Boil over a fairly high heat, keeping the pan uncovered and stirring from time to time. Taste and add salt if required, then stir in 3 tablespoons of olive oil and the Parmesan cheese. Add a little freshly ground pepper. Stir and serve at once.

Pasta Tubes with Broccoli
Sedanini con Broccoletti

To serve 4

1¾lb young broccoli

4-6 shallots

a little parsley

2 sprigs fresh fennel

5 tbsp olive oil

3 cups small pasta tubes (sedanini)

a handful of grated Pecorino cheese

Preparation and cooking time: about 30 minutes

Wash the broccoli and divide it into flowerets. Chop the stalks into lengths of about 1½-2 inches. Cook the broccoli in a saucepan of boiling water for 7-8 minutes. Leave uncovered. While the broccoli is cooking, finely slice the shallots. Chop the parsley and fennel together and sauté with the shallots in the olive oil, using a large iron or copper-plated skillet.

Remove the broccoli from the pan with a slotted spoon and, without draining too thoroughly, place it in the skillet with the other ingredients. Fry the broccoli in turn without mixing – simply shake the pan. Add freshly ground pepper. Into the same water used for the broccoli, and there should be at least 6¼ pints, pour the pasta and cook until it is *al dente*. Drain and sauté in the pan with the broccoli, sprinkling with the Pecorino cheese. Serve at once.

Pasta with broccoli

Seafood Pasta Twists

Fusilli "Marechiaro"

To serve 6

1¼lb firm, ripe tomatoes

1 medium onion

1 garlic clove

1 small green bell pepper

olive oil

¼ lb canned mussels

6 fresh basil leaves

a little sugar

1¼ lb pasta twists (fusilli)

1 sprig fresh parsley

Preparation and cooking time: about 1 hour

Remove the stalks from the tomatoes, wash, dry and coarsely chop them and put them through the finest disk of a food processor or purée them in a blender. Chop the onion finely with the garlic and bell pepper and sauté the mixture gently in ¼ cup of olive oil, taking care not to let it brown. Add the drained mussels, giving them a few moments to absorb the flavors, then add the tomatoes and the torn-up basil leaves. Salt cautiously, then add the pepper and a good pinch of sugar. Stir and simmer for 30 minutes over a moderate heat with the lid half on.

Meanwhile, take a large pan and bring a gallon of water to the boil. Add salt and, after a moment, plunge in the pasta and cook until just *al dente*. Drain, and add the prepared sauce plus 3 tablespoons of olive oil and a little more pepper. Stir carefully, turn into a heated tureen, sprinkle with chopped parsley and serve.

Pasta Quills with Yellow Pepper Sauce
Mezze Penne al Peperone

To serve 4

1 large yellow bell pepper

1 medium onion

6 tbsp olive oil

1 garlic clove

5-6 fresh mint leaves

4 fresh basil leaves

½lb peeled tomatoes

1 cup light stock (or use a bouillon cube)

3 cups small pasta quills (mezze penne)

2 tbsp grated Pecorino cheese

Preparation and cooking time: 1¼ hours

Broil and peel a ripe, yellow bell pepper, then cut it into 1-inch cubes. Finely slice the onion and soften with the pepper cubes in 5 tablespoons of olive oil, taking care not to brown any of the ingredients. Then add a large garlic clove, with the green core removed, 5-6 leaves of fresh mint and 4 fresh basil leaves, all finely chopped.

Stir, and fry slowly for a few minutes, then put the tomatoes through a food processor, using a fine disk, and add these. Add the stock (made with a bouillon cube if necessary) and a little salt and pepper and cook in a partly covered pan for about 35 minutes, when the sauce will be just about reduced and well-cooked. Now put half the sauce through the food processor, using the fine disk, and return the puréed sauce to the pan containing the remainder. Mix well together.

Cook the pasta in salted boiling water until just slightly firm. Drain, add a tablespoon of olive oil, then the prepared sauce and the grated Pecorino cheese. Stir and serve.

Pasta with yellow pepper sauce

Garlic, Oil and Hot Pepper Sauce for Long, Hollow Macaroni
Aglio, Olio e Peperoncino per Fusilli Lunghi Bucati

6 garlic cloves

2 hot chili peppers

1 lb hollow macaroni

⅞ cup good olive oil

½ cup grated Parmesan cheese

½ cup grated Pecorino cheese

Chop the garlic and chili peppers coarsely and liquidize them with ½ cup of cold water. Add this to a panful of salted hot water, bring to the boil and simmer for 15 minutes, then filter the liquid through a fine strainer into a second pan. Boil the pasta in this and, when it is cooked *al dente*, drain it and add the olive oil and the two cheeses, stirring well.

■PASTA & PIZZA■PASTA & PIZZA■

Basil Sauce for Pasta Caps
Sugo al Basilico per Orecchiette

5-6 fresh basil leaves

1 garlic clove

¼ cup shortening (or ¼ cup butter)

3 tbsp olive oil

¾lb pasta caps (orecchiette)

2 tbsp grated Parmesan cheese

1 tbsp grated Pecorino cheese

Wash the basil and chop it with the garlic. Heat the shortening and olive oil and fry the basil and garlic very gently, adding a generous quantity of freshly ground pepper. Cook and drain the pasta, tip it into the sauce and sprinkle with the two cheeses before serving.

Cream Sauce for Fluted Macaroni

Salsa alla Crema per Pipe Rigate

2 slices ham

⅜ cup cream

2 egg yolks

⅜ cup butter

⅓ cup grated Parmesan cheese

3 cups fluted macaroni (pipe rigate)

Chop the ham finely and place it in the serving bowl. Warm the cream, take it off the heat, incorporate the egg yolks and add it to the ham. Flake the butter and stir it into the other ingredients with the grated Parmesan cheese and freshly ground pepper. Cook and drain the pasta and stir it into the prepared sauce.

Small pasta dumplings in egg sauce

Pasta Dumplings with Cheese Sauce

Gnocchi alla Bava

To serve 4

1½lb potatoes

1 cup flour

2 egg yolks

nutmeg

2oz block of Parmesan cheese

¼ cup butter

⅜ cup light cream

Preparation and cooking time: about 30 minutes

Boil the potatoes in salted water, drain, peel and mash them. Add the flour, 1 egg yolk, a little salt and nutmeg. Knead together and divide the dough into small gnocchi shapes. Give them an interesting texture by rolling them on the back of a grater.

Remove the rind from the cheese and dice it. Put it in a pan with the melted butter and the cream. Place on a low heat

or in a *bain-marie* and stir with a wooden spoon until the cheese has melted. Add the other egg yolk and a generous grinding of pepper and stir briskly.

Cook the gnocchi in plenty of salted boiling water until they rise to the surface and are *al dente*. Drain. Pour the sauce over the boiled gnocchi and serve at once.

■PASTA & PIZZA■PASTA & PIZZA■

Small Pasta Dumplings in Egg Sauce

Gnocchietti Sardi in Salsa d'Uova

To serve 8

2 eggs

¼lb ham

¼lb mushrooms

¼ cup capers

12 green olives, pitted

5 dill pickles/gherkins, finely sliced

1-1¼lb small pasta dumplings (gnocchi)

2 tbsp vinegar

⅜ cup olive oil

⅜ cup fresh Quartirolo cheese

Preparation and cooking time: about 30 minutes

Hard-boil the eggs and cool them under running water. Cut the ham into tiny cubes, discarding any fat. Place the mushrooms, capers, olives and dill pickles in a salad bowl.

Heat plenty of water in a large saucepan and add salt as it comes to the boil.

Cook the gnocchi until *al dente*, drain well and spread on a tray to cool. Shell the eggs and then finely crumble the yolks into a bowl. Moisten with the vinegar and season with a little salt and pepper. Gradually blend in the olive oil.

Place the cold pasta and the diced ham in the salad bowl with the other ingredients. Dress with the prepared sauce and stir well. Dice the fresh Quartirolo cheese and stir it into the salad. Serve.

Hollow Spaghetti with Caviar

Bucatini al Caviale

To serve 1

small piece onion

½ garlic clove

3 tbsp olive oil

1½oz caviar

a little vodka

3 tbsp fish stock

Worcestershire sauce

2 tbsp light cream

¼ lb hollow spaghetti (bucatini)

fresh basil for garnish

Preparation and cooking time: about 30 minutes

Finely chop together the onion and half garlic clove. Soften in a pan with 2 tablespoons of olive oil, without browning. Next add the caviar and let it heat for a few moments, without frying; stir with a wooden spoon.

Moisten with a sprinkling of vodka and let it evaporate almost completely, keeping the heat very low. Pour in the hot fish stock, letting it reduce almost entirely before adding a sprinkling of Worcestershire sauce and, off the heat, 2 tablespoons of cream. Mix gently and keep the sauce warm in a *bain-marie*.

Heat 2 pints of water in a saucepan, adding salt when it starts to boil. Plunge in the pasta and cook until *al dente*. Drain and season, first with a tablespoon of olive oil, then with the caviar sauce. Garnish the dish with fresh basil and serve immediately.

Hollow spaghetti with caviar

Pasta Riviera-Style

Gramigna della Riviera

To serve 4

1 small onion

olive oil

about ½lb zucchini

½ bouillon cube

about ¼lb ham, in 2 thick slices

¾lb gramigna pasta

grated Parmesan cheese

chopped fresh parsley

Preparation and cooking time: about 30 minutes

Finely chop the onions and fry gently in 2 tablespoons of olive oil. Trim the zucchini, halve lengthwise and then, holding the 2 halves together, slice finely. Add the slices of zucchini to the pan, together with half a crumbled bouillon cube. Lower the heat and cook gently until the zucchini are tender, being careful not to overcook them.

Cut the ham into thin strips, discarding any fat. Cook the pasta until *al dente* in plenty of salted boiling water, drain thoroughly and pour into a tureen. Stir in the zucchini mixture and the ham, and serve immediately with grated Parmesan cheese. Top with chopped parsley if desired.

Milk Sauce for Thin Spaghetti

Salsa al Latte per Spaghettini

1 small onion

butter

¼lb smoked bacon

2 egg yolks

cornstarch

1 cup milk

¾ cup grated Parmesan cheese

1-2 sprigs fresh parsley

¾-1lb thin spaghetti (spaghettini)

Slice the onion finely, place it in a large pan with 2 tablespoons of butter and sweat it gently, taking care it does not brown. Cut the bacon into short narrow strips, add it to the onion and cook until it becomes transparent. Beat the egg yolks with a large pinch of cornstarch, gradually add the milk, then half the cheese and the chopped parsley, and season with salt and pepper. Add this to the bacon and onions and bring to the boil. Cook and drain the pasta and tip it into the pan with the sauce. Before serving, sprinkle with the remaining grated Parmesan cheese.

Cold Pasta in Pizzaiola Sauce

Mezze Penne alla Pizzaiola

To serve 8

1 garlic clove

⅜ cup olive oil

about 1¼lb tomatoes

½lb Mozzarella cheese

1¼lb small pasta quills (mezze penne)

a little oil

5 anchovy fillets in oil

2 tbsp capers

ground oregano

a few fresh basil leaves for garnish

Preparation and cooking time: about 30 minutes

Place the garlic clove in a bowl with the olive oil and leave to infuse for a few minutes. Wash and dry the tomatoes and slice them, cutting each slice into 4 pieces. Dice the Mozzarella cheese.

Cook the pasta until *al dente* in salted boiling water. Drain thoroughly and spread out on a tray. Sprinkle with a little oil and leave to cool.

Drain the anchovy fillets and chop them coarsely. When the pasta is cold, place it in a large salad bowl and stir in the pieces of tomato, the cubes of Mozzarella cheese, the chopped anchovy fillets and the capers. Sprinkle with plenty of dried oregano and a pinch of salt. Dress with the oil in which the garlic had been soaking. Stir thoroughly, garnishing with a few leaves of fresh basil and serve.

Oriental Sauce for Pasta Tubes

Sogo all'Orientale per Sedanini Rigati

1 medium onion

1 garlic clove

4-5 sprigs fresh parsley

olive oil

5oz canned tuna

12 canned anchovy fillets in oil

¾lb fluted pasta tubes (sedanini rigati)

½ bouillon cube

1 tsp soy sauce

grated Parmesan cheese

Chop the onion, garlic and parsley finely together. Sweat the mixture in 6 tablespoons of olive oil, then add the tuna and anchovies. Fry gently, using a fork to break up the fish. Cook and drain the pasta when it is *al dente* and tip it into the pan with the sauce, keeping the heat fairly high. Dissolve the bouillon cube and soy sauce in ⅔ cup of the pasta cooking water, add this and let it soak in for a couple of minutes. Serve sprinkled with plenty of Parmesan cheese.

■PASTA & PIZZA■PASTA & PIZZA■

Herb Sauce for Thin Noodles

Sugo di Biete per Trenette

1¾lb fresh herbs, basil, thyme, oregano, parsley

⅜ cup good olive oil

1 large garlic clove

1-1¼lb thin noodles (trenette)

½ cup grated Emmental cheese

Clean the herbs. Put the oil to heat in a small pan with the crushed garlic, and discard the garlic when it has browned. Boil plenty of salted water, add the herbs, cover and bring back to the boil, then add the trenette and cook until *al dente*. Drain the herbs and pasta, dress with the garlic-flavored oil and the grated Emmental cheese and stir well.

Cold pasta in pizzaiola sauce

Pasta Thimbles with Sausage and Carrot

Ditali Rigati con Salsiccia e Carota

To serve 4-5

¼lb carrots

1 celery heart

¼lb onions

butter

olive oil

½lb sausages

½ bouillon cube

½ cup dry rosé wine

¾lb fluted pasta thimbles

grated Parmesan cheese

Preparation and cooking time: about 1 hour

Clean the carrot and celery then cube them and cook for about 12 minutes in boiling salted water. Finely chop the onion and soften it in 2 tablespoons of butter, melted together with 2 tablespoons of olive oil. Skin the sausages and mash the meat with a fork. Add to the lightly fried onion, season with the half crumbled bouillon cube and moisten with the rosé wine. When the wine has evaporated, add the drained cubed vegetables and remove from the heat.

Meanwhile cook the pasta in plenty of salted boiling water until *al dente*. Drain it and pour the sausage and vegetable sauce over it then pour it into a warmed tureen and serve with grated Parmesan.

Orecchiette with Würstchen

Orecchiette Nord-Sud

To serve 4

a bunch of parsley

3 large boiling sausages

¾lb orecchiette pasta

5 tsp butter

3 tbsp olive oil

1 tbsp cornstarch

½ cup milk

½ bouillon cube

grated Pecorino cheese

Preparation and cooking time: about 20 minutes

Wash and dry the parsley, then coarsely chop together with the sausages, first cut up into smaller pieces. Cook the pasta in salted boiling water until it is *al dente*.

Melt the butter in a large skillet together with the olive oil. When the fat is hot, add the parsley and sausage. Dissolve the cornstarch in a little cold water and stir this into the mixture in the skillet. Then pour in the cold milk and flavor with the bouillon cube.

Cook until the sauce is smooth and consistent. Drain the pasta and pour it into the skillet off the heat. Mix carefully then pour the contents of the skillet into a preheated soup tureen and serve at once with the Pecorino cheese sprinkled on top.

Ligurian-style Butterfly Pasta

Farfallette alla Ligure

To serve 4

¼lb small tender borage leaves

4 medium-sized artichokes

¼lb onions

a little parsley

1 large garlic clove

olive oil

⅔ cup stock (or use bouillon cube)

1 sprig fresh thyme

¾lb small pasta butterflies (farfallette)

a handful of grated Peccorino cheese

Preparation and cooking time: 45 minutes

Wash and drain the borage, then coarsely chop. Clean the artichokes, keeping the leaves, cut them in half and then in thin slices. Chop the onions together with the garlic and parsley and sauté in 5 tablespoons of olive oil in a pan. Add the artichokes and borage, stir and fry gently for a few seconds. Boil the stock and pour this into the pan. Flavor with a pinch of thyme and a little freshly ground pepper.

Cover the pan and simmer for about 20 minutes over a moderate heat, until the artichokes are tender and have absorbed all the liquid. Taste and adjust the seasoning. Cook the pasta until it is *al dente* in plenty of salted boiling water. Drain and stir in 2 tablespoons of olive oil, serve with the artichoke and borage sauce and with the grated Pecorino cheese.

*Orecchiette with Würstchen (left); **thin noodles with basil sauce** (right)*

Toasted Flour Sauce for Macaroni

Condimento di Farina Tostata per Maccheroni

1 heaped tablespoon flour

2 heaped tablespoons grated Parmesan cheese

pepper

1 large onion

7 tbsp butter

3 cups macaroni

Pre-heat the oven to 325°F. Put the flour in a small baking tray and brown it in the oven. Spread it out on a plate and add the grated Parmesan cheese and some pepper. Chop the onion finely and fry it in the butter in a covered pan over a low heat, so that the onion becomes slightly golden. Cook and drain the pasta, sprinkle with the flour mixture and then pour on the butter and onion.

Thin Noodles with Basil Sauce

Trenette al Pesto

To serve 4

2 garlic cloves

2 tsp pine-nuts

about 18 fresh basil leaves

½ tbsp Pecorino cheese

½ tbsp grated Parmesan cheese

¼ cup olive oil

2oz fresh French beans

1 potato

¾lb thin noodles (trenette)

Preparation and cooking time: about 45 minutes

Preheat the oven to 350°F. Chop the garlic and place in a mortar with a little salt. Lightly toast the pine-nuts in the oven for 3-4 minutes and leave to cool. Wash and dry the basil leaves and add them one at a time to the mortar, alternating them with a few pine-nuts. Pound with a pestle, gradually adding the grated cheeses. Continue pounding until the ingredients have blended to form a green paste. Transfer the mixture to a bowl and gradually stir in enough olive oil to form a smooth paste.

Heat plenty of water in a saucepan. Top and tail the beans and cut them into small pieces. Dice the potato. Salt the water as soon as it comes to the boil and cook the beans for 10 minutes. Add the diced potato and the pasta. Cook the pasta until *al dente* and drain it, reserving 2 tablespoons of the cooking liquid to dilute the basil sauce. Dress the pasta with the basil sauce, stir well and serve if you like with more grated Parmesan cheese.

Curry Sauce for Hollow Spaghetti

Salsa al Curry per Bucatini

2 large onions

3-4 slices smoked bacon

¼ cup butter

3 tbsp olive oil

⅜ cup Marsala, Port or Madeira wine

½ bouillon cube

1 tsp curry powder

¾-1 lb hollow spaghetti (bucatini)

Slice the onion finely and dice the bacon. Melt the butter with the oil in a wide pan, add the onion and bacon and lightly brown them. Pour in the fortified wine, stirring with a wooden spoon, then lower the heat and simmer for about 10 minutes. Stir from time to time, gradually adding the crumbled half-bouillon cube and the curry powder. Cook and drain the pasta, tip it into the sauce, stir and serve.

Pasta Ribbons with Piquant Tuna Sauce

Fettuccine Ricce al Tonno

To serve 4-5

½ small onion

1 garlic clove

1 sprig parsley

3 tbsp olive oil

6oz canned tuna in oil

5 tsp butter

1½ tbsp flour

1¼ cups stock (or use 1 bouillon cube)

white pepper

1 small pimiento in vinegar

10 capers in vinegar

¾ lb scalloped pasta ribbons (fettucine)

Preparation and cooking time: about 40 minutes

Chop the onion with 1 garlic clove and a parsley sprig. Lightly fry them in the oil in a small pan without browning. When the onion is softened, drain the tuna and mash it roughly with a fork, then add it to the lightly fried mixture and leave on the heat for a few more minutes.

Prepare a smooth Béchamel sauce by melting the butter in another pan, stirring in the flour and adding the hot stock; season with a grinding of white pepper. Mix the sauce with the tuna mixture and keep the sauce warm in a hot *bain-marie*. Roughly chop the drained pimiento and the drained capers and then add them to the sauce. Cook the pasta in salted boiling water until *al dente*. Drain well and pour the tuna sauce over it. Pour the pasta into a large warmed tureen or serving dish and serve at once.

The pasta suggested is the one which is most suited to this type of sauce; however, you can also obtain excellent results by using other kinds of wide egg noodles such as pappardelle.

Pasta ribbons with piquant tuna sauce

Pasta Butterflies with Chicken and Shrimp Sauce

Farfalle con pollo e Gamberetti

To serve 1

½ small onion

1 tbsp butter

small chicken breast

few shelled shrimp

1 tbsp Cognac

2 tbsp dry white wine

⅜ cup chicken stock

½ tsp cornstarch

¼ cup cream

1 cup pasta butterflies (farfalle)

1 sprig parsley and 1 shrimp for garnish

Preparation and cooking time: about 40 minutes

Finely chop the onion and soften it gently, without browning, in the butter. Meanwhile, finely mince the trimmed chicken breast and shrimp. Add them to the onion and let them cook over a low heat, stirring frequently with a wooden spoon. Then moisten with the Cognac and, when it has evaporated almost entirely, pour in the white wine.

. When the wine has been absorbed almost completely, pour in the cold chicken stock, in which you have dissolved half a teaspoon of cornstarch, and the cream. Stir and simmer gently on a very low heat for a few minutes, then liquidize in the blender to obtain a smooth and creamy sauce. Season with pepper, adjust the salt to taste and keep it warm in a *bain-marie*.

Heat 2 pints of water in a saucepan and salt it when it starts to boil. Plunge in the pasta and cook until *al dente*. Drain and pour over the chicken and shrimp sauce. If you like, garnish with a sprig of parsley and a shrimp. Serve at once.

Pasta butterflies with chicken and shrimp sauce

Pasta with Tuna and Bell Peppers

"Sedani" al Tonno e Peperone

To serve 4

1 small onion

olive oil

1 red bell pepper weighing about ¾lb

4oz canned tuna

¾lb short macaroni

¾ cup ready-made tomato sauce

1 bouillon cube

1 sprig fresh parsley

a little grated Pecorino cheese

Preparation and cooking time: about 25 minutes

Finely chop the onion and fry gently in 3 tablespoons of olive oil until transparent. Meanwhile wash the pepper and cut it in half, discarding the stalk and seeds. Cut it into short, thick strips and add them to the onion and cook for a few minutes.

Drain the tuna, break it into pieces with a fork and add it to the pan. Cook the pasta until *al dente* in plenty of salted boiling water. Add the tomato sauce and the crumbled bouillon cube to the tuna mixture and cook on a low heat.

Drain the pasta, pour it into a tureen and dress with the prepared sauce. Top with chopped parsley and serve immediately with the grated Pecorino cheese.

■PASTA & PIZZA ■PASTA & PIZZA■

Mascarpone Sauce for Thin Noodles

Sugo al Mascarpone per Tagliolini

¼lb raw ham

⅝ cup Mascarpone cheese

1 tbsp Worcestershire sauce

¾lb thin noodles (tagliolini)

¼ cup grated Parmesan cheese

¼ cup grated Gruyère cheese

Cut the ham into fine strips. Warm the Mascarpone in a wide saucepan with the Worcestershire sauce and the ham over a low heat, stirring with a wooden spoon. Boil the noodles in salted water until *al dente*, drain them, tip them into the sauce, add the grated cheeses, stir round and serve at once.

Orecchiette with Tomato and Sausage Ragout

Orecchiette con Pomodoro e Salsiccia

To serve 4-5

1 small onion

1 stick celery

1 small carrot

2oz bacon

6 tbsp butter

1 garlic clove

1 sprig basil

3-4 sprigs parsley

¼lb skinned sausages

½ cup dry white wine

flour

1lb ripe tomatoes

1lb orecchiette pasta

olive oil

4 tbsp mild Pecorino cheese, grated

Preparation and cooking time: about 2 hours

Finely chop together the onion, celery and carrot and fry with the diced bacon in the butter in a small saucepan. Add a large garlic clove (to be removed and thrown away later), a sprig of basil and 3-4 sprigs of parsley, tied in a small bunch. Add the sausage meat mashed with a fork. Moisten with the wine and let it evaporate almost completely. Then sprinkle with a teaspoon of flour. Chop the tomatoes and purée them. Add them to the pan. Stir, salt and pepper lightly and cook over a very low heat for about 1½ hours, moistening when the sauce becomes too thick with a small amount of hot water or stock.

About 30 minutes before the ragout is ready cook the pasta until *al dente* in plenty of salted boiling water. Drain the orecchiette and mix immediately with 3 tablespoons of olive oil. Add the ragout, discarding the garlic and the small bunch of seasoning herbs. Sprinkle with the Pecorino cheese, mix once more and serve.

Pasta Ribbons with Mushrooms

Fettuccia Riccia ai Funghi

To serve 1

1 thick slice onion

a few fresh sprigs of parsley

1 garlic clove

2 tbsp butter

1 cep mushroom

1 tbsp dry Marsala wine

¼ bouillon cube

½ tsp cornstarch

2 tbsp milk

¼lb scalloped pasta ribbons (fettuccia)

Preparation and cooking time: about 30 minutes

Finely chop together the onion, a few parsley sprigs and a small garlic clove. Soften in the butter, melted in a small pan. Meanwhile, scrape the dirt from the stem of a very fresh, firm cep mushroom and wash or wipe the cap with a damp cloth. Slice thinly and add the slices to the onion mixture. Sauté for a few minutes, stirring gently with a wooden spoon.

Next, moisten with the dry Marsala wine and season with a quarter of a bouillon cube. Dissolve half a teaspoon of cornstarch in the cold milk and add it to the slices of mushroom, stirring with a wooden spoon. Leave the sauce on a very low heat for 4-5 minutes.

Heat water in a saucepan and salt it when it starts to boil. Plunge in the pasta and cook until *al dente*. Drain, and pour over the mushroom sauce to which you have added, at the last moment, half a teaspoon of chopped parsley.

Pasta ribbons with mushrooms

Pasta with Lentils
Pasta e Lenticche

To serve 6

½lb dried lentils

¼lb potatoes

2 sage leaves

1 large garlic clove

a little parsley

¼lb peeled tomatoes

olive oil

2 bouillon cubes

¼lb pasta shells

3 tbsp grated Parmesan cheese

Preparation and cooking time: 2½ hours

Pick over the lentils to make sure there are no impurities or grit. Wash under warm running water and place in a saucepan. Peel and dice the potatoes and put these in too. Chop the sage, garlic and parsley and add these too. Purée the tomatoes and add these together with 3 tablespoons of olive oil. Stir and pour in 4½ pints of cold water and bring to the boil. Turn the heat down to the minimum as soon as the mixture starts to boil, add the bouillon cubes, cover and simmer for about 2 hours, stirring from time to time.

When the cooking is completed, purée a ladleful of the mixture and return the purée to the pan.

Stir in and bring back to the boil. Then add the pasta, stir and cook until the pasta is *al dente*. Remove from the heat, add a little freshly ground pepper, 3 tablespoons of olive oil and the Parmesan cheese. Serve, and sprinkle each portion with chopped parsley.

Spaghetti with Frankfurters and Olives
Spaghetti con Würstel e Olive

To serve 4

¼lb onions, chopped

butter

olive oil

4 skinless frankfurter sausages, sliced

brandy

8 green olives, pitted and sliced

½ bouillon cube

cornstarch

¾lb spaghetti

¼ cup grated Parmesan cheese

Preparation and cooking time: about 30 minutes

Sauté the onions in a large knob of butter and 2 tablespoons of olive oil. Add the slices of frankfurter sausage and cook for a few minutes. Sprinkle generously with brandy and flambé. Add the olives and cook for a further 2-3 minutes.

Pour on about ⅔ cup of boiling water and add the crumbled half bouillon cube. Dissolve a large pinch of cornstarch in 2 tablespoons of cold water and pour into the pan, stirring constantly. Simmer for about 10 minutes or until the liquid has reduced to form a light, creamy sauce.

Cook the spaghetti in plenty of salted boiling water, drain and cover with the sauce. Sprinkle with grated Parmesan cheese and serve immediately.

Roman-style Pizza
Pizza alla Romana

To serve 1

flour

½lb bread or pizza dough

2 fresh medium tomatoes, peeled

3oz Mozzarella cheese

a pinch of oregano

3 fresh basil leaves, chopped

2 tbsp grated Pecorino cheese

olive oil

Preparation and cooking time: 30 minutes plus any defrosting time

Preheat the oven to 400-425°F
Flour a pastry-board and roll the dough, defrosted if necessary, into a ball, then flatten it out to an 8-inch round. Lightly oil a baking tray and place the dough on it. With your fingertips, press down the dough just inside the edge to give it a slightly raised edge.

De-seed the tomatoes and finely slice them. Spread over the pizza. Lightly sprinkle with salt and pepper, a pinch of oregano and the basil. Sprinkle the Pecorino on top and pour over a thin trickle of olive oil. Bake in the oven for 12-14 minutes until the pizza is golden brown. Pour over a thin trickle of oil before serving hot.

Roman-style pizza

Artichoke Turnovers
Panzarotti di Carciofi

To serve 4

1lb pizza dough

6 small artichokes

1 small onion

½ garlic clove

butter

olive oil

a little chopped parsley

¼ bouillon cube

¼lb salami

¼lb Emmental cheese

oil for frying

Preparation and cooking time: about 1¼ hours

Defrost the dough if necessary. Clean the artichokes, removing the stalks (they can be used for another recipe) and the tips. Remove the outer leaves until you reach the heart. Cut in half and remove the choke using a small corer.

Finely slice the onion and garlic and fry in a large knob of butter and 2 tablespoons of olive oil. Add the artichoke hearts. After a few seconds add the parsley, crumble in the bouillon cube, add a little pepper and about 6 tablespoons of boiling water. Shake the pan, cover and simmer for 25 minutes, moistening with more boiling water if necessary. The artichokes should be tender and dry in the end. Plunge the pan into cold water to cool.

Cut the salami into 12 sticks, likewise the Emmental cheese. Roll out the pizza dough to ⅛ inch and from this cut out 12 5-inch rounds, kneading and rolling out the trimmings again. On each round of dough place half an artichoke heart, a stick of salami and a stick of Emmental. Then fold in two and press down the edges to seal.

Heat plenty of oil in a deep-frying pan and when it is hot, fry the turnovers a few at a time, until they are brown all over. Remove from the pan with a slotted spoon and drain on paper towels. Serve at once.

Corn, Ham and Olive Pizza
Schiacciata di Maïs, Prosciutto e Olive

To serve 4

1 small onion, peeled

1½ garlic cloves

olive oil

½ lb peeled tomatoes

sugar

6 green olives in brine

¼lb ham in one slice

2oz rindless Emmental cheese

2 tbsp butter

1 cup canned yellow corn

a pinch of ginger

11oz pizza dough

a pinch of oregano

Preparation and cooking time: about 15 minutes plus any defrosting time

Preheat the oven to 400°F. Finely slice the onion and garlic clove. Fry in a saucepan with 3 tablespoons of olive oil without browning. Then put the tomatoes through a food processor with the medium disk, and add these to the pan with a little salt and a pinch of sugar. Mix and simmer gently for about 15 minutes.

Pit and quarter the olives. Cut the ham into short strips. Finely slice the Emmental cheese. Heat a skillet with the butter and ½ garlic clove. Fry the corn for a few seconds and season with a pinch of ginger.

Roll out the dough, defrosted if necessary, into a 10-inch round and place on an oiled baking tray. Pour over the tomato sauce and pour the corn on top. Arrange the ham, olives and cheese over the pizza and sprinkle with oregano. Pour on a thin trickle of olive oil. Bake for about 15 minutes until golden brown. Transfer to a serving plate or a wooden chopping board and serve immediately, with a seasonal mixed salad.

Piquant Mini-Pizzas
Pizzette Piccanti

To serve 6

6 frozen mini-pizzas

olive oil

capers in wine vinegar

6 anchovy fillets in oil

12 stuffed green olives

Preparation and cooking time: about 20 minutes

Preheat the oven to 400°F. Place the mini-pizzas on an oven tray and moisten each one with a little oil, then place them in the oven, still frozen, for 7-8 minutes. In the meantime drain the capers, the anchovies and the olives, and slice the olives into small rounds.

About 2 minutes before the pizzas are ready, when the cheese has melted but not browned, remove them from the oven and place on each one 4-5 capers, 1 fillet of anchovy, and 2 sliced olives. Moisten with a little oil, and put them back in the oven for the last 2 minutes, taking care that they do not brown too much.

Remove the mini-pizzas from the oven and, after arranging them on a serving plate or tray, serve them hot as an appetizer or cut into quarters, with an apéritif.

Corn, ham and olive pizza (far right)

Egg Pizza

Pizza all'Uovo

To serve 4

flour

¾-1 lb pizza dough

olive oil

¾lb firm, ripe tomatoes

oregano

1 medium zucchini

¼lb Mozzarella cheese

slice lean ham

a few fennel leaves

2 tbsp grated mild Pecorino cheese

1 egg

Preparation and cooking time: about 45 minutes plus any defrosting time

Preheat the oven to 400°F. Flour a pastry-board and roll the dough, defrosted if necessary, into a ball, then flatten it out to a round about 12 inches in diameter. Lightly oil a baking pan and place the dough on it. With your fingertips, press down the dough just inside the edge all the way round to give it a raised edge.

Blanch the tomatoes in boiling salted water for a few seconds and peel them. Cut them in half, remove the seeds, then chop them coarsely. Season them with salt, pepper and a pinch of oregano. Trim and finely slice the zucchini. Bring back to the boil the water in which the tomatoes were blanched, and put in the zucchini slices for a bare 2 minutes. Remove them with a slotted spoon and drain carefully. Lay them out to dry on a large plate covered with a double layer of paper towels. Dice the Mozzarella into small cubes of about ½ inch. Cut the ham into equal matchstick-sized lengths.

Spread the tomatoes over the surface of the pizza dough and arrange the rounds of zucchini around the outside edge, slightly overlapping each other. Then make a circle of Mozzarella, followed by the ham. Place a few young fennel leaves on the ham. Pour over a trickle of olive oil and sprinkle with the grated Pecorino cheese. Bake in the oven for about 15 minutes.

Meanwhile, heat a skillet with 2 tablespoons of olive oil. Break the egg into a bowl, keeping the yolk intact. When the oil is hot, put in the egg and cook slowly until the white is firm. Cut the egg out with a smooth round cookie cutter 4 inches in diameter. Sprinkle very lightly with salt and remove from the pan with a flexible spatula. Remove the pizza from the oven and place the egg in the center. Garnish with more fennel leaves and serve immediately.

Mushroom Pizza

Pizza ai Funghi

To serve 4

¾lb mushrooms

juice of 1 lemon

olive oil

1 garlic clove

flour

1lb bread dough

a little chopped parsley

Preparation and cooking time: 45 minutes

Preheat the oven to 400-425°F. Peel or wipe the mushrooms and trim the stalks. As they are ready, put them in a bowl of cold water to which the lemon juice has been added. Heat 3 tablespoons of olive oil in a skillet. Crush the garlic and put it in the hot olive oil. Fry until the garlic browns and then remove from the skillet. Slice the mushrooms directly into the hot oil and sauté for 3-4 minutes, seasoning with salt and pepper.

Flour a pastry-board and roll the dough into a ball, then flatten it out to a round about 12 inches in diameter. Lightly oil a baking tray and place the dough on it. With your fingertips press down the dough just inside the edge to give it a bigger crust. Spread the mushrooms over the pizza and pour over a trickle of olive oil. Sprinkle with chopped parsley and place in the oven for about 15 minutes. Serve hot from the oven, cut into quarters.

■PASTA & PIZZA■PASTA & PIZZA■

Farmhouse Pizza with Ham and Cheese

Pizza Rustica con Prosciutto e Formaggio

To serve 8

¾ lb puff pastry

flour

butter

breadcrumbs

¼ lb ham, sliced

1 large firm tomato

2oz Mozzarella cheese

a few sprigs fresh parsley

2 large fresh basil leaves

2 eggs

5 tbsp whipping cream

½ cup grated Emmental cheese

nutmeg

a pinch of powdered marjoram

Preparation and cooking time: about 1¼ hours plus any defrosting time

Preheat the oven to 375°F. Defrost the pastry if frozen. Roll it out on a lightly floured pastry-board until it is large enough to line a shallow, buttered 11 x 7-inch pie dish. Prick the pastry with a fork, sprinkle the base with breadcrumbs and then make an even layer of ham.

Now prepare the filling: Blanch the tomato in lightly salted boiling water for a few seconds then immerse it in cold water. Peel, cut in half and remove the seeds. Cut the tomato into irregular pieces. Dice the Mozzarella cheese and finely chop the parsley with the basil. In a bowl, whisk the eggs with the cream, the grated Emmental cheese, salt, pepper and a little grated nutmeg. Add a pinch of marjoram and then put the chopped tomato into the bowl together with the diced Mozzarella and the chopped parsley and basil. Mix well and pour into the pie dish. Bake in the lower part of the oven for about 35 minutes and serve hot from the oven.

Farmhouse pizza

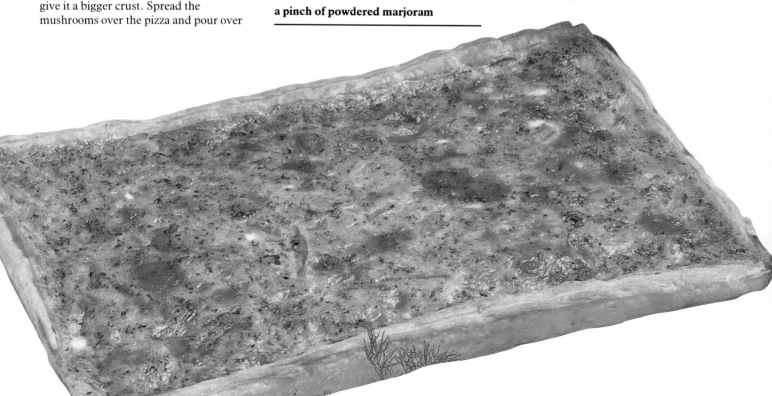

Pizza with Capers
Pizza "in Fiore"

To serve 4-6

7 tbsp olive oil

1 package ready-made pizza mix

a little flour

¼lb Mozzarella cheese

1 thick slice ham

24 capers in vinegar

a few fresh basil leaves

Preparation and cooking time: about 40 minutes

Oil a 10-inch round baking pan. Pour the pizza mix into a bowl, add the amount of cold water indicated on the package and 2 tablespoons of olive oil; knead until you obtain a smooth, elastic dough. Roll out on a lightly floured pastry-board until large enough to cover the bottom and come part-way up the sides of the pan. Spread the tomato from the package over the dough, salt and sprinkle with any herbs included in the package.

Preheat the oven to the temperature indicated on the package. Slice the Mozzarella cheese and place the slices like wheel spokes on the tomato sauce; cut the slice of ham into little squares and place them with the well-drained capers between the slices of Mozzarella cheese.

Pepper lightly and sprinkle with 3-4 tablespoons of olive oil. Place the pizza in the preheated oven for the length of time shown on the package; then put it on a serving board, garnish with fresh basil leaves and serve immediately, cutting it into 4 or 6 slices in front of the guests.

*Pizza of many flavors (above); **pizza with capers** (below)*

Naples-style Pizza
Pizza alla Napoletana

To serve 1-2

flour

7oz pizza dough

olive oil

2-3 fresh or canned medium tomatoes, peeled

a pinch of oregano

2-3 large fresh basil leaves

1 garlic clove, green shoot removed

Preparation and cooking time: about 30 minutes, plus any defrosting time.

Preheat the oven to 400-425°F. Flour a pastry-board and roll the dough into a ball, then flatten it out to an 8-inch round. Lightly oil a baking tray and place the dough on it. With your fingertips, press down the dough just inside the edge to give it a raised edge.

Chop the tomatoes, season with a little salt and a pinch of oregano and spread over the pizza. Wipe the basil leaves with a damp cloth and finely chop them before sprinkling them over the tomato. Finely chop or slice half a garlic clove and sprinkle this on too. Do not spread these ingredients right to the edges of the dough. Drizzle on plenty of good olive oil and bake for about 12 minutes. Serve straight from the oven on a flat, preheated plate.

Pizza of Many Flavors

Pizza Capricciosa

To serve 4

flour

¾-1 lb pizza dough

½ lb peeled tomatoes

a pinch of oregano

¼ cup diced Mozzarella cheese

3 fresh basil leaves, chopped

20 fresh mussels

6 artichoke hearts in oil, cut into quarters

6 black olives, pits removed and cut into quarters

5 tbsp clams

8 tbsp baby mushrooms in oil

3 tbsp capers

2 thin slices ham, cut into strips

a few slivers Emmental cheese

a little chopped parsley

olive oil

Preparation and cooking time: about 40 minutes plus any defrosting time

Preheat the oven to 400-425°F. Flour a pastry-board and roll the dough, defrosted if necessary, into a ball, then flatten it out to a 12-inch round. Lightly oil a baking tray and place the dough on it. With your fingertips, press down the dough just inside the edge to give it a raised edge. De-seed the tomatoes and slice finely. Spread over the pizza. Lightly sprinkle with salt and flavor with a pinch of oregano.

Top the pizza in 8 divisions with 8 separate toppings: the Mozzarella cheese, sprinkled with the chopped basil, mussels, artichoke hearts, olives, clams, the well-drained mushrooms, the well-drained capers and finally the strips of ham and slivers of Emmental. Sprinkle with the parsley and pour over a trickle of olive oil. Bake for about 15 minutes and serve at once.

Naples-style pizza

Tortelloni with Zucchini
Tortelloni di Zucchini

To serve 6

1 lb zucchini

1¾ cups tomatoes

2¾ cups all-purpose flour

½ cup button mushrooms

¼ cup butter

¼ cup grated Parmesan cheese

5 eggs

fresh basil

garlic

dried marjoram

olive oil

nutmeg

Preparation and cooking time: 2 hours

1) Clean and dice the zucchini. Clean and slice the mushrooms. Heat ¼ pint of oil in large fry pan with a garlic clove (to be removed before brown). Add the mushrooms and the zucchini and cook for 20 minutes. Allow to cool and then blend them with a food processor. Stir in the Parmesan, 2 egg yolks, a sprinkle of marjoram, a level tablespoon of flour, a sprinkle of nutmeg and salt and pepper.

2) Mix the remaining flour with salt and 3 eggs, and work into a dough.

3) Cut the strips into 2 inch squares. Put a teaspoon of the zucchini mixture onto each square.

4) Fold the tortelloni into triangles, and firmly seal the edges with your fingertips.

5) Peel and dice the tomatoes, melt the butter in a large fry pan and add the tomatoes, salt and 7 chopped basil leaves (or 1 teaspoon dry basil).

6) Cook the sauce for 5 minutes. Meanwhile bring to the boil a large pan of salted water. Drop in the tortelloni. Drain them when still underdone (*al dente*) and add to the sauce. Cook together for a few minutes.

Transfer to a soup tureen and serve hot.

1

2

3

4

5

6

SEAFOOD

Italy's long coastlines on the Adriatic and Mediterranean provide a wealth of fish, shellfish and seafood, including white and red fish varieties, scampi, octopus, tuna and squid. A *fritto misto* (mixed fried fish) of locally available seafood is an Italian speciality not to be missed. In imaginative combinations and with delicious sauces, the following recipes make the most of a delicious variety of seafoods.

Golden Jumbo Shrimp
Gamberoni Dorati

To serve 4

12 fresh jumbo shrimp

1 small leek

1 small stalk celery

1 small carrot

1 garlic clove

a few sprigs fresh parsley

4 tbsp dry white wine

flour

1 large egg

breadcrumbs

oil for frying

1 bay leaf

1 lemon

Preparation and cooking time: about 40 minutes plus 1 hour's marination

Peel the shrimp and lay them in a shallow bowl. Finely slice the leek, celery and carrot and arrange on top of the shrimp. Coarsely chop the garlic, removing the green shoot if necessary, with the parsley and add these to the shrimp. Pour over the wine and lightly sprinkle with salt. Cover the dish with plastic wrap and leave to marinate for 1 hour in a cool place or the least cold part of the refrigerator.

Remove the shrimp from the marinade, shaking off the other ingredients without wiping them, then dip them first in the flour, next in the beaten egg and finally in the breadcrumbs. Ensure that the shrimp are coated all over with these ingredients. Heat the oil with a bay leaf in a skillet, and when it is hot, pour in the shrimp and fry until they are golden brown all over. Use 2 forks to turn them over carefully while cooking.

Drain the shrimp from the oil and lay them on a plate covered with a double layer of paper towels to absorb any excess oil. Then arrange on a serving dish, sprinkle lightly with salt and garnish with slices of lemon.

Golden jumbo shrimp

Mixed Shellfish
"Capriccio" Marino

To serve 4

12 scallops

½lb shrimp

1-1¼lb mussels

5 tbsp olive oil

3 garlic cloves

a little lemon juice

1 small onion

a small bunch of parsley

5 tsp butter

¼ cup brandy

⅜ cup dry white wine

½ bouillon cube

Worcestershire sauce

Preparation and cooking time: about 45 minutes

Open the scallops using an oyster knife and remove the molluscs from their shells. Carefully separate the membranes which surround the fish and rinse the molluscs under running water to remove any sand.

Carefully peel the shrimp. Scrub the mussel shells and rinse under running water. Place the mussels in a skillet with 2 tablespoons of olive oil, 2 cloves of garlic and a few drops of lemon juice. Cover the skillet and heat briskly to open the shells. Remove the molluscs from their shells and place on a plate. Strain the cooking juices.

Finely chop the onion, a garlic clove and a small handful of parsley and fry gently in the butter and 3 tablespoons of olive oil. Add the scallops, shrimp and mussels and cook for a few minutes. Pour over the brandy and dry white wine. Season with the crumbled half bouillon cube and a generous dash of Worcestershire sauce. Add 3-4 tablespoons of the strained mussel cooking juices and simmer until a light sauce has formed. Stir in a little chopped parsley and serve.

Gray Mullet with Shellfish

Cefali con Crema di Molluschi

To serve 4

¾lb mussels

½lb clams

4 grey mullet, together weighing about 2lb

2 garlic cloves

a handful of parsley

1 bay leaf

olive oil

1 small onion

⅔ cup sparkling white wine

a pinch of cornstarch

¼ bouillon cube

breadcrumbs

1 sprig rosemary

Preparation and cooking time: about 1 hour plus 1 hour's soaking

Scrape the mussel shells clean with a knife and then leave to soak in cold water for about 1 hour, together with the clams. Cut off the fins and clean the mullet. Rinse and dry thoroughly.

Place the mussels and clams in a skillet with 2 lightly crushed garlic cloves, a few sprigs of parsley and a small bay leaf. Pour in 2 tablespoons of olive oil, cover the pan and heat gently to open the shells. Remove from the heat and leave to cool. Remove the molluscs from their shells and strain the juices.

Finely chop the onion and a small handful of parsley and fry gently in 4 tablespoons of olive oil. Add the molluscs and cook for a few minutes. Pour over half the sparkling wine and 4-5 tablespoons of the strained juices in which the cornstarch has been dissolved. Season with the crumbled quarter bouillon cube and simmer for a few minutes. Place in the blender and blend vigorously. Pour back into the pan and keep hot.

Coat the mullet in breadcrumbs. Heat 5 tablespoons of olive oil and a sprig of rosemary in a skillet and fry the mullet until golden brown on both sides. Sprinkle with salt and pepper and pour over the remaining sparkling wine. Allow the wine to evaporate and then transfer the fish to a warmed dish. Top with the creamed shellfish and garnish as desired.

Mixed shellfish

Taranto Style Mussels
Cozze Tarantine

To serve 4

1-1¼lb tomatoes

2½ lb fresh mussels

1 garlic clove

plenty of olive oil

¾ lb potatoes

½ lb zucchini

¾ lb onion

2 tbsp grated Pecorino cheese

1 sprig fresh parsley

Preparation and cooking time: about 1¾ hours

Parboil the tomatoes and then peel and slice them thinly, discarding the seeds. Scrape and rinse the mussels and place them in a skillet with the sliced garlic clove and 2 tablespoons of olive oil. Cover the pan and heat briskly to open the shells. Discard the empty half of each shell and place the half containing the mollusc on a plate. Strain the cooking juices into a bowl.

Peel and wash the potatoes and slice them, not too thinly. Top and tail the zucchini and cut them into slices about ⅛ inch thick. Slice the onion very finely.

Preheat the oven to 325°F. Grease a large ovenproof pan or dish with plenty of olive oil and line the bottom of it with a quarter of the onion rings. Arrange all the potato slices on top in one layer. Add another layer of onion rings and sprinkle with salt. Arrange half the mussels on top of the onion rings. Add half the tomatoes and season with pepper and a tablespoon of grated Pecorino cheese. Add another layer of onion rings, then all the zucchini slices and then the rest of the onion. Sprinkle with salt. Add another layer of mussels and top with the remaining tomato and a little pepper.

Sprinkle with another tablespoon of grated Pecorino cheese and pour on all the strained mussel juices and 5-6 tablespoons of oil. Add a few young leaves of parsley and cover the pan with a lid or with aluminum foil. Bake in the oven for about 1 hour or until the potatoes and zucchini are tender. Serve.

Octopus with Tomatoes and Olives
Moscardini, Pomodori e Olive

To serve 4-6

2¼lb fresh small octopuses

1 tender rib celery

1 small onion

1 sprig fresh parsley

2 small garlic cloves

¼ cup olive oil

1-1¼lb tomatoes

1 piece lemon rind

8 green olives in brine, pitted

celery leaves for garnish

Preparation and cooking time: about 2½ hours

Remove the "beak", eyes and viscera from the octopuses' body pouches and discard them. Wash and drain the octopuses. Trim the celery rib and chop it finely with the onion, parsley and garlic. Heat the olive oil in a saucepan and lightly fry the chopped vegetables. Trim, wash and chop the tomatoes and process them in a blender. Add them to the pan, stir the mixture and bring it slowly to the boil.

Beat the octopus tentacles with a wooden meat mallet and stir them into the boiling sauce. Add a piece of lemon rind. Season with a little salt and pepper and bring the mixture back to the boil. Lower the heat, cover the pan and cook for about 1¾ hours, stirring occasionally. If the sauce reduces too much, pour on a little boiling water.

Stir in the olives and cook for 15 minutes more. Test and adjust the seasoning according to taste. Serve topped with a few finely chopped celery leaves.

Stuffed Bream
Pagellini alla Ghiotta

To serve 4

8 small fresh bream

1-2 sprigs fresh parsley

2-3 leaves fresh basil

2 tbsp capers

2 anchovy fillets in oil

a little oregano

7 tbsp fresh white breadcrumbs

1 egg

1 egg, hard-boiled

olive oil

⅓ cup dry white wine

Preparation and cooking time: about 1¼ hours

Cut the fins off and scale and clean the fish. Rinse under running water and dry thoroughly. Finely chop 1 sprig of the parsley, the basil, the capers and the drained anchovy fillets. Stir in a little oregano and 4 tablespoons of breadcrumbs and bind the mixture with a beaten egg. Season with salt and pepper. Stuff the bream with the prepared mixture and sew up with kitchen twine.

Preheat the oven to 375°F. Mix the remaining breadcrumbs with the crumbled yolk of the hard-boiled egg and a tablespoon of olive oil. Arrange the bream in a well-greased ovenproof serving dish. Brush them with olive oil and sprinkle with a little salt. Top with the bread and egg mixture and a little finely chopped parsley. Sprinkle with olive oil and cook in the oven for 25-30 minutes. Pour on the white wine and cover with foil. Return to the oven for about 10 minutes to finish cooking and serve immediately.

Octopus with tomatoes and olives and Taranto style mussels

Red Mullet and Hake with Anchovies

Triglie e Merluzzetti all'Acciuga

To serve 5

5 red mullet, together weighing ¾lb

5 baby hake, together weighing ¾lb

4-5 tbsp olive oil

1 garlic clove

1 sprig parsley

2 anchovy fillets

2 tbsp breadcrumbs

oregano

1 tbsp lemon juice

1 lemon, sliced

a little dry white wine

Preparation and cooking time: about 45 minutes

Scale and de-fin the mullet. Gut the hake and mullet and rinse well under running water and dry.

Oil an ovenproof dish which is large enough to hold all the fish without any overlap. Preheat the oven to 375°F.

Finely chop a large garlic clove, a sprig of parsley and 2 well-drained anchovy fillets and place them in a shallow bowl. Add 2 tablespoons of breadcrumbs, a little oregano and a generous pinch of salt and pepper. Mix.

In another shallow bowl, beat a tablespoon of lemon juice with 3 tablespoons of olive oil and a large pinch of salt to form a smooth sauce. Dip the fish one by one in the sauce and then sprinkle them with the breadcrumb mixture. Arrange on the ovenproof dish, alternating the 2 different types of fish.

Place half-slices of lemon between the heads of the fish and sprinkle with a little olive oil. Cook in the oven for about 15 minutes, pouring on a little white wine halfway through cooking. Serve.

Fried Mixed Seafood

Frittura "Misto Mare"

To serve 4

⅔ cup mayonnaise

juice of ½ lemon

Worcestershire sauce

1 tsp mustard

paprika

1 sprig parsley, finely chopped

2 gherkins, finely chopped

1 tbsp capers, finely chopped

oil for frying

¾lb mixed seafood

½lb squid rings

Preparation and cooking time: about 30 minutes

Mix the mayonnaise and lemon juice and season with a splash of Worcestershire sauce, the mustard and a pinch of paprika. Add the chopped parsley, gherkins and capers to the mayonnaise. Blend to a smooth sauce. Check and adjust seasoning to taste. Pour into a serving bowl or jug.

Heat plenty of oil in a skillet and fry the mixed seafood and squid briskly until crisp and golden (2-3 minutes should be enough). Drain well on paper towels and arrange on a warm plate. Garnish and serve with the prepared sauce.

Red mullet and hake with anchovies

Bream San Marco

Orata "San Marco"

To serve 6

1 gilt-head bream, weighing about 3¼lb

1 small onion, thinly sliced

1 small carrot, thinly sliced

1 small stalk celery, thinly sliced

3 tbsp butter

1 garlic clove

1 small bay leaf

½ cup dry white wine

½ cup fish stock

2-3 whole black peppercorns

olive oil

a handful of fresh parsley

3 anchovy fillets in oil

Worcestershire sauce

1 tbsp mustard

juice of ½ lemon

Preparation and cooking time: about 1 hour

Prepare the fish: Remove the fins, scale carefully and gut. Rinse and dry. Sauté the onion, carrot and celery in 1 tablespoon of the butter. Add the lightly crushed garlic clove and the bay leaf and pour on the white wine and fish stock. Add the whole peppercorns, half-cover the pan and simmer gently until almost all the liquid has been absorbed.

Preheat the oven to 400°F. Arrange half the vegetables on a large sheet of buttered aluminum foil. Lay the fish on top and cover with the remaining vegetables. Season with a pinch of salt and a little olive oil. Wrap the foil around the fish, place on a baking pan and cook in the oven for about 30 minutes.

Meanwhile, finely chop a handful of parsley and the anchovy fillets and place them in a bowl. Add a generous dash of Worcestershire sauce, the mustard, lemon juice and 4 tablespoons of olive oil. Mix carefully, test and adjust the seasoning to taste.

Take the fish from the oven, unwrap it and cut off the head and tail. Discard the vegetables. Divide the fish in half and remove all the bones. Arrange the two fillets on a warmed dish, cover with the prepared sauce, garnish and serve while still hot.

Fried Bogue
Boghe in Tegame

To serve 4

8 bogue, each weighing about 6oz

a handful of parsley

2 garlic cloves

4 basil leaves

4 anchovy fillets in oil

oregano

breadcrumbs

flour

milk

olive oil

3 sage leaves

2 sprigs rosemary

½ cup dry white wine

juice of ½ lemon

Preparation and cooking time: about 45 minutes

Cut off the fins and scale and clean the fish. Wash under cold running water and dry thoroughly.

Finely chop the parsley, garlic, basil and anchovies and place in a bowl. Add a pinch of salt, a pinch of oregano, some freshly ground black pepper and the breadcrumbs, mixing thoroughly. Stuff the fish with the mixture and close the openings without sewing them up. Roll the fish in flour, then in milk and finally in breadcrumbs.

Heat a large quantity of olive oil in a pan which is able to hold all the fish. Add the sage and rosemary. When the oil is very hot, put in the fish. Allow them to fry and brown on one side then, using a spatula, turn them and cook the other side. Then pour in the wine and the strained juice of half a lemon. Shake the pan, add salt, pepper, and cook until the liquid has reduced by half.

Transfer the fish to a warm serving dish, pour over the liquid from the pan and serve at once. For garnish you can use Venus clams, opened over a high heat, then seasoned with very finely chopped parsley and garlic, a little olive oil, and freshly ground black pepper.

Mussels and Jumbo Shrimp
Datteri e Mazzancolle "Sapore di Mare"

To serve 4

1¼lb mussels

12 jumbo shrimp

1 shallot

1 small carrot

1 stalk celery

1 garlic clove

2 whole black peppercorns

¼ bay leaf

3-4 tbsp dry white wine

3-4 tbsp olive oil

1 tbsp brandy

½ tsp cornstarch

a few chives

Preparation and cooking time: about 1¼ hours

Thoroughly scrub the mussels and soak them in cold salted water for at least 30 minutes. Peel the shrimp and place in a small saucepan. Add the chopped shallot, the carrot and celery, a lightly crushed garlic clove, peppercorns and a quarter of a bay leaf. Pour on 2¼ cups of water and the wine. Season with a little salt, half-cover the pan and simmer gently for about 15 minutes. Strain the liquid into a skillet and leave the shrimp to cool.

Thoroughly drain the mussels and place them in the skillet with the strained liquid. Cover the pan and heat briskly to open the shells. Place the mussels on a plate, cover and keep hot.

Strain the remaining liquid into a bowl. Wash and dry the skillet and heat 3-4 tablespoons of olive oil in it. Fry the shrimp gently for a few minutes and then pour on a tablespoon of brandy. When the brandy has evaporated, add the strained liquid. Stir in half a teaspoon of cornstarch dissolved in 2 tablespoons of cold water. Simmer for a few minutes and then add the mussels. Stir and cook for 3-4 minutes. Sprinkle with the chopped chives and serve with hot toasted slices of home-made bread.

Fried Shrimp with Herbs

Gamberetti in "Scapece"

To serve 4-6

oil for frying

1-1¼lb shrimp, peeled and washed

flour

2 shallots

2 fresh sage leaves

1 sprig fresh chervil

⅜ cup olive oil

⅝ cup white wine vinegar

⅝ cup dry white wine

2-3 whole black peppercorns

1 bay leaf

parsley for garnish

Preparation and cooking time: about 1 hour plus 12 hours' chilling

Heat plenty of oil in a large skillet. Coat the shrimp in flour and fry them rapidly in the oil until crisp and golden. Drain on paper towels and sprinkle with salt.

Finely chop the shallots, 2 large sage leaves and a few small leaves of chervil and sauté in the olive oil. Pour on the vinegar and white wine and add the peppercorns, bay leaf and a little salt. Simmer on a moderate heat for about 10 minutes.

Meanwhile, arrange the shrimp in a serving dish, strain the prepared sauce and pour it over the shrimp. Leave to cool at room temperature and then cover the dish and chill in the refrigerator for at least 12 hours before serving. Garnish with a few leaves of parsley and serve.

*Fried bogue (left); **fried shrimp with herbs** (top right) and **mussels and jumbo shrimp***

Hake in Velvety Sauce with Herbs

Naselli Supremi

To serve 6

3 very fresh hake, each weighting ¾-1lb

1 medium onion

1 stick celery

3 garlic cloves

2 bay leaves

fresh parsley

6 black peppercorns

1 cup dry white wine

flour

½ cup vegetable oil

2 fresh basil leaves

1 sprig fresh tarragon

6 tbsp butter

½ cup fresh whipping cream

Preparation and cooking time: about 2 hours

Remove the fins from the fish and clean them. Wash and dry the fish, cut off their heads, remove all the bones, and skin the fillets. Put the heads, bones, and skin in a small saucepan with the halved onion, the chopped celery, 2 crushed garlic cloves, 2 bay leaves, 4-5 parsley sprigs, and 6 black peppercorns, the white wine, and 2½ cups of cold water, salt lightly and bring slowly to the boil. Skim the liquid and simmer it, uncovered, for about 15 minutes. Strain it through a fine sieve.

Roll the 6 fillets of hake in the flour and shake off the excess, then fry them gently in the heated vegetable oil and 1 lightly crushed garlic clove. When they are cooked and lightly browned, remove the fillets and drain them on paper towels. Preheat the oven to 400°F.

Finely chop a handful of parsley with 2 basil leaves and the leaves of a sprig of tarragon. In a small saucepan melt 4 tablespoons of the butter, and mix in ⅓ cup of flour; pour on to this *roux* 2½ cups of the prepared fish stock, pouring it in a trickle, stirring constantly to obtain a smooth sauce. Bring to the boil stirring all the time; remove from the heat, mix in the cream and the chopped herbs, taste and, if necessary, adjust the seasoning.

Pour a third of the sauce into an ovenproof pan large enough to contain the fish fillets, arrange them in the dish and cover them with the remaining sauce, then sprinkle with the rest of the butter, melted in a *bain-marie*. Place the pan in the oven for about 15 minutes, then serve.

Lenten pie

Lenten Pie

Sfogliata di Magro

To serve 6-8

¾ lb puff pastry

1 medium onion

1 large garlic clove

a little parsley

4 tbsp olive oil

¾lb frozen squid (rings and tentacles)

3 tbsp dry white wine

½lb peeled tomatoes

1¾ cups frozen peas

about ¼ cup butter

2½ tbsp flour

½ cup milk

nutmeg

2 eggs

breadcrumbs

Preparation and cooking time: 1¾ hours plus any thawing time

Defrost the pastry if using frozen. Slice the onions, chop a large garlic clove and a small bunch of parsley and soften them in the oil. Then add the frozen squid, lower the heat to simmer, cover the pan and allow to thaw, stirring from time to time. Now add the wine, put the tomatoes through a food processor and add these, with the frozen peas. Add a little salt and pepper, stir, then cook in a covered pan over a moderate heat for about 30 minutes, when the squid and the peas should be quite tender and the liquid thickened. Preheat the oven to 400°F.

While the squid and pea mixture is cooling, prepare a thick Béchamel sauce. Melt 2 tablespoons of butter in a pan, add the flour and cook for a minute or two; pour in the boiling milk, add salt and nutmeg and cook gently for a few minutes. Add the sauce to the squid and peas, then the beaten eggs and a little salt.

Line a buttered 9-inch round pie dish with the puff pastry. Prick the base and sprinkle with a heaping tablespoon of breadcrumbs, then pour in the prepared mixture and bake for about 30 minutes.

Fried Sardines with Cheese

Sarde al Formaggio, Fritte

To serve 4

16 large fresh sardines

⅜ cup cold milk

2½ cups fresh breadcrumbs

½ cup grated Parmesan cheese

oil for frying

1 bay leaf

1 large garlic clove

Preparation and cooking time: about 1 hour

Lighly scale then gut the sardines. Wash quickly under running water and dry. Slit right down to the tail and remove the backbone and all the small bones, but leave on the head and the tail. Sprinkle with salt and pepper and dip them in the milk. Mix the breadcrumbs and grated Parmesan cheese and thoroughly coat the sardines in this mixture. Lay the sardines on a large tray.

Heat oil in a large skillet and add a bay leaf and the crushed garlic. When the garlic has browned and the oil is very hot, remove the garlic and bay leaf and put in the sardines, a few at a time. Fry until they are golden brown, turning them with a spatula. Remove them from the pan and drain them on a dish covered with a double thickness of paper towels, then arrange them on a preheated serving dish. Keep them warm while you cook the others. Garnish as you please. Serve immediately.

Swordfish Rolls

Involtini di Pesce Spada

To serve 4

1 small onion

olive oil

8 thin slices swordfish, weighing about ½lb, and a further ¼lb swordfish scraps

2 fresh basil leaves

1 tbsp chopped parsley

⅔ cup breadcrumbs

2oz Provolone cheese, finely diced

1 egg

juice of ½ lemon

oregano

Preparation and cooking time: about 1 hour

Finely slice the onions and fry gently in 3 tablespoons of olive oil until transparent. Add the finely chopped swordfish scraps and cook until slightly browned. Add the chopped basil and parsley. Stir and cook for a few minutes and then add the breadcrumbs. Cook for a little longer and then mash to a paste.

Add the Provolone cheese, the egg and a little salt and pepper and mix thoroughly. Adjust the seasoning to taste. Leave to cool.

Lightly beat the slices of swordfish with a meat mallet and spread the prepared mixture on them. Roll them up and secure the rolls with kitchen twine or wooden toothpicks. Preheat the broiler. Brush the rolls with olive oil and broil them, turning occasionally to ensure that they cook evenly.

Pour 6 tablespoons of olive oil into a bowl and, stirring with a fork or whisk, blend in 3 tablespoons of boiling water, the juice of half a lemon, a pinch of oregano, and a little salt and pepper. Arrange the swordfish rolls on a warmed dish and serve with the prepared sauce.

Fried sardines with cheese

Mussels with a Sea Tang

Cozze al Sapore di Mare

To serve 6

6½lb fresh mussels

4-6 shallots

½ celery heart

1½ cups mushrooms

a handful of parsley

1 tbsp chopped chives

2 tbsp butter

⅝ cup dry white wine

nutmeg

⅓ tsp cornstarch

a few drops lemon juice

Preparation and cooking time: about 1½ hours

Scrape the mussels with a small knife under running water, then leave them in a bowl of salted cold water for at least 30 minutes. Meanwhile, finely chop the shallots with the celery, mushrooms and a handful of parsley. Add the finely chopped chives and fry in 2 tablespoons of butter, taking care not to let the ingredients brown. Then put the mussels into the pan, pour in the wine, season generously with freshly ground black pepper and a little grated nutmeg. Cover the pan and allow the mussels to open over a high heat, shaking the pan from time to time.

Remove from the heat as soon as the mussels have opened. Take the mussels from their shells and place on a serving dish. Filter the liquid from the pan through a cheesecloth, then heat the liquid until it has reduced by half. Add the rest of the butter, softened, in small pieces. Dissolve the cornstarch in 2 or 3 tablespoons of cold water and a few drops of lemon juice and add this too. Simmer gently for a few seconds then pour over the mussels and sprinkle generously with chopped parsley. Serve immediately, garnishing the dish to taste.

Gourmet Fried Fish
Tracine del Gourmet

To serve 4

16 small weevers or star-gazers, weighing about 2lb in all

flour

4 jumbo shrimp

4 shallots

2-3 sprigs parsley

4 tbsp olive oil

½ cup dry white wine

½lb peeled tomatoes

⅜ cup fish stock

2 fresh basil leaves

½ bay leaf

oil for frying

Preparation and cooking time: about 1 hour

Remove the fins and the dangerous spines around the gills and gut the fish. Wash the fish rapidly and dry them carefully. Coat them one by one in the flour and shake off the excess. Shell the shrimp.

Chop the shallots finely with the leaves of 2-3 sprigs of parsley, then sauté very gently in 4 tablespoons of olive oil, taking care not to brown. Add the shrimp, fry them for a few moments, then moisten them with the white wine and let it evaporate by a third before putting the peeled tomatoes in the pan, after passing them through the food processor using the finest disk. Also add the fish stock, 2 leaves of basil and half a bay leaf, and salt and pepper to taste, then cook over a fairly high heat for about 15 minutes. Stir from time to time and moisten with a little boiling water if necessary.

While the shrimp mixture is cooking, heat plenty of oil in a large skillet, fry the whole fish, drain them well when tender and lay them on a plate covered with a double sheet of paper towels. Salt them and arrange them on an appropriate serving dish. Pour the shrimp mixture over them, having removed the basil and bay leaf, and serve immediately.

Scallops au Gratin
Capesante Gratinate

To serve 4

a few sprigs parsley

2 small garlic cloves

16 scallops

4 tbsp butter

olive oil

fresh white breadcrumbs

⅜ cup dry white wine

16 green olives in brine

2 tbsp flour

⅔ cup fish stock

⅓ cup fresh cream

1 egg yolk

2 tbsp Emmental cheese

Preparation and cooking time: about 1¼ hours

Chop the parsley and garlic finely. Wash the scallops and heat them gently in a skillet until the shells open. Remove the molluscs and discard the grayish flesh and the little black sac which is attached to each. Rinse and drain carefully. Scrub the shells clean under running water, dry and reserve.

Heat 2 tablespoons of the butter and 2 tablespoons of oil in an ovenproof dish and fry the chopped parsley and garlic for a few minutes. Coat the scallops in the breadcrumbs, put them in the pan and fry them briskly until golden on both sides. Sprinkle with the wine and season with salt and pepper to taste.

While the wine is evaporating, prepare the sauce by heating the remaining butter in a separate saucepan. Stir in the flour, then add the fish stock and cream. Cook gently for a few minutes. Remove the sauce from the heat and add the egg yolk. Preheat the oven to 425°F.

Once the wine has reduced by at least two thirds, return the scallops to their shells, pour the juice from the pan over them and put a sliced, pitted olive on the top of each one. Cover the scallops with the sauce and sprinkle with the Emmental cheese. Place in the oven for 4-5 minutes. Serve immediately.

Squid in Rhine Wine
Calamaretti in Carpione, alla Renana

To serve 4

1lb cleaned squid

flour

frying oil

1 large onion

olive oil

2 garlic cloves

1 bay leaf

4 whole black peppercorns

3 tbsp white wine vinegar

1⅓ cups white German wine

1 bouillon cube

Worcestershire sauce

Preparation and cooking time: about 1 hour plus 12 hours' refrigeration

Rinse the squid and drain them well, then flour them and fry a few at a time in very hot oil. When crisp and golden, lift them out with a slotted spoon and drain them on paper towels.

Slice the onion very finely and sauté it in 5 tablespoons of olive oil with 2 whole garlic cloves; discard the garlic when it is brown. Add the bay leaf and peppercorns and, after a few moments, the vinegar, the wine, the crumbled bouillon cube and a dash of Worcestershire sauce. Allow to simmer, uncovered, over a moderate heat until the liquid has been reduced to about one third. Discard the peppercorns.

Place the fried squid in a deep dish and pour the liquid, with the onion, over them. Leave to cool at room temperature, then cover the dish with plastic wrap and keep in a cool place (or the least cold part of the refrigerator) for at least 12 hours before serving, carefully turning the squid over after 6 hours.

Monkfish with an Aromatic Sauce

Pescatrice in Salsa Aromatica

To serve 6

1 small onion

1 small stalk celery

1 small carrot

2 tbsp butter

3 tbsp olive oil

2 garlic cloves

2 bay leaves

¼ lb shrimp, unpeeled

1⅛ cups dry white wine

1 tsp tomato paste

1 tsp cornstarch

½ bouillon cube

1 monkfish weighing about 1¾ lb, head removed

1 sprig rosemary

2 or 3 sage leaves

Worcestershire sauce

celery leaves for garnish

Preparation and cooking time: about 1¼ hours

Preheat the oven to 400°F. Finely slice the onion, celery and carrot. Heat in a saucepan with the butter and 2 tablespoons of olive oil. Add a lightly crushed garlic clove and a small bay leaf. Fry gently but do not brown. Then put in the shrimp and sauté for a few minutes. Pour in half the wine and simmer until the wine has almost evaporated. Dissolve the tomato paste and the cornstarch in about ⅝ cup of cold water, pour into the pan and stir. Crumble in the bouillon cube and simmer until the liquid has reduced by half.

Remove the bay leaf and blend the mixture at maximum speed for a couple of minutes. Filter the mixture through a fine strainer, taste and add salt if required. Keep the sauce hot over a double boiler.

Clean the fish and remove the dorsal and ventral fins, then brush all over with olive oil, sprinkle with salt and place in a dish large enough to hold the whole fish. Surround with a sprig of rosemary, sage leaves, a garlic clove and a small bay leaf. Put in the oven for about 30 minutes, moistening from time to time with the remaining white wine.

Towards the end of the cooking, add a dash of Worcestershire sauce. Place the fish on a preheated serving dish and pour over some of the sauce. Serve the rest in a sauceboat. Sprinkle chopped celery leaves over the fish for garnish.

Marine Style Clams

Cappe Chione alla Marinara

To serve 6

24 fresh clams

1 bay leaf

8 white peppercorns

2-3 sprigs fresh parsley

1 small onion

1 garlic clove

3 tbsp olive oil

2 egg yolks

5 tbsp whipping cream

Preparation and cooking time: about 40 minutes plus at least 2 hours' soaking

Soak the clams in plenty of lightly salted cold water for a long time, frequently turning them and changing the water at least twice. Finally wash them well, one by one, under running water, placing them in a saucepan as they are done.

Cover them with cold water and add the bay leaf, peppercorns and almost all the parsley. Bring gradually to the boil, keeping the lid on but stirring from time to time. Take them off the heat, lift them out, rinse again in the cooking water if there is any trace of sand and keep them covered in a large deep serving dish.

Chop the onion and garlic finely and fry them gently in the oil, taking care not to brown them. Pour in the white wine and half a glass of the clams' cooking water strained through a cloth. Simmer for 5 or 6 minutes then thicken with the egg yolks beaten together with the cream. Taste the sauce (which will be fairly runny), adjust the seasoning, pour it over the clams, sprinkle with chopped parsley and serve at once.

It is essential that all the sand is removed from the clams and that they should not be overcooked – being somewhat leathery, they would then become inedible.

Monkfish in an aromatic sauce (top left); marine style clams (left)

Cheesy Fishcakes with Parsley Sauce

Polpette di Pesce

To serve 6

1 dry bread roll

4-5 sprigs fresh parsley

2 garlic cloves

¼ lb Provolone cheese

1¼lb filleted fish (whiting, swordfish, hake)

1 small lemon

2 eggs

breadcrumbs

flour

oil for frying

2 tbsp butter

1 cup fish stock

Preparation and cooking time: about 45 minutes

Soften the bread in warm water. Wash the parsley, reserving 2 tablespoons of it, and chop it finely with a garlic clove. Grate the cheese. Chop the fish coarsely, making sure it contains no bones or bits of skin. Grate the lemon rind. Squeeze the bread well to get rid of the water and put all these ingredients together in a bowl with the 2 eggs. Season with freshly ground pepper and salt to taste.

Mix the ingredients thoroughly and add sufficient breadcrumbs to make a mixture that can be made into 12 sausage shapes with your hands. Roll them separately in the flour, coating them evenly but not too thickly. Heat a large skillet with plenty of oil, then fry the fishcakes gently, turning them frequently so that they are cooked through and nicely browned on all sides. When they are done, lift them from the pan with a slotted spatula, drain them for a moment on paper towels, arrange them on a serving dish and keep them warm.

Crush a garlic clove and brown it in the butter in a small pan. Discard the garlic and add 2 tablespoons of flour to the butter, mixing until smooth with a wooden spoon or a small whisk. Gradually add the boiling fish stock and

bring to the boil, stirring continuously. Remove from the heat, flavor with a teaspoon of the lemon juice and add 2 tablespoons of chopped parsley. Use this sauce to coat the 12 fishcakes and serve them at once, garnished to taste.

■SEAFOOD■SEAFOOD■SEAFOOD■

Carp Poached in Court-Bouillon

Carpa in Court-Bouillon

To serve 6

1 large onion

1 celery heart

1 carrot

1 small lemon

3 cloves

1 bay leaf

5-6 whole black peppercorns

2¼ cups dry white wine

1 rainbow carp, weighing 4lb

⅝ cup butter

Preparation and cooking time: about 1¾ hours

Clean and slice the onion, celery, carrot and lemon. Place them in a pan with the cloves, bay leaf, peppercorns, the wine and 10 pints of water. Salt sparingly and boil over a moderate heat for about 1 hour. Strain the liquid into a fish kettle and leave it to become tepid.

Clean the carp carefully, rinse and drain it and put it in the now cool court-bouillon. Return to the heat and cook for about 30 minutes from the time it comes to the boil. It should simmer very gently, otherwise the fish will break up. Remove the fish kettle from the heat but leave the fish in the broth for another 10 minutes or so. Clarify the butter in a small pan (warm it gently until floating impurities can be skimmed off and others sink to the bottom); pour off the clear part and keep it warm in a *bain-marie*.

Meanwhile, lift out the carp, drain it well, carefully remove the skin and arrange it on a suitable dish. Serve at once accompanied by the butter in a warm sauceboat.

Deep-fried Dogfish with Egg Sauce

Palombo in Frittura con Salsa d'Uova

To serve 4

2 eggs, hard-boiled

1 baby onion

1 large sprig fresh parsley

juice of 1 lemon

½ cup olive oil

oil for frying

¾-1lb dogfish fillets in batter

Preparation and cooking time: about 30 minutes

Mash the hard-boiled egg yolks. Finely chop the baby onion and the parsley and add to the egg yolks. Season with a pinch of salt and pepper and stir in the lemon juice a little at a time. Gradually pour in the olive oil, stirring constantly. Bind the sauce with 2 teaspoons of water and pour into a sauceboat.

Heat plenty of oil in a large skillet and fry the dogfish fillets until golden brown. Drain on paper towels. Arrange on a dish and serve immediately with the egg sauce.

Carp poached in court-bouillon and cheesy fishcakes with parsley sauce

Swordfish Skewers
Spiedini di Pesce Spada

To serve 4

1 red and 1 yellow bell pepper, each weighing about ¾ lb

2 thick slices of swordfish, together weighing 1¼lb

flour

olive oil

1 garlic clove

½ cup dry white wine

Worcestershire sauce

Preparation and cooking time: about 1 hour

Broil the peppers, turning them often, to scorch the skins. Wrap them individually in paper towels and set them aside for a few minutes. Peel, cut them in half, remove the seeds and stem, then cut them into 1½-inch squares.

Remove the skin from the swordfish and cut each slice into 16 small pieces of similar size. Thread 8 pieces on a long wooden skewer, alternating with the pepper squares, and beginning and ending with a pepper square. Make 4 skewers. Roll each skewer in the flour, shaking off the excess. Arrange the skewers side by side in a large skillet containing 5 tablespoons of hot oil. Flavor with a slightly crushed garlic clove. Let the skewers of fish brown well, then sprinkle with the white wine and season with a generous dash of Worcestershire sauce and some salt. Let the wine evaporate almost completely and serve on a heated plate, garnished to your taste.

Hake with Tomato Sauce
Filetti di Nasello Infuocati

To serve 6

3 hake, each weighing about ¾lb

milk

flour

olive oil

½lb firm ripe tomatoes

⅔ cup fish stock

2 basil leaves

granulated sugar

1 garlic clove

½ green pepper; scorched and peeled

1 tsp cornstarch

Preparation and cooking time: about 1 hour

Dip the filleted hake first in lightly salted cold milk, then roll them in flour. Heat 5 tablespoons of olive oil in a skillet large enough to hold all the fish. When the oil is hot add the fillets and brown, adding salt and pepper to taste. As soon as they are cooked, remove the fillets from the pan and arrange them fanwise on a heatproof dish, without overlapping them. Cover with foil and keep them warm.

Chop and purée the tomatoes, then whisk them together with the fish stock. Strain the mixture through a fine sieve into the skillet used to fry the fillets. Add 2 basil leaves, a pinch of sugar, a slightly crushed garlic clove, salt, pepper, and the finely chopped sweet pepper. Simmer for about 10 minutes, then thicken the sauce with a teaspoon of cornstarch dissolved in 5 tablespoons of cold water; stir and simmer for a few more minutes. Discard the garlic and basil. Pour the sauce over the fish fillets and serve at once, garnishing as you wish.

Seafood Pilau
Pilaf Marinaro

To serve 4

½lb cod fillets

1½ bouillon cubes

1 medium onion

olive oil

¾lb rice

a little powdered saffron

1 small leek

2 garlic cloves

¼lb shrimp

dry white wine

Worcestershire sauce

a few tender celery leaves

Preparation and cooking time: about 30 minutes

Cut the cod fillets into ¾-inch cubes. Preheat the oven to 400°F. Boil 2½ cups of water with 1 bouillon cube. Finely chop the onion and sauté it in 4 tablespoons of olive oil, in an ovenproof pan. Add the rice and cook it for a few moments, color it with the saffron, stir, and immediately pour on the boiling stock. Bring back to the boil, then put the dish in the oven for about 15 minutes, until the rice has absorbed the liquid completely.

Meanwhile cut the leek into rings and finely chop the garlic. Put them both in a skillet with 3 tablespoons of olive oil and sauté them gently. Then put the cubes of cod and the prawns in the pan. Cook them over a fairly vigorous heat. Flavor with large a dash of Worcestershire sauce. Remove the rice from the oven and mix it with the seafood. Scatter over a few tender celery leaves, coarsely chopped, then serve.

Hake with tomato sauce (top) and swordfish skewers

Cold Skate and Scorpion Fish in Green Sauce

Razza e Scorfano in Verde

To serve 6

1 scorpion fish, weighing about 1lb

1 wing of skate, weighing about 1lb

1 small onion

1 small carrot

1 stalk celery

a bunch of parsley

1 garlic clove

1 bay leaf

2-3 whole black peppercorns

⅔ cup dry white wine

3 gherkins

30 capers

3 anchovy fillets in oil

1 slice white bread soaked in white wine vinegar

olive oil

1 lemon, sliced

1 hard-boiled egg

Preparation and cooking time: about 1¼ hours

Preheat the oven to 375°F. Cut off the fins, scale and clean the scorpion fish. Rinse both fish under running water and place in an ovenproof dish. Add the chopped onion, carrot and celery, 4-5 chopped sprigs of parsley, a sliced garlic clove, a small bay leaf and 2-3 whole black peppercorns. Pour over the wine and ⅔ cup of water, add a little salt and bring to the boil. Cover the dish and place in the pre-heated oven for about 15 minutes. Remove from the oven and leave to cool.

Prepare the sauce: put the gherkins, capers, anchovy fillets, bread, a small handful of parsley, a generous pinch of salt and pepper and 6 tablespoons of olive oil in the blender. Blend to form a smooth sauce and then pour into a bowl. If the sauce seems too thick, add a little more olive oil.

Remove all the meat from the skate and scorpion fish, discarding the skin and bones, and flake coarsely. Place a slice of lemon in the bottom of each of 6 small dishes and divide the fish between them. Top with the prepared sauce and garnish with slices of hard-boiled egg. Serve.

■SEAFOOD■SEAFOOD■SEAFOOD■

Stuffed Cod

"Picaia" di Merluzzo

To serve 6-8

4 fresh cod fillets, weighing about 1¾ lb in all

3 large garlic cloves

large bunch fresh parsley

⅔ cup very fine breadcrumbs

½ cup grated Parmesan cheese

2 eggs

2 tbsp olive oil

Preparation and cooking time: about 1¼ hours

Preheat the oven to 375°F. Lightly beat the cod fillets and overlap them a little so as to form a rectangle with an even edge. Sprinkle with salt and pepper. Finely slice a large garlic clove and scatter over the cod. Wash and dry the parsley and chop it very finely together with 2 garlic cloves. Place in a bowl. Add the breadcrumbs and Parmesan cheese, a pinch of salt and a generous sprinkling of freshly ground pepper. Mix well and add the eggs and olive oil. Work into a smooth mixture and spread this evenly over the fish, stopping short of the edges.

Using the blade of a long knife, raise the slab of fish, from the shorter edge, and roll it up tightly enough to keep the stuffing inside. Wrap the roll in a double sheet of oiled aluminum foil, sealing the ends and then the upper edges. Tie up with kitchen string, as for a roast. Place the roll in a casserole dish that is just the right size and bake in the oven for about 45 minutes, carefully turning the roll from time to time. Serve either hot by itself or cold with mayonnaise garnished to taste.

Cold Fish Mousse

Sformato di Pesce, Freddo

To serve 8

4 envelopes plain gelatin

4oz monkfish, cut into walnut-sized pieces

flour

butter

olive oil

½lb onions

2 garlic cloves

½lb shrimp, peeled and heads removed

½ cup dry white wine

2½ cups fish stock

Preparation and cooking time: about 40 minutes plus overnight refrigeration

Dissolve the gelatin in a little cold water. Lightly flour the monkfish pieces and cook them very gently in 2 tablespoons of butter and 2 tablespoons of olive oil, without browning them. Add a little salt and leave on a plate to cool. Finely chop the onion with the garlic and sauté in the skillet the monkfish was cooked in. Add the shrimp and brown gently, stirring from time to time with a wooden spoon. Pour over the white wine and allow to evaporate. Season with salt and pepper. Then pour in the fish stock, stir and bring slowly to the boil.

Pour the contents of the pan into a blender and leave on maximum speed for a couple of minutes. Strain the mixture into a bowl. Stir in the gelatin, mixing until you are sure it has completely dissolved. Line the bottom and sides of a 5-cup rectangular baking pan with foil. Pour in the fish purée and sink the pieces of monkfish into it. Leave to cool at room temperature, then cover with a piece of plastic wrap and refrigerate overnight. Before serving, turn out the mousse on to a dish and garnish as you please. Serve at once.

Cold fish mousse (top) and *stuffed cod*

Stuffed Squid
Calamari Ripieni di Magro

To serve 4

8 medium squid

a handful of parsley

3 garlic cloves

¼lb shrimp

1¾ cups breadcrumbs

2 tbsp grated Pecorino cheese

2 eggs

7 tbsp olive oil

1 small onion

⅜ cup dry white wine

¾ cup fish stock

1 tsp cornstarch

Preparation and cooking time: about 1½ hours

Separate the tentacles from the body of each squid. Empty the body pouches and discard the dark outer skins. Discard the eyes and "beaks" and wash and drain both the tentacles and pouches.

Finely chop a handful of parsley and 2 large garlic cloves and place in a bowl. Peel and chop the shrimp and add to the parsley and garlic. Stir in the breadcrumbs, grated Pecorino cheese, eggs and 3 tablespoons of olive oil. Season with salt and pepper according to taste and blend thoroughly. Stuff the pouches of the squid with the prepared mixture and stitch up the opening.

Finely chop the onions, a garlic clove and a small handful of parsley and fry gently in 4 tablespoons of olive oil. Add the stuffed squid and their tentacles and fry gently for a few minutes, turning once. Pour over the white wine and allow it to evaporate rapidly on a brisk heat. Pour in the fish stock in which a teaspoon of cornstarch has been dissolved.

Move the pan to make sure that nothing is sticking and then cover it.

Lower the heat and simmer for about 40 minutes, moving the pan occasionally and adding a little more fish stock if necessary. By the end of cooking, the squid should be fairly dry and the sauce well reduced.

Transfer to a warmed dish and serve topped with a little chopped parsley.

Stuffed squid

Savory Anchovies
Acciughe "in Savore"

To serve 4-6

1¾ lb very fresh anchovies

flour

oil for deep-frying

2 large onions

2 large garlic cloves

1 sprig fresh rosemary

1 bay leaf

3-4 peppercorns

a piece of cinnamon stick

⅜ cup olive oil

⅝ cup white wine vinegar

2 cups dry white wine

1 bouillon cube

1 leek, green part only, for garnish

Preparation and cooking time: about 1½ hours plus 36 hours' marination

Remove the heads from the anchovies, slit and gut the fish. Wash them rapidly under running water and drain carefully. Flour them, a few at a time, and shake off any excess flour. Heat plenty of oil in a deep-frying pan and when it is hot, fry the anchovies until they are perfectly browned all over. Drain from the oil and lay on a plate covered with a double layer of paper towels to absorb the excess oil. Lightly sprinkle with salt.

Meanwhile, finely slice the onions. Make a small cheesecloth bag and place inside the lightly crushed garlic, rosemary, bay leaf, peppercorns and cinnamon. Secure the bag firmly. Heat the olive oil in a skillet and put in first the bag of herbs and then the onion. Fry gently, stirring with a wooden spoon. As soon as the onions begin to brown, pour in the vinegar and the wine. Mix and bring slowly to the boil, then turn down the heat and cover the pan. Leave to simmer for about 15 minutes. Add salt 5 minutes before removing the pan from the heat.

Crumble in the bouillon cube. Remove the herb bag and squeeze it out well.

Place the anchovies and the boiling marinade in a deep dish and leave to cool, first at room temperature and then in the least cold compartment of the refrigerator for at least 36 hours. Be sure to cover the dish. Before serving, slice the leek into thin rings and use for garnish.

■SEAFOOD■SEAFOOD■SEAFOOD■

Spider Crab "Julie"
Grancevole "Giulie"

To serve 4

4 medium-sized spider crabs

a large handful of parsley

2 garlic cloves

2 tbsp breadcrumbs

3 tbsp olive oil

juice of 1 lemon

Preparation and cooking time: about 1½ hours plus 3 hours' soaking

Soak the crabs in cold water, preferably running, for about 3 hours. Then simmer for about 20 minutes in a half-covered pan. Preheat the oven to 325°F.

Remove the crabs from the pan and leave to cool. Then empty the shells completely, juices as well as meat. Chop the meat and put it in a large bowl. Add the juices, the parsley, finely chopped with the garlic, salt, pepper, half the breadcrumbs, olive oil and the strained lemon juice. Mix with care and fill the 4 crab shells with the mixture. Sprinkle with the remaining breadcrumbs. Cook in the oven for about 30 minutes, then serve.

Savory anchovies

Baked Stuffed Sea Bass
Spigola Farcita, al Forno

To serve 8

1 small onion

2 garlic cloves

a few sprigs parsley

5 tbsp olive oil

¼lb cod fillet

1 slice white bread soaked in milk

1 egg

10 shrimp

15 mussels

breadcrumbs

1 sea bass, weighing about 2¾ lb

2-3 bay leaves

3-4 tbsp dry white wine

Preparation and cooking time: about 1½ hours

Chop the onion, 1 garlic clove and the parsley and sauté in 3 tablespoons of oil. Leave to cool. Cut the cod fillet into small pieces, drain the milk from the bread and then place the sautéed mixture, the cod, bread, egg and a pinch of salt and pepper in the blender. Blend briskly for a couple of minutes. Shell the shrimp, dice them and add to the blended mixture.

Scrape and wash the mussel shells and place them in a skillet with a tablespoon of oil, a garlic clove and a few leaves of parsley. Cover the pan and place on a high heat to open the shells. Shell the mussels and add to the blended mixture. Strain the mussels' cooking juices through cheesecloth and reserve. If the stuffing seems too liquid, add some breadcrumbs and leave to stand in a cool place. Preheat the oven to 400°F.

Cut the fins off the bass, scale it, wash it under running water and dry it. Remove the spine, bones and entrails and clean the inside of the fish with paper towels. Stuff the bass with the prepared mixture and sew up the opening. Brush the fish with olive oil and coat it thoroughly in breadcrumbs.

Place 2 or 3 bay leaves in the bottom of a well-oiled ovenproof pan, put the fish in the pan and bake in the oven for about 30 minutes. Turn the fish once or twice during cooking, being careful not to damage it, and sprinkle it with 3-4 tablespoons each of white wine and the cooking liquid from the mussels. Serve the fish cut into large slices.

■SEAFOOD■SEAFOOD■SEAFOOD■

Aromatic Stewed Clams
Telline in Umido Aromatico

To serve 4

2½lb clams

a handful of fresh parsley

1 garlic clove

4 fresh basil leaves

5 tbsp olive oil

¾-1 lb firm ripe tomatoes

extra basil leaves for garnish

Preparation and cooking time: about 40 minutes plus 1 hour's soaking

Wash the clams well under cold running water then soak them in a bowl of cold salted water for about 1 hour to release any sand. Meanwhile, finely chop the parsley with the garlic, removing the green shoot first, and the basil. Put the herbs in a large skillet with the olive oil and cook over a moderate heat. Do not allow to brown.

Blanch the tomatoes in boiling water, peel and chop them. Add them to the skillet and stir with a wooden spoon. Cook for about 10 minutes then drain the clams thoroughly and put these in too. Stir, and cover the skillet for a few minutes until the clams have opened. Then remove the lid and simmer gently, stirring from time to time. After 5-6 minutes season with freshly ground pepper, taste and correct the seasoning if necessary. Serve in a warmed bowl or serving dish, garnished with fresh basil.

Sea Bream with Herbs
Pagellini alle Erbe

To serve 6

12 small sea bream

4oz canned tuna in oil

parsley

1 tbsp capers

1 garlic clove

1 tbsp breadcrumbs

1 egg

2 bay leaves

olive oil

rosemary

1 sprig each fresh chervil and marjoram

¼ cup dry white wine

Preparation and cooking time: about 1¼ hours

Wash the fish one at a time under cold running water, then dry them thoroughly both inside and out. Preheat the oven to 400°F.

Finely chop the well-drained tuna with a handful of parsley, the capers and half a garlic clove. Place the minced mixture in a small bowl, add the breadcrumbs, a little salt and a generous grinding of pepper, then bind with the egg. Fill each fish with the mixture, then sew up the openings.

Put 2 crushed bay leaves and the fish into an oiled rectangular ovenproof dish. Brush them with olive oil and season with salt, white pepper, and a small sprig of rosemary. Finely chop the chervil leaves and the marjoram and sprinkle the herbs over the fish.

Put them in the oven for about 20 minutes. Halfway through the cooking time moisten them with the wine. Serve them from the same dish.

Aromatic stewed clams (top); **baked stuffed sea bass** (bottom)

Sea Bream with Mussel Sauce

Pagelli con Salsa di Cozze

To serve 4

¾-1 lb fresh mussels

1½ garlic cloves

olive oil

1 lemon

1 small bay leaf

1 small onion

3-4 sprigs fresh parsley

a little dry white wine

½ tsp cornstarch

Worcestershire sauce

4 sea bream, each weighing about ½lb

1 tbsp breadcrumbs

Preparation and cooking time: about 1¼ hours

Preheat the oven to 375°F. Scrape the mussel shells under cold running water using a small sharp knife. Then put the mussels in a skillet with a lightly crushed garlic clove, a trickle of olive oil, a slice of lemon cut into segments and a small bay leaf. Cover the pan and place over a high heat to open the mussels.

Once they have opened, remove the mussels from their shells and strain the juices into a bowl. Finely chop the onion with the half garlic clove and a little parsley, and fry gently in 1 tablespoon of olive oil, taking care not to let the mixture brown. Then put in the mussels and, after a few seconds, pour in a little wine. Dissolve the cornstarch in the cold juices from the mussels and add to the pan. Stir and simmer for a few seconds. Flavor with a dash of Worcestershire sauce, then remove from the heat.

Oil an ovenproof dish that is just the right size to hold the bream. Scrape the fish, wash rapidly under running water and dry. Place in the dish and sprinkle with salt and pepper. Pour over the mussel sauce and sprinkle with 1 tablespoon of breadcrumbs and chopped parsley. Pour over a trickle of olive oil and lay a sheet of aluminum foil over the dish without sealing it. Bake in the oven for about 20 minutes, then serve.

Hake with Tomato and Beans

Nasello con Pomodoro e Fagioli

To serve 4

1 large hake, weighing about 1¾ lb, fins and gills removed and gutted

5 heaping tbsp breadcrumbs

1 garlic clove

3-4 sprigs fresh parsley

a few celery leaves

1 egg

1 small onion

olive oil

1¾ cups canned white beans

1¾ cups canned tomatoes

2 large fresh basil leaves

Preparation and cooking time: about 1½ hours

Preheat the oven to 375°F. Rinse the gutted fish quickly under running water and dry. Put 4 heaping tablespoons of breadcrumbs in a bowl and chop half the garlic clove together with 2-3 sprigs of parsley and a few celery leaves. Add this mixture to the bowl and bind with the egg. Season with salt and pepper. Stuff the fish with this mixture and sew up the opening.

Finely chop the onion with the remaining half garlic clove and fry in 3 tablespoons of olive oil. Drain the beans thoroughly, rinse and add to the onions, stirring with a wooden spoon. After a few minutes, add the tomatoes, mashed finely, the basil, salt and pepper. Mix and simmer for 5-6 minutes. Place the hake in an oiled ovenproof dish and pour the tomato and bean sauce all around the fish. Brush with a little olive oil and sprinkle with salt and the remaining tablespoon of breadcrumbs. Cover the dish with a sheet of aluminum foil and cook in the oven for about 25 minutes. Remove the foil 10 minutes before the fish is cooked and baste with some of the sauce. Sprinkle the cooked fish with chopped parsley and serve.

Seafood Kebabs

Spiedini del Mare

To serve 4

16 jumbo shrimp, unpeeled

16 scallops, shelled

8 green olives in brine

16 canned baby onions in oil

very fine breadcrumbs

½ garlic clove

olive oil

3 tbsp dry white wine

Preparation and cooking time: about 1 hour

Preheat the oven to 425°F. Peel the shrimp. Remove the beards and the darker flesh from the scallops then rinse rapidly, drain and dry thoroughly. Remove the pits from the olives, dry them and cut them in half widthwise. On 8 wooden skewers alternate an onion, a shrimp, half an olive and a scallop, then another onion, followed by a shrimp, then an olive and a scallop. Roll the kebabs in the breadcrumbs, pressing lightly to coat the ingredients evenly all over.

Rub the bottom of an ovenproof dish with garlic, grease it with olive oil, then place the kebabs in it, well apart. Pour over a thin trickle of olive oil and season with salt and pepper. Cook in the oven for about 10 minutes. Splash over the wine, and cook for a couple of minutes more before serving.

Hake with tomato and beans (top), *sea bream with mussel sauce* (center) and *seafood kebabs*

Florentine-style Fillet of Perch

Filetti di Pesce Persico Fiorentina

To serve 4

2¼lb fresh young spinach

4 tbsp butter

5 tbsp olive oil

nutmeg

flour

1 cup milk

1 garlic clove

2 sage leaves

16 small or 8 large fillets of perch, weighing about 2 lb in all, divided in half lengthwise

breadcrumbs

parsley for garnish

Preparation and cooking time: about 1¼ hours

Preheat the oven to 475°F. Wash the spinach thoroughly under running water. Cook in an uncovered saucepan with only the water that remains on the leaves after washing and a little coarse cooking salt for about 10 minutes, until the leaves are tender, occasionally stirring with a wooden spoon. Drain the spinach and cool under running water. Then squeeze it dry and chop coarsely.

Heat 2 tablespoons of butter and 2 tablespoons of the olive oil in a large skillet, and as soon as the fat is hot, put in the spinach and fry lightly, seasoning with a little salt, pepper and nutmeg. Then sprinkle in the flour and heat the milk before pouring that in too. Stir and simmer for a few seconds, then transfer the contents of the pan to a heatproof dish and keep warm in the oven with the door open.

Flour the fish and shake them to remove any excess. Clean and dry the pan that was used for the spinach and melt the rest of the butter and 3 tablespoons of olive oil in it, flavoring with the lightly crushed garlic and the sage leaves. Fry the fish until golden brown and season with a little salt and pepper.

Remove from the pan and arrange on the bed of spinach. Strain the juices in the pan and pour over. Sprinkle lightly with breadcrumbs and bake for a couple of minutes. Serve garnished with parsley.

■SEAFOOD■SEAFOOD■SEAFOOD■

Trout in Herbed Breadcrumbs

Trote al Pangrattato Aromatico

To serve 4

4 cleaned trout

2 large sprigs fresh rosemary

1 sprig fresh parsley

1 sprig fresh sage

1 garlic clove

4 slices fresh white bread

juice of ½ lemon

a little olive oil

lemon slices for garnish

Preparation and cooking time: about 50 minutes plus thawing

Defrost the trout if frozen. Drain well and dry on paper towels. Finely chop the leaves of 1 rosemary sprig, 1 parsley sprig, 3 sage leaves and a garlic clove. Crumble the bread and reduce it to fine breadcrumbs by rubbing it between your fingers. Mix the breadcrumbs with the chopped herbs and place on a large plate or tray.

Preheat the oven to 375°F. Slice the trout lengthwise and open them out. Sprinkle the insides with a little salt and pepper. Rub with a little lemon juice and brush with a little olive oil.

Coat the fish thoroughly in the herbed breadcrumbs, place them on a lightly oiled baking pan and cook in the oven for about 20 minutes or until golden brown. Arrange the trout on a warmed dish, garnish with parsley and slices of lemon and serve.

Florentine-style fillet of perch (right); trout in herbed breadcrumbs (below)

Adriatic Salt Cod with Potatoes
Baccalà dell'Adriatico

To serve 6

2 large potatoes

1 small onion

1 garlic clove

5-6 tbsp olive oil

18oz tomatoes, peeled

½ bay leaf

a pinch of sugar

1¼lb salt cod, soaked to soften and then dried

a few fresh basil leaves

Preparation and cooking time: about 1½ hours

Preheat the oven to 375-400°F. Boil a large saucepanful of water and add a little salt when it begins to boil. Peel, wash and dry the potatoes, and cut them into horizontal slices about ⅛ inch wide. Boil them for about 3 minutes. Drain and leave to cool.

Meanwhile, finely chop the onion together with the garlic. Heat 3 tablespoons of olive oil in a small saucepan and fry the onion and garlic. Peel the tomatoes and put them through the fine disk of a food processor, and add to the saucepan. Season with salt, pepper, half a bay leaf and a pinch of sugar. Mix and simmer for about 15 minutes, leaving the pan uncovered.

Cut the cod into equal pieces. Pour 2 tablespoons of olive oil into an ovenproof earthenware dish and make layers of potatoes and cod. Pour a little tomato sauce between each layer and sprinkle with the chopped basil. Pour a trickle of olive oil over the top and bake in the oven for about 1 hour. Before serving, sprinkle with more basil, freshly ground pepper and a little olive oil.

Adriatic salt cod with potatoes (top) and *fried salt cod in beer batter*

Trout with Tuna Fish

Trota Tonnata

To serve 6-8

1 large trout, weighing about 3½lb

6oz canned tuna in oil

1¼ cups fresh breadcrumbs

a few sprigs parsley

3 eggs

½ cup grated Parmesan cheese

olive oil

2 sprigs rosemary

2 garlic cloves

½ cup dry white wine

Preparation and cooking time: about 1½ hours

Preheat the oven to 375°F. Remove the fins from the trout and clean it. Wash quickly under cold running water, then pat dry. Open the fish out flat and fillet it, taking care not to crush the flesh in the process.

Now prepare the stuffing: drain the tuna throroughly and mash it. Add ¾ cup of the breadcrumbs and the parsley, washed, dried and finely chopped. Bind the mixture with the eggs and the Parmesan cheese, and season with a little salt and freshly ground pepper. Stuff the trout with the mixture and sew it up. Brush the entire surface of the trout with olive oil, sprinkle with the rest of the breadcrumbs and lay on a baking tray with the rosemary and lightly crushed garlic (which should remain under the trout during cooking).

Bake for about 45 minutes, turning the trout over halfway through. Splash a little wine over from time to time. Remove the trout from the oven and leave to rest for about 5 minutes. Then place on a serving dish, garnished to taste.

White Bream with Tomatoes and Peas

Sarago "Verderosso"

To serve 4

1 white bream weighing about 2½lb

2 bay leaves

1 sprig rosemary

1 garlic clove, lightly crushed

6 tbsp butter

1 onion

1 lb peeled tomatoes

2 basil leaves

a pinch of sugar

1¾ cups frozen young peas

Preparation and cooking time: about 1¼ hours

Remove the fins from the bream and scale and gut it. Wash rapidly under running water and pat dry. Stuff the fish with a bay leaf, the rosemary, the garlic and pepper. Melt 4 tablespoons of the butter. Arrange the bream in an ovenproof dish and pour over the melted butter. Leave for about 30 minutes, turning it over a couple of times.

Meanwhile, preheat the oven to 375°F. Chop the onion and gently sauté in the remaining butter in a pan. Then put the tomatoes through a food processor using the finest disk and add these to the onions. Add the basil, sugar and a little salt. Put in the frozen peas and bring to the boil. Simmer for 20-25 minutes, keeping the pan partly covered and stirring from time to time with a wooden spoon.

Put the bream in the oven for about 25 minutes, turning it once, with great care, halfway through the cooking. After this, cover it with a sheet of aluminum foil. Finally, arrange the fish on a preheated serving dish and bring to the table accompanied by the simmering tomato and pea sauce.

Fried Salt Cod in Beer Batter

Filetti di Baccalà Fritti

To serve 4

1 cup flour

1 egg

1 tbsp olive oil

1¼ cups lager

1½lb salt cod, soaked to soften and then dried

¼ cup butter

1 garlic clove

¼ cup grated Parmesan cheese

oil for frying

1 sprig fresh parsley for garnish

Preparation and cooking time: about 1½ hours

Put the flour in a dish together with ½ teaspoon of salt. Mix and make a well in the center. Separate the egg and put the yolk in the well; reserve the white. Add 1 tablespoon of olive oil and as much lager as is required to make a smooth batter that is not too runny. Take care not to let it become lumpy. Cover the dish and set aside for 1 hour.

Cut the cod into equal pieces. Heat the butter and garlic in a skillet which is large enough to contain all the fish in a single layer. As soon as the butter has melted, put in the pieces of cod and fry over a moderate heat, turning them over carefully to allow them to absorb the flavor. Remove the skillet from the heat and sprinkle over the Parmesan. Cover and leave to cool.

Heat plenty of light frying oil in a deep pan over a low heat. Whisk the egg white until it is stiff and carefully fold it into the batter using an up-and-down movement rather than a circular one. Dip the cod fillets in the batter, one at a time, and shake off any excess so they do not drip. When the oil is hot, drop them in and fry until they are golden brown and crisp all round. Remove and shake off as much oil as possible, then lay them on a plate covered with kitchen paper to absorb any remaining oil. Arrange them on a hot serving dish, garnish with the chopped parsley and serve.

Seafood Soufflé

Sformato Marino

To serve 8

1¼ lb cod fillets

1¾ cups ripe tomatoes

1 large onion

⅓ cup black olives, stoned and chopped

⅓ cup fresh breadcrumbs

⅓ cup butter

4 eggs

garlic

fresh basil

Preparation and cooking time: 1½ hours plus any defrosting time and soufflé cooling

1) Slice the cod fillets with a sharp knife. Lay them on a dish previously rubbed with garlic. Cover the cod with basil.

2) Bring to the boil a medium sized pan of salted water. Clean the tomatoes and drop them into the boiling water. Cook for two minutes and remove with a draining spoon.

Peel and finely chop the tomatoes and the onion. Melt 4 tablespoons of butter in a fry pan, add the chopped onion and fry gently.

3) Stir in the chopped tomatoes.

4) Stir in the cod. Season with salt and pepper and cook for 15 minutes, stirring occasionally.

5) Remove from the heat and add the olives and the breadcrumbs.

6) Add the eggs. Stir well and leave for a few minutes.

7) Meanwhile, grease a 10 x 8 inch ovenproof dish and pour in the mixture.

Cook in a *bain-marie* (**8** and **9**) for 1 hour in the oven at 375°F.

8) Pour some hot water into another larger oval pan.

9) . . . and immerse the smaller pan in it.

When cooked leave to cool and then turn out on to a serving dish. Garnish with finely sliced cucumber and radishes.

1

2

3

4

5

6

7

8

9

VEGETABLES

Vegetables are frequently served as a separate course in Italy. Often with their own accompaniments and sauces, vegetables Italian-style make ideal vegetarian dishes or imaginative side-dishes to meat, fish or poultry main courses. Vegetables such as asparagus, a northern speciality, and artichokes, are comparatively cheap and plentiful, and so relatively widely used in Italy.

Asparagus Quiche
Torta salata di Asparagi

To serve 8

½lb puff pastry

2¼lb fresh asparagus

¼lb raw ham, thinly sliced

¼lb Emmental cheese

¼ cup butter

3 eggs

⅜ cup cream

¼ cup grated Parmesan cheese

ground nutmeg

a few sprigs fresh parsley for garnish

Preparation and cooking time: about 1½ hours plus any thawing time

Defrost the pastry if using frozen. Trim and wash the asparagus and tie in a bundle with kitchen string. Stand the bundle upright in a saucepan of enough salted boiling water to come halfway up the bundle and cook for about 15 minutes or until tender. Remove the string and spread the asparagus out to dry on paper towels.

Roll out the pastry and use it to line a greased 9½-inch flan dish. Line the bottom with the slices of raw ham and cover with the thinly sliced Emmental cheese. Chop the asparagus and fry it gently in the butter, then arrange it on top of the cheese.

Preheat the oven to 375°F. Beat the eggs with the cream, the grated Parmesan cheese, a pinch of salt and pepper and a little ground nutmeg. Pour this mixture into the pie shell. Cook in the lower part of the oven for about 40 minutes. Place the quiche on a large plate, surround it with sprigs of parsley and serve.

Navy Beans with Onion Sauce
Bianchi di Spagna con Salsa di Cipolla

To serve 4

1¾ cups canned navy beans

1 small onion

5 tsp butter

1 tsp cornstarch

scant ½ cup milk

10 capers

sprig fresh parsley

Preparation and cooking time: about 30 minutes

Rinse the beans thoroughly under warm running water and drain. Chop the onion finely, almost to a paste. Melt the butter in a small saucepan and fry the onion without browning over a low heat for about 15 minutes. Add a tablespoon of warm water, if necessary, to keep the onion soft and to stop it drying out. Sprinkle the cornstarch over the onion and blend in well. Dilute gradually with the cold milk to obtain a smooth, consistent sauce. Season with a pinch of salt and simmer over a low heat, stirring constantly, for 5-6 minutes. Remove from the heat and blend at maximum speed until the sauce is completely smooth, then put it in a bowl.

Drain the capers thoroughly, chop them coarsely and add to the chopped parsley. Pour the beans into a serving dish and pour over the onion sauce. Sprinkle with the chopped parsley and capers and serve. This makes a delicate accompaniment to boiled meat dishes.

Asparagus quiche (left); navy beans with onion sauce (above right) and potatoes with herb butter

Potatoes with Herb Butter

Patate al Burro Aromatico

To serve 4

1¼lb medium-sized potatoes

2 tbsp butter

ground thyme

nutmeg

1 sprig fresh parsley for garnish

Preparation and cooking time: about 1 hour

Preheat the oven to 375°F. Peel the potatoes and cut into slices about ¼ inch thick, using a knife with a serrated blade to give them a scalloped surface. Rinse under cold running water to eliminate most of the excess starch. Heat a large saucepanful of water and add salt when it begins to boil. Put in the potatoes and bring back to the boil, then simmer for about 10 minutes until they just begin to soften.

Meanwhile, prepare the herb butter: Soften the butter and cut into small knobs and place in a bowl. Cream with a wooden spoon and when you have obtained a smooth cream, combine with a pinch of salt, plenty of freshly ground pepper, a pinch of thyme and a little grated nutmeg. Blend these ingredients

thoroughly.

Remove the potatoes from the water with a slotted spoon and lay out to dry on paper towels. Grease a round ovenproof dish with a tablespoon of the herb butter, spreading it thickly on the bottom. Arrange the potatoes in it, overlapping them a little. Cover with more slivers of herb butter and bake in the oven for about 30 minutes until the surface is golden brown. Remove the dish from the oven and leave for a couple of minutes. Sprinkle with the chopped parsley and serve.

Bell Peppers with Scrambled Egg

Peperoni e Uova

To serve 4

1 yellow and 1 red fresh bell pepper, together weighing about 1lb

½lb firm, ripe tomatoes

3-4 large fresh basil leaves

4 tbsp olive oil

1 garlic clove

2 eggs

1 tsp grated Pecorino cheese

Preparation and cooking time: about 45 minutes

Wash and dry the bell peppers and cut them in half lengthwise, discarding the stalks and seeds. Cut them again lengthwise into strips about ¾ inch thick.

Parboil the tomatoes in lightly salted water. Peel them and cut them in half, discarding the seeds. Chop into small pieces. Wipe the basil leaves with a damp cloth.

Heat the olive oil and the lightly crushed garlic clove in a skillet. Discard the garlic as soon as it has browned. Place the bell peppers in the skillet and fry gently until tender (about 15 minutes), stirring occasionally during cooking. Stir in the tomatoes and basil leaves and

season with a little salt and pepper. Cook on a low heat for a further 15 minutes, adding a little boiling water if the mixture becomes too dry.

Beat the eggs with a pinch of salt and pepper and stir them into the vegetables. Keep stirring until the eggs have scrambled. Remove from the heat and serve sprinkled with the grated Pecorino cheese.

Stuffed baked eggplants (below) and *bell peppers with scrambled eggs* (bottom)

Stuffed Baked Eggplants

Melanzane dello Skipper

To serve 4

2 large eggplants, together weighing about 1½lb

1 small onion

2-3 fresh basil leaves

1 garlic clove

5 tbsp olive oil

½lb firm ripe tomatoes

½ bouillon cube

4 heaping tbsp breadcrumbs

1 tbsp chopped parsley

2 tbsp grated Pecorino cheese

Preparation and cooking time: about 1¾ hours.

Wash the eggplants and halve them lengthwise. Scoop out the flesh, leaving a border of about ½ inch and being careful not to damage the skin. Cut the flesh into small pieces.

Chop the onion and basil and fry gently with a whole garlic clove in 4 tablespoons of olive oil. Stir in the pieces of eggplant and cook for a few minutes.

Chop the tomatoes finely, process them in a blender and add them to the pan. Season with the crumbled half-bouillon cube and a little pepper. Cover the pan and cook on a moderate heat for about 20 minutes, stirring occasionally. Remove from the heat and leave to cool. Discard the garlic. Blend in 3 heaping tablespoons of fresh breadcrumbs, the chopped parsley and grated Pecorino cheese.

Preheat the oven to 375°F. Stuff the eggplants with the prepared mixture and place them in an oiled ovenproof serving dish. Sprinkle with a tablespoon of breadcrumbs and a little olive oil. Cover the dish with aluminum foil and cook in the oven for about 1 hour. Remove the aluminum foil after about 45 minutes so that the eggplants can brown slightly on top. Serve either hot or cold.

Baby Onions and Grapes with Marsala

Cipollette e Uva al Marsala

To serve 4-5

about 4 dozen green grapes

1¾lb baby onions

butter

1 garlic clove

1 bay leaf

½ cup dry Marsala wine

granulated sugar

1 tbsp white wine vinegar

½ bouillon cube

½ tsp cornstarch

Preparation and cooking time: about 1¼ hours

Peel the grapes carefully, using a knife with a short, thin blade. Remove the outer skin and any imperfections from the onions, wash them, then plunge them into salted boiling water and boil them for about 10 minutes.

In the meantime melt a large knob of butter in a skillet and add the lightly crushed garlic clove and a small bay leaf. Next add the well-drained onions and brown them lightly, moving the pan continuously. Moisten with the Marsala wine, add a good pinch of sugar and the vinegar and flavor with the crumbled half bouillon cube.

Cover and let the liquid reduce by about half, then remove the garlic and bay leaf, add the grapes and half a teaspoon of cornstarch dissolved in 2 tablespoons of cold water. Stir gently and keep the preparation on a rather high heat until the liquid has thickened and formed a dense sauce. At this point pour the onions and grapes into a deep serving dish and serve at once.

Mediterranean Zucchini

Zucchini Mediterranea

To serve 4

¾-1 lb small tender zucchini

2-3 sprigs fresh parsley

capers

1 garlic clove

oregano

6 tbsp olive oil

Preparation and cooking time: about 30 minutes

Boil a large saucepanful of salted water. Trim the zucchini and cut into lengths of about 2 inches. Cut each piece vertically in half and then into small sticks. Put the zucchini into the boiling water and boil for a few minutes until they are cooked but still firm. Remove with a slotted spoon and lay them to cool on paper towels.

Trim and wash the parsley then dry with a clean cloth. Drain the capers and peel a small garlic clove. Coarsely chop these ingredients together and put in a bowl. Season with a pinch of salt and a small pinch of freshly ground pepper and flavor with a pinch of dried oregano. Pour in the olive oil and mix well. Arrange the cold zucchini on a small serving dish and pour over the dressing, mixing the salad at the table. This tasty and light vegetable dish may be served with a wide variety of meals.

Grandma's chick peas (top) *and*
Mediterranean zucchini

Grandma's Chick Peas
Ceci Della Nonna

To serve 4

1 cup canned chick peas

2 tbsp olive oil

2 small tomatoes, peeled and broken up coarsely with a fork

½ bouillon cube

1 small green pimiento

1 small onion

Preparation and cooking time: about 30 minutes

Rinse the chick peas thoroughly under warm running water, then leave to drain. Heat 2 tablespoons of olive oil in a skillet and as soon as it is hot, put in the tomatoes. Crumble in the half bouillon cube and fry over a low heat until some of the liquid from the tomatoes has evaporated.

Meanwhile, drain the pimiento and cut into strips no longer than ½ inch. Slice the onion into fine rings, beginning at the center where it is widest and using a very sharp knife. Add the chick peas and pimiento to the tomatoes and fry for a few minutes, so that the chick peas are just heated up. Then turn the mixture into a bowl and arrange the onion rings on top. Sprinkle with freshly ground pepper and serve.

■ VEGETABLES ■ VEGETABLES ■

Broccoli with Olives
Broccoletti alle Olive

To serve 6

3lb fresh broccoli

olive oil

2 garlic cloves

12 green olives in brine

anchovy paste

2 tbsp white wine vinegar

Preparation and cooking time: about 30 minutes

Bring a large saucepan of water to the boil and add salt. Wash the broccoli, dividing it into flowerets and cutting the tender part of the stalks into small pieces. Cook in the boiling water for about 6 minutes until just *al dente*. Drain and allow to cool on paper towels.

Heat 5 tablespoons of olive oil in a large skillet and fry the whole garlic cloves; remove when golden brown. Fry the broccoli in the garlic-flavored oil for a few minutes, tossing gently to prevent sticking. Pit the olives, quarter them and add to the broccoli, together with 4 inches of anchovy paste dissolved in the wine vinegar. Cover the skillet and cook on a low heat for a few minutes. Serve on a hot dish.

■ VEGETABLES ■ VEGETABLES ■

Ring of Spinach
Corona di Spinaci

To serve 6

1¼lb frozen spinach

1 small onion

6 tbsp butter

4 eggs

½ cup milk

nutmeg

½ cup grated Parmesan cheese

breadcrumbs

Preparation and cooking time: about 1 hour

In a saucepan bring some water to the boil, salt it, then plunge in the frozen spinach and cook until defrosted. Drain, rinse under cold running water and squeeze well. Chop the onion and soften it in 4 tablespoons of the butter, melted in a large skillet. Finely chop the spinach and cook with the onions for a few minutes then remove from the heat to a bowl to cool completely. Preheat the oven to 350°F.

In another bowl beat the eggs with the milk, season with salt and pepper and a good pinch of nutmeg. Add the egg mixture and the grated Parmesan cheese to the spinach. Adjust the salt to taste, then pour the mixture into a ring mold, well buttered and sprinkled with breadcrumbs, about 3 cups in capacity and 9 inches in diameter.

Put the mold in the preheated oven for about 30 minutes. Rest it for 5 minutes before unmolding it on to a warmed serving dish. Serve garnished, if you like, with fresh tomato sauce.

Ring of spinach

Crepes with Mushrooms and Artichokes

Crespelle con Funghi e Carciofi

To make 16 crepes

---

3 artichokes

---

juice of ½ lemon

---

1 small onion

---

1 garlic clove

---

a few sprigs parsley

---

8 tbsp butter

---

olive oil

6oz mushrooms

⅔ cup stock (or use a bouillon cube)

---

dried thyme

1½ cups flour

3¼ cups milk

---

nutmeg

---

2 eggs and 1 egg white

¾ cup grated Parmesan cheese

Preparation and cooking time: about 2 hours

Clean the artichokes and put them in a bowl of cold water with the juice of half a lemon. Finely chop the onion with a garlic clove and a few sprigs of parsley and fry in a knob of butter and 2 tablespoons of olive oil. Drain the artichokes and chop, cut up the mushrooms and add both to the pan. Stir and leave for a few minutes. Then pour in the stock, add a little salt, pepper and a pinch of thyme.

Cover and simmer over a medium heat for about 30 minutes, until the mushrooms and artichokes are tender and the liquid has almost entirely evaporated.

Purée the contents of the pan. Make a thick Béchamel sauce with 3 tablespoons of butter, the same amount of flour and 1 cup of milk. Season with salt and nutmeg. Add this to the mushroom and artichoke purée, together with an egg yolk and ½ cup of Parmesan cheese. Taste and add salt if necessary.

Now make the crepes: beat the 2 whole eggs and the egg white in a bowl, sift in 1 cup of flour and add a pinch of salt. Dilute with 1¼ cups of milk, beating with a whisk to prevent lumps forming. Brush the bottom of a skillet with a little oil and heat it well. Pour in a ladleful of the crepe batter and shake the pan rapidly to spread it evenly over the bottom of the pan. Slowly cook one side until it is golden then toss and brown the other side. Turn on to a plate and continue to make 15 more crepes. Spread them with the mushroom and artichoke mixture and fold them over. Preheat the oven to 400°F.

Prepare a Béchamel sauce with 2 tablespoons of butter and ¼ cup of flour and the rest of the milk, and when it is boiling, pour it into a round dish about 11 inches in diameter, spreading it evenly. Arrange the crepes in the dish, pour over the rest of the butter, melted, and sprinkle with the remaining grated Parmesan cheese. Bake in the oven for about 15 minutes, then serve.

Peppers and potatoes

Spinach Pie with Olives

Spinacina alle Olive

To serve 6-8

1lb frozen spinach

¼ cup butter

1½ tbsp flour

½ cup milk

¼ cup grated Parmesan cheese

4oz puff pastry

2 eggs, lightly beaten

ground nutmeg

1 tbsp breadcrumbs

4 walnuts, chopped

2 slices Piccadolce cheese, diced

Preparation and cooking time: about 1 hour plus any thawing time

Chop the spinach and sauté in 2 tablespoons of butter. Cook briskly until the moisture has evaporated and then place in a bowl. Prepare a Béchamel sauce with 1 tablespoon of butter, the flour and the milk. Stir the spinach and Parmesan cheese into the sauce and leave to cool.

Meanwhile, defrost the pastry if using frozen, roll out thinly and use to line a greased 8-inch square baking pan.

Stir the eggs into the Béchamel sauce and season with salt, pepper and a little ground nutmeg. Pierce the pastry with a fork and sprinkle with the breadcrumbs.

Preheat the oven to 375°F. Pour half the prepared mixture into the pan, sprinkle with the chopped walnuts and cover with the rest of the sauce. Trim off any excess pastry. Bake the pie in the bottom of the oven for 35-40 minutes. Sprinkle the pie with the diced Piccadolce cheese and cook for a further 5 minutes or until the cheese has melted. Turn on to a plate and serve immediately.

Spinach pie with olives

Peppers and Potatoes

Peperoni e Patate "Minuetto"

To serve 4-5

2 potatoes of equal size, together weighing about ¾lb

2 red bell peppers

¼lb onions

1 large garlic clove

4 basil leaves

olive oil

a little stock (or use bouillon cube)

a little chopped parsley

Preparation and cooking time: about 1 hour

Peel the potatoes, wash them and cut them in slices about ¼ inch thick. Cut each slice with a round, smooth pastry cutter about 1½ inches in diameter.

Heat salted water in a small saucepan; as soon as it starts to boil plunge in the potato discs and boil for 3-4 minutes, then drain them with a slotted spoon and lay them to dry and cool on a tray covered with a double sheet of paper towels. Wash and dry the peppers, cut them in half and clean them; divide each half into 3 strips.

Slice the onion and a large garlic clove very thinly; finely chop the basil leaves. Heat 5 tablespoons of olive oil in a pan, and soften the garlic and onion, without browning them. Next add the pieces of pepper and, after 5 minutes, the potato discs. Lightly fry the vegetables, adding salt, pepper and the basil. Once in a while moisten with a little hot stock.

When the potatoes and peppers are cooked and tender (they will take about 20 minutes) arrange the mixture on a serving plate, sprinkle with the chopped parsley and serve immediately.

■ VEGETABLES ■ VEGETABLES ■

Braised Baby Scallions with Runner Beans

Cipollette e Fagiolini Brasati

To serve 4

½lb runner beans

¾-1lb baby scallions

butter

½ bouillon cube

marjoram

Preparation and cooking time: about 1¼ hours

Trim the beans and wash well, and do the same with the baby scallions. Chop them both into 1¼ inch pieces. Melt the butter, add the vegetables and sauté them, taking care they do not brown. Salt sparingly, add pepper, and flavor with the crumbled half bouillon cube and a pinch of marjoram. Stir well with a wooden spoon, add ¾ cup of boiling water and bring back to the boil.

Lower the heat, cover the pan and cook for about 45 minutes or until the vegetables have absorbed all the liquid and are tender and well flavored. If any liquid remains, raise the heat to dry it off. Turn into a heated vegetable dish and serve at once.

Ham and Zucchini Pie
Sfogliata di Prosciutto e Zucchine

To serve 6

¾lb puff pastry

3 tbsp olive oil

1 garlic clove

¾lb zucchini

½ bouillon cube

powdered thyme

a little butter

1 tbsp breadcrumbs

¼lb raw ham, thinly sliced

4 eggs

½ cup grated Parmesan cheese

Preparation and cooking time: 40 minutes plus any thawing time

Defrost the puff pastry if using frozen. In a skillet heat the oil and sauté the garlic clove. Trim and wash the zucchini then slice them very finely. After discarding the garlic, cook the zucchini in the skillet until tender, seasoning with half a bouillon cube and a pinch of thyme.

Meanwhile preheat the oven to 375°F and butter a pie dish 9 inches in diameter. Divide the puff pastry into two unequal portions. Roll out the larger one and line the dish with it, then sprinkle over a tablespoon of breadcrumbs and cover with the ham. Beat 3 of the eggs with the Parmesan cheese, add a pinch each of salt and pepper. Arrange the zucchini in the pie dish in one layer then pour over the eggs.

Roll out the other piece of pastry and cover the pie, sealing all round the sides and brushing the surface with a beaten egg. Prick the pastry with a fork and put it in the oven for 35-40 minutes so that it bakes through. Remove the pie from the oven, let it rest for a few minutes, then turn it out onto a serving dish and serve at once.

Carrots with Cream
Carote alla Crema di Latte

To serve 4

1¼lb carrots

2 shallots

4 tbsp butter

⅔ cup milk

1 tsp cornstarch

½ bouillon cube

nutmeg

4 tbsp single cream

a little parsley

Preparation and cooking time: about 45 minutes

Peel the carrots, wash and drain them well, then cut them into thin sticks about 1½ inches long. Cook for about 10 minutes in salted boiling water.

Meanwhile finely chop the shallots and soften, without browning, in the butter, melted in a large skillet. Remove the carrot sticks with a slotted spoon and drain well, add them to the shallots and sauté them for a few minutes, turning them gently with a spatula.

Dissolve the cornstarch in the cold milk then add it to the carrots, pouring it in a trickle and stirring with a wooden spoon. Season the mixture with half a crumbled bouillon cube and a grinding of nutmeg, then add the cream, stirring carefully.

Leave to simmer for a few minutes on a very low heat, stirring occasionally, until the mixture is creamy. Salt to taste and serve garnished with a few parsley leaves.

Ham and zucchini pie

Tasty Baked Zucchini
Zucchine "Infornate"

To serve 6

1¼lb fresh zucchini

flour

oil for frying

¼ lb ham

¼lb Mozzarella cheese

olive oil

4-5 fresh basil leaves

1½ cups canned tomatoes, finely mashed

oregano

Preparation and cooking time: about 1½ hours

Trim the zucchini and cut them in half lengthwise. Cut them again lengthwise into strips about ⅛ inch thick. Sprinkle with salt and place on a tilted plate for about 30 minutes to drain off some of the juices.

Rinse the zucchini strips under running water, dry them and coat them in flour. Heat plenty of oil in a skillet and fry the zucchini until golden brown. Drain on paper towels.

Preheat the oven to 375°F. Cut the ham into short, thin strips and the Mozzarella cheese into slightly larger strips. Oil the bottom of a 9½-inch round pie dish and sprinkle with 4-5 chopped fresh basil leaves. Line the dish with strips of zucchini and cover them with some of the crushed tomato, a little oregano and some of the strips of ham and cheese. Continue layering in this way until all the ingredients have been used up.

Cook in the oven for about 20 minutes. Remove from the oven and leave to stand for at least 15 minutes before serving.

Carrot and Walnut Fritters
Frittelline di Carote e Noci

To serve 4

1lb baby carrots

4 tbsp flour

4 tbsp butter

1 egg

2oz walnuts, coarsely chopped

oil for frying

Preparation and cooking time: about 40 minutes

Cook the carrots in salted boiling water until tender. Drain and cool on paper towels. Purée the carrots in a blender and dry out the purée in a pan on a low heat if it seems too liquid. Stir in the flour and season with a pinch of salt and pepper. Stir in the melted butter and the egg yolk.

Beat the egg white until stiff and fold it gently into the carrot mixture. Add the walnuts. The mixture should be soft and slightly sticky. Divide the mixture into fritters about the size of a large walnut.

Heat plenty of oil in a large skillet and cook the fritters on a moderate heat. Turn the fritters during cooking so that they brown on all sides. Drain on paper towels and keep warm. Arrange on a warmed plate and serve hot.

Spicy Eggplant
Melanzane Infuocate

To serve 4

1lb eggplant

olive oil

1 small piece chili pepper

1 garlic clove, finely chopped

1 large sprig fresh parsley, chopped

Preparation and cooking time: about 50 minutes

Peel the eggplant, discarding the stalks, and cut them into ½-inch cubes. Place in a colander, sprinkle with salt and leave to drain for about 30 minutes.

Heat ⅔ cup of olive oil in a skillet and add the piece of chili pepper. Stir in the chopped garlic and half the parsley and fry gently. Dry the eggplant cubes and add to the pan. Cook on a low heat for about 20 minutes, stirring occasionally to prevent sticking.

Season with salt and discard the chili pepper. When they are tender, place the eggplant in a warmed dish, sprinkle with the remaining parsley and serve.

Tasty baked zucchini

Stewed Leeks
Porri Stufati

To serve 4

4 large fresh leeks

1 small onion

olive oil

2 tomatoes, peeled and cut into small pieces

½ cup light stock (or use bouillon cube)

Preparation and cooking time: about 50 minutes

Trim and clean the leeks, discard the outer leaves and cut in half lengthwise. Finely slice the onions and fry gently in 3 tablespoons of olive oil until transparent. Add the leeks, turning them gently until coated in the oil. Stir in the tomatoes. Pour on the stock and simmer on a low heat for about 40 minutes or until the leeks are tender. Turn the leeks occasionally during the cooking and add a little more stock if necessary. Taste and adjust the seasoning.

Carefully place the leeks and onions in a serving dish and cover with the cooking liquid. Serve hot as an accompaniment to red or white meat.

■ VEGETABLES ■ VEGETABLES ■

Asparagus in Batter
Asparagi in Pastella, Fritti

To serve 6

3-3½lb fresh asparagus

1 cup flour

1 egg yolk

¾ cup fresh cream

5 egg whites

oil for frying

Preparation and cooking time: about 1 hour

Peel and trim the asparagus and tie into a bundle with kitchen twine. Stand the bundle upright in a saucepan containing a little salted boiling water and cook for about 15 minutes or until tender. Remove the twine and spread the asparagus out to dry on paper towels.

Meanwhile prepare the batter: sift the flour into a bowl and add the egg yolk and a little salt. Gradually blend in the cream, stirring with a whisk. Beat the egg whites with a pinch of salt until stiff and then fold them into the batter mixture.

Cut the asparagus pieces in half, dip them in the batter and fry them in the hot oil until golden brown. Drain the asparagus on paper towels, arrange on a plate and sprinkle with salt. Serve immediately while still hot and crisp.

■ VEGETABLES ■ VEGETABLES ■

Treviso-style Broiled Radicchio
Radicchio all'Uso Trevisano

To serve 4

1¾lb radicchio

olive oil

black peppercorns

Preparation and cooking time: about 20 minutes

Remove the roots and any damaged leaves from the radicchio heads which should all be about the same size. Wash the heads one at a time under running water and drain thoroughly. Dry with a cloth and divide them in half, or into 4 if they are very big, lengthwise.

Wrap them in the cloth again and squeeze gently to remove any water that may still be inside. Then brush every surface with olive oil and season with salt and freshly ground black pepper. Heat the broiler then place the radicchio halves under it, at a fairly high temperature. Turn them over two or three times with a spatula. If possible, cook on a barbecue over glowing embers, and in this case, turn more frequently.

When the radicchio is cooked and crunchy, remove from the broiler, arrange on a heated oval serving dish and serve at once. You can also cook the radicchio in an iron skillet, proceeding as for the broiler. For a more delicate flavor, heat butter as well as olive oil in the pan, and cook with the lid on.

Wax Beans with Cheese Sauce
Cornetti Gialli con Salsa al Formaggio

To serve 4-6

1¼lb wax beans

4 tbsp butter

olive oil

flour

¾ cup stock (or use bouillon cube)

⅓ cup fresh whipping cream

1 egg yolk

¼ cup grated Emmental and Parmesan cheese

ground nutmeg

Preparation and cooking time: about 1 hour

Heat a pan of water. Break off the ends of the beans and wash them thoroughly. As soon as the water is boiling drop them in and cook for about 20 minutes; they should be very tender. Drain them and sauté them in a large knob of the butter and 2 tablespoons of olive oil, keeping the heat low and the pan covered. Stir occasionally and cook for about 10 minutes.

Meanwhile melt the remaining butter in another pan, fold in 2 tablespoons of flour and stir to prevent lumps forming; dilute with the hot stock and bring slowly to the boil. Remove the sauce from the heat, stir in the cream beaten with the egg yolk, the grated Emmental and Parmesan cheeses, a little salt and ground nutmeg. Stir well after the addition of each ingredient. Arrange the beans in a shallow dish, pour over the sauce, toss them gently and serve.

These beans make an ideal side dish for delicate main courses such as fillet of sole, veal escalopes, chicken and turkey breasts, roast saddle or medallions of rabbit. French beans can be prepared with the same cheese sauce.

Asparagus with Anchovies

Asparagi Verdi all'Acciuga

To serve 4

2¼ lb fresh asparagus

anchovy paste

Worcestershire sauce

2 tbsp white wine vinegar

5 tbsp olive oil

10 anchovy fillets for garnish

5 green olives, pitted and halved, for garnish

1 lemon, sliced, for garnish

Preparation and cooking time: about 1 hour

Trim the asparagus and rub gently to remove the outer skin. Wash, tie in a bundle and stand upright in a saucepan of salted boiling water (the water should come about halfway up the asparagus). Cook for about 15 minutes or until tender.

Drain and untie the asparagus and cut into 3-inch lengths. Spread out to dry on paper towels.

Prepare the sauce: Place 3 inches of anchovy paste in a bowl with a pinch of salt and a generous dash of Worcestershire sauce. Add the wine vinegar and stir with a fork until the salt has completely dissolved. Blend in the olive oil, stirring vigorously.

Arrange the hot asparagus in a warmed serving dish, dress with the prepared sauce and mix carefully. Garnish with the anchovy fillets wrapped round the halved olives and with half-slices of lemon. Serve immediately.

Filled Zucchini Chunks
Tronchetti di Zucchine

To serve 3

3 equal-sized zucchini

a little milk

1 slice very fresh white bread

¼lb ground lean beef

1 tbsp pine-nuts

handful of parsley

2 garlic cloves

¼ cup grated Parmesan cheese

1 egg yolk

ground nutmeg

5 tbsp olive oil

¼ cup meat stock

2 tbsp tomato juice

Preparation and cooking time: about 1¼ hours

Having trimmed off the ends, wash and dry the zucchini, then cut each one into 3 chunks of equal size. Remove most of the pulp of each one (keep it for a soup or a cream of vegetables), making sure not to cut the outside green part.

Prepare the stuffing: soak the slice of white bread in a small amount of milk, then squeeze it and crumble it in a bowl. Add the ground meat, the pine-nuts, the finely chopped parsley mixed with half a garlic clove, the Parmesan cheese and the egg yolk. Mix everything together thoroughly, add salt and pepper and season with ground nutmeg.

Use this mixture to stuff the 9 pieces of zucchini without overfilling them. Preheat the oven to 400°F. Heat 4 tablespoons of oil in a skillet and sauté a garlic clove. When the oil is hot, remove the garlic and throw it away, then place the chunks of zucchini in the pan and fry them lightly on each side. Next arrange them in an ovenproof dish, just big enough to contain them all in one layer; moisten them with the stock mixed with the tomato juice and a tablespoon of oil. Cover the dish and put it in the oven for about 40 minutes, uncovering the dish for the last 10 minutes. Transfer the zucchini to a serving dish.

Yellow Peppers with Aromatic Sauce
Peperoni Gialli con Trito d'Aromi

To serve 4

4 yellow bell peppers

1 garlic clove

anchovy paste

15 capers in vinegar

few sprigs parsley

1 sprig fresh watercress

Worcestershire sauce

5 tbsp olive oil

Preparation and cooking time: about 40 minutes plus at least 2 hours' resting

Wash and dry the peppers, then broil them to scorch the skins, turning them over. Then wrap them individually in a double sheet of paper towel and leave them to rest for about 10 minutes. Remove the paper and peel them completely, keeping them under running water. Dry and divide each pepper into 3 large strips, removing at the same time the seeds and the stem. Arrange the strips in a bowl, overlapping them slightly, and prepare the dressing.

Crush the garlic clove in a small bowl, add 1½ inches of anchovy paste and the finely chopped capers, parsley sprigs and watercress leaves, a pinch of salt, a few drops of Worcestershire sauce and 5 tablespoons of olive oil. Pour the sauce over the pepper strips, cover the dish with plastic wrap and leave it for at least 2 hours in a cool place. Serve the peppers sprinkled with chopped parsley in 2 or more small serving bowls.

Golden Eggplant Slices
Melanzane "Indorate"

To serve 4-5

2 eggplants, each weighing about 12oz

2 eggs

2oz Pecorino cheese, grated

2 cups fresh breadcrumbs

flour

vegetable oil for frying

Preparation and cooking time: about 40 minutes plus 1 hour's resting

Wash and dry the eggplants and cut them in slices about ½ inch thick. Lay them on a large tray covered with paper towels and sprinkle them with salt to bring out their bitter juices. Leave them to rest in a cool place for about 1 hour, then wash and dry the slices.

Beat the eggs in a bowl with a pinch of salt and pepper. Mix the Pecorino cheese with the breadcrumbs. Roll each slice of eggplant in the flour, then dip it in the beaten eggs and then in the mixture of breadcrumbs and Pecorino cheese, making sure that each coating covers the slice completely. Heat plenty of vegetable oil in a skillet; place the slices of eggplant in the pan a few at a time and brown. Remove them with a slotted spoon and, after draining, place them on a plate covered with a double sheet of paper towels to absorb the excess oil; continue to fry the others. Finally arrange the eggplant slices on a serving dish.

Filled zucchini chunks (top left), *yellow peppers with aromatic sauce* (top right) *and golden eggplant slices*

Potato Rings
"Bomboloni" di Patate

To serve 10

¾-1lb potatoes

about 5 cups plain flour

3 eggs

8 tbsp butter

3 packages yeast

a little milk

oil for deep-frying

sugar

cinnamon

Preparation and cooking time: about 1 hour plus 1½ hours' rising

Boil the potatoes, then peel them and mash immediately. As they cool, sift about 4½ cups of flour, make a well in the center and add the mashed potato, the whole eggs (not straight from the refrigerator), a pinch of salt and the softened butter, cut in small pieces. Dissolve the yeast in ½ cup of warm milk, add to the other ingredients and work the mixture in well. Dip your hands in flour to prevent the mixture sticking to them as you knead, but do not use too much, to avoid altering the proportions.

As soon as the dough is soft and pliable, cut it into pieces and form them one at a time into long rolls with a diameter of about ¾ inch. Cut these into lengths of about 6 inches and form them into rings. Place them on 3 or more trays, lined with dish-towels sprinkled lightly with flour, and keep them well spaced, so that they will not stick together when they rise. Cover the small rings with paper towels and leave to rise in a warm place (about 80°F) for about 1½ hours.

Place a deep skillet, fitted with a basket and containing plenty of oil, on the heat and when it is very hot, but not boiling, plunge the rings into it 2 or 3 at a time, turning them several times during cooking. The heat must be kept moderate, otherwise the outside of the rings may brown, while the inside is still uncooked. As soon as they are ready, lift them out of the oil, using a slotted spoon, and drain well, then spread them out on a plate covered with paper towels and proceed to cook the others. In a deep plate, mix some sugar with a little ground cinnamon and dip the hot rings in this, then serve immediately.

Asparagus au Gratin
Asparagi Gratinati

To serve 4

2½ lb fresh asparagus

6 tbsp butter

3 tbsp flour

1 cup meat stock

1 egg yolk

¼ cup whipping cream

¾ cup grated Parmesan cheese

Preparation and cooking time: about 1 hour 20 minutes.

Trim, peel and wash the asparagus and tie in a bundle with kitchen twine. Stand the bundle upright in a saucepan of enough salted boiling water to come halfway up the asparagus and cook for about 15 minutes. Drain, discard the twine and spread the asparagus out to dry and cool on absorbent paper towels. Preheat the oven to 400°F.

Lightly butter a rectangular ovenproof dish which will hold the asparagus lengthwise. Melt 3 tablespoons of the butter in a saucepan and stir in the flour to form a smooth *roux*. Gradually add the boiling stock and bring back to the boil, stirring constantly. Remove the pan from the heat and blend in the egg yolk and cream.

Arrange half the asparagus in the ovenproof dish and sprinkle on about ¼ cup of the grated Parmesan cheese. Pour over half of the prepared sauce and sprinkle with about ¼ cup of Parmesan cheese. Form a second layer in the same way using the remainder of the sauce and cheese.

Melt the remaining butter and pour it over the asparagus. Cook in the oven for about 15 minutes and serve immediately.

Asparagus with Vinaigrette
Asparagi Bianchi alla Castellana

To serve 4

3½lb fresh asparagus

anchovy paste

1 tsp mustard

1 tbsp white wine vinegar

5 tbsp olive oil

Preparation and cooking time: about ¾ hour

Tail, scrape and wash the asparagus and tie in a bundle with kitchen twine. Stand the bundle upright in a saucepan of enough salted boiling water to come halfway up the asparagus and cook for about 12 minutes or until tender. Drain, discard the twine and spread the asparagus out to dry on paper towels.

Place in a bowl a generous pinch of salt and pepper, about 1 inch of anchovy paste, a teaspoon of mustard and a tablespoon of wine vinegar. Stir with a fork until the salt has completely dissolved. Add 5 tablespoons of olive oil, stirring constantly.

Serve the asparagus, either hot or warm, with the prepared sauce.

Asparagus au gratin and asparagus with vinaigrette

Brussels Sprouts with Ham and Cream

Cavolini di Bruxelles con Panna e Prosciutto

To serve 6

2¼lb Brussels sprouts

1 medium onion

1 garlic clove

2 tbsp butter

1 tbsp olive oil

slice of ham, weighing about ¼ lb

½ cup whipping cream

½ bouillon cube

nutmeg

Preparation and cooking time: 1¼ hours

Remove the outer leaves from the Brussels sprouts, trim the stalks and make 2 deep cuts in the shape of a cross in the base. Place them in a lightly salted bowl of cold water while you heat a large saucepanful of water. When it begins to boil add a little salt and put in the sprouts. Boil them for about 12 minutes. Remove from the water with a slotted spoon, shaking off as much water as possible, and lay them on paper towels to drain and cool.

Meanwhile, finely slice the onion and gently fry in the butter and olive oil in a large skillet, together with the lightly crushed garlic clove. Take care not to let them brown. Quarter the Brussels sprouts and cut the ham into strips. Add these to the onions in the skillet. Fry together for a few seconds, shaking the pan frequently. Heat the cream, without boiling it, and add to the other ingredients. Shake the skillet again to mix them, then cover and simmer for about 10 minutes, adding a little boiling water if necessary. Finally, remove the garlic and adjust the salt. Sprinkle on a little grated nutmeg, arrange in a hot ovenproof dish and serve.

Braised brussels sprouts (top); soybean sprouts with parmesan (center) and brussels sprouts with ham and cream

Soybean Sprouts with Parmesan

Germogli di Soia alla Parmigiana

To serve 4

¾lb soybean sprouts

¼ cup butter

1 garlic clove

½ bouillon cube

¼ cup grated Parmesan cheese

Preparation and cooking time: about 30 minutes

Preheat the oven to 400°F. Heat a large saucepanful of water and add a little salt when it begins to boil. Wash the soybean sprouts thoroughly under cold running water then drain and put into the boiling water for about 1 minute. Remove with a slotted spoon, place in a colander and leave to drain thoroughly.

Heat the butter in a large skillet and put in a lightly crushed garlic clove. Once this is brown, remove it. Now put in the bean sprouts and crumble in the half-bouillon cube. Mix carefully and fry gently for a few minutes. Arrange in an ovenproof dish in layers, sprinkling a little Parmesan cheese and milling a little fresh pepper over each layer. Cook in the oven for about 10 minutes then serve.

■ VEGETABLES ■ VEGETABLES ■

Braised Brussels Sprouts

Cavolini di Bruxelles, Stufati

To serve 6

2¼lb Brussels sprouts

about ½ cup butter

juice of 1 lemon

1 tbsp grated Parmesan cheese

Preparation and cooking time: about 1¼ hours

Preheat the oven to 350°F. Remove the tough outer leaves from the Brussels sprouts and trim the stalks. Cut each one into quarters and leave to soak in a large

bowl of lightly salted cold water for about 30 minutes. Drain well and arrange in a buttered, fairly heavy, heatproof dish which can also be used as a serving dish. Dot the rest of the butter among the Brussels sprouts. Sprinkle with salt and pepper and pour over the strained lemon juice.

Cover the dish with a tightly fitting lid and cook in the oven for about 30 minutes or a little longer, depending on the size and freshness of the sprouts. From time to time turn the sprouts over then replace the lid. The Brussels sprouts should end up perfectly cooked and dry. Remove from the oven, sprinkle with a tablespoon of Parmesan cheese, mix with care and serve.

■ VEGETABLES ■ VEGETABLES ■

Vegetable and Ham Casserole

Verdure al Forno con Prosciutto Cotto

To serve 4

3 fennel bulbs

4 young carrots

¾lb asparagus tips

¼ cup butter

⅝ cup whipping cream

¼ lb ham

2 tbsp grated Parmesan cheese

Preparation and cooking time: about 1 hour 20 minutes

Preheat the oven to 350°F. Clean the fennel, cut them in half and slice them thinly. Scrape the carrots and cut them into fine rings. Cut the asparagus into small pieces. Rinse them all thoroughly and leave to drain. Butter an ovenproof dish and arrange the vegetables in layers. Add salt and cover them with the cream.

Dot with the remaining butter, cover the dish with a sheet of aluminum foil, and cook in the oven for about 50 minutes. Meanwhile, cut the ham into strips and, when the vegetables are cooked, mix it with them. Sprinkle with the Parmesan cheese and replace in the oven, uncovered, for another 10 minutes. Serve hot.

Country Style French Beans

Fagiolini alla Moda Paesana

To serve 4

¾ lb French beans

1 small onion

1 small carrot

1 stalk celery

1 large garlic clove

2 slices bacon, diced very small

2 tbsp butter

2 tbsp olive oil

½lb peeled tomatoes

1 small bay leaf

2 or 3 sprigs parsley

2 fresh basil leaves

a pinch of sugar

¼ cup grated Parmesan cheese

Preparation and cooking time: about 45 minutes

Preheat the oven to 400°F. Boil the beans in salted water until tender then lay them out to cool and dry on a tea-towel. Finely chop the onion, carrot, celery and garlic, removing the green shoot from the garlic. Gently fry together with the bacon in the butter and oil. Rub the tomatoes through a sieve, or put them through the finest disk of a food processor and add to the pan. Tie the bay leaf, parsley and basil leaves together and add these too. Season with a little salt and pepper and add a pinch of sugar.

Simmer for about 10 minutes with the pan half-covered, then add the beans and leave them to absorb the flavors for about 10 minutes, tossing frequently. Remove the herbs and pour the contents of the pan into an ovenproof dish that is also a serving dish. Sprinkle with the grated Parmesan cheese and bake in the oven for about 10 minutes, then serve at once.

French Beans and Onions

Fagiolini Cipollati

To serve 4

¾-1lb French beans

½lb onions

½ sprig rosemary

1 garlic clove

2 tbsp butter

olive oil

2-3 tbsp dry Marsala wine

½ bouillon cube

nutmeg

⅔ cup light stock

1 tsp cornstarch

Preparation and cooking time: about 45 minutes

Cook the beans in salted boiling water until tender, drain and lay out to cool and dry on a dish-towel. Slice the onions very thinly and finely chop the rosemary leaves together with the garlic. Gently fry the onion in the butter and 3 tablespoons of olive oil, taking care not to let them brown. Add the beans and leave for a few minutes.

Pour in the Marsala wine. Allow to evaporate then crumble in the bouillon cube and season with a little grated nutmeg. Dissolve the cornstarch in the cold stock and pour into the pan. Shake the pan and cover, turn the heat down and leave the beans to simmer until the sauce has become thick. Taste and correct seasoning with salt, then place the beans on a serving dish and serve piping hot.

French Beans with Crab

Fagiolini al Granchio

To serve 6

1½lb French beans

6oz canned crab meat

1 tender lettuce heart

2 anchovy fillets in oil

a handful of parsley

5 or 6 mushrooms in oil

1 tbsp white wine vinegar

¼ cup mayonnaise

1 tsp mustard

Worcestershire sauce

Preparation and cooking time: 30 minutes

Boil the beans in salted water until tender, then drain and lay them out to dry on a large tray covered with a double layer of paper towels. Crumble the crab meat finely. Remove the tender leaves from the lettuce heart one at a time, wash and dry thoroughly.

Now prepare the sauce: Finely chop the anchovy fillets with the parsley and mushrooms. Put these in a bowl and incorporate first the vinegar and then the mayonnaise, flavoring with the mustard and a dash of Worcestershire sauce. Mix with great care after each addition. You should obtain a smooth, fairly runny sauce. In a salad bowl mix the beans and crab meat, arrange the lettuce leaves around the outside and serve accompanied by the sauce. Pour the sauce over the beans and crab at table.

French beans with crab (top left), *French beans and onions* (lower left) and *country style French beans* (upper right)

Potato and Mushroom Bake

Teglia di Patate e Funghi

To serve 6-8

¾lb fresh mushrooms

1¾lb potatoes, approximately equal in size

---

a bunch of parsley

3-4 fresh basil leaves

---

1 small garlic clove

---

3 tbsp breadcrumbs

---

3 tbsp grated Pecorino cheese

---

6 tbsp olive oil

Preparation and cooking time: about 1½ hours

Preheat the oven to 350°F. Trim the mushroom stalks and wipe the caps with a damp cloth. Slice them vertically, not too finely. Peel, wash and dry the potatoes, then cut them into slices about ¼ inch thick. Wash and dry the parsley and wipe the basil leaves with a damp cloth. Coarsely chop the herbs together with the garlic. Place these ingredients in a bowl and add the breadcrumbs and the Pecorino cheese; season with salt and a little freshly ground pepper. Mix with the fingertips.

Into a round ovenproof dish 10 inches in diameter pour 1 tablespoon of olive oil to grease the dish. Make a layer of potato slices, placing them close together without piling them on top of each other. Sprinkle with a pinch of salt and place half the mushrooms on top of the potatoes. Spread half the herb mixture on top. Then pour over 2 tablespoons of olive oil. Make another layer of potatoes and sprinkle with salt. Place the remaining mushrooms on top and spread the rest of the herb mixture on the mushrooms. Pour 4 tablespoons of olive oil over and cover with a sheet of aluminum foil.

Bake for about 1 hour. Ten minutes before removing from the oven, take off the aluminum foil and let the surface brown a little. Remove the pie from the oven and serve.

Potato and mushroom bake

Artichokes Stuffed with Ham

Carciofi Ripieni al Prosciutto

To serve 4

---

4 artichokes

---

juice of 1 lemon

---

a little flour

2oz lean ham

---

5 tbsp butter

½ cup milk

¼ bouillon cube

¼ cup grated Emmental cheese

---

3 tbsp Parmesan cheese

Preparation and cooking time: about 1¼ hours

Trim the artichokes and remove the tough outer leaves, but reserve the tender central flesh of the stalks. Cut the artichokes in half lengthwise, scoop out and discard the chokes. Place the halves in a bowl of water with half the lemon juice.

Bring a large saucepan of water to the boil. Add salt, the rest of the lemon juice and the flour dissolved in a little cold water. Add the artichokes and stalks and cook for about 20 minutes or until the outer leaves are tender. Drain and cool on paper towels.

Preheat the oven to 375°F. Finely chop the artichoke stalks and the ham. Prepare a Béchamel sauce with 2 tablespoons of butter, a tablespoon of flour and the milk. Blend in the crumbled quarter bouillon cube and the grated Emmental cheese. Stir in the chopped ham and artichoke stalks.

Fill the artichoke halves with the prepared sauce and arrange them in a buttered ovenproof pan. Pour on 2 tablespoons of melted butter, sprinkle with the grated Parmesan cheese and bake in the oven for about 20 minutes or until golden brown. Serve hot.

Bismark-style Leeks
Porro alla Bismarck

To serve 4

16 leeks, not too large and all about the same size

½ cup butter

⅜ cup grated Parmesan cheese

4 eggs

Preparation and cooking time: about 40 minutes

Trim the leeks, removing the roots, the tops of the leaves and discarding the outer layer. Boil water in a narrow saucepan which is deep enough to immerse the white part of the leeks (an asparagus pan is ideal). Add salt when the water begins to boil. Tie the leeks together in bunches of 4 and put them in the boiling water. Boil them for about 10 minutes. Remove them when they are tender but still firm. Untie them and place 4 leeks on each of 4 plates. Melt ¼ cup of the butter and, as soon as it is hot (it is essential not to let it brown), pour a little over each plate of leeks. Sprinkle with grated Parmesan cheese and keep warm in the lit oven with the door open.

Melt the remaining butter in a large skillet and break in the eggs. Salt the whites only and cook until the whites have completely set while the yolks remain runny. Remove carefully with a spatula and place an egg in the center of the white part of the leeks on each plate. Serve at once. This is an ideal accompaniment for very light meat or fish dishes, or it can be served as a course on its own.

Savoy Cabbage with Onions
Verza Cipollata

To serve 4

¾lb savoy cabbage

6oz onions

4 tbsp cooking fat

rosemary

1 garlic clove

olive oil

1 bouillon cube

ground nutmeg

a little dry white wine

Preparation and cooking time: about 45 minutes

Bring a large saucepan of water to the boil and add salt. Wash and drain the cabbage and boil for about 5 minutes. Meanwhile slice the onions thinly. Blend the fat with a few leaves of rosemary and a garlic clove and fry gently in 2 tablespoons of olive oil. Add the onions and cook until transparent.

Drain the cabbage, slice thickly and add to the onions. Flavor with half a crumbled bouillon cube, pepper and a pinch of nutmeg, and sprinkle with a little white wine. Cover the pan and allow the wine to evaporate, stirring occasionally. Test and adjust the seasoning to taste. Serve immediately.

■ VEGETABLES ■ VEGETABLES ■

Broiled Asparagus Bundles
Asparagi in Gabbia, Grigliati

To serve 4

24 fresh asparagus spears

2 tbsp butter

16 thin slices smoked bacon

Preparation and cooking time: about 45 minutes

Peel and trim the asparagus and tie in a bundle with kitchen string. Stand the bundle upright in a saucepan of enough salted boiling water to come halfway up the asparagus and cook for about 12 minutes or until tender. Remove the string and spread the asparagus out to dry and cool on kitchen paper.

Divide the asparagus into 8 bundles of 3 spears each and brush with the melted butter. Wrap each bundle in 2 slices of bacon. Brown gently under the broiler, turning carefully with a spatula so that they cook evenly. Place on a warmed dish and serve.

■ VEGETABLES ■ VEGETABLES ■

Stuffed Tomatoes
Pomi Dorati con Riso

To serve 4

1 bouillon cube

4 tomatoes, of equal size, together weighing about 1lb

5 tbsp butter

2 tbsp chopped onion

½ cup frozen young peas

½ cup rice

5 tbsp butter

1 tbsp flour

1 cup milk

½ cup grated Parmesan cheese

fresh basil leaves for garnish

Preparation and cooking time: about 1 hour

Preheat the oven to 350°F. Prepare some stock by heating ¾ cup of water with half the bouillon cube. Wash and dry the tomatoes, cut them in half horizontally, sprinkle the insides with a pinch of salt and turn them upside down on a tray covered with paper towels. Melt 5 teaspoons of the butter in an ovenproof dish and put in the onion. Lightly fry, then add the peas and the rice. Then pour in the boiling stock and bring back to the boil. Cover the pan with a lightly buttered sheet of aluminum foil and place in the oven for 15 minutes.

Meanwhile, in a small pan prepare a Béchamel sauce by melting 5 teaspoons of butter, stirring in the flour and adding the milk; flavor with the other ½ bouillon cube. Remove the rice from the oven and fluff up with a fork, incorporating a little butter. Leave to cool. Dry the tomatoes with paper towels and arrange in a buttered ovenproof dish. Add two-thirds of the Béchamel sauce to the rice as well as ⅓ cup grated Parmesan cheese. Fill the tomato halves with the mixture, heaping it up to make dome shapes. Pour over the rest of the Béchamel and sprinkle over the Parmesan. Place in the oven for about 20 minutes, until the surface of the tomatoes is slightly golden. Serve garnished with fresh basil.

Stuffed tomatoes

Peas and Carrots with Bacon

Piselli e Carote "Affumicate"

To serve 6

1 small leek, white part only

butter

olive oil

¼lb ham

2oz smoked bacon

¾lb frozen peas

1lb young carrots

½ bouillon cube

2 garlic cloves

thyme

ground nutmeg

Preparation and cooking time: about 1¼ hours

Chop the leek and sauté it in 2 tablespoons of butter and a tablespoon of olive oil, but do not let it brown. Dice the ham and bacon, add them to the leek and fry gently for a few moments, then add the still frozen peas and the carrots, cut into ⅔-inch cubes. Sauté gently until tender, then add 2½ cups of water and flavor with the crumbled half bouillon cube, the crushed garlic and a pinch each of thyme and ground nutmeg.

Bring to the boil, reduce the heat, put on the lid and cook for about 45 minutes, or until everything is tender and has absorbed all the liquid (if the liquid boils away during cooking, add more hot water). Remove the garlic and serve hot.

Broiled asparagus bundles (top)

Cauliflower with Tomato and Garlic Sauce

Cavolfiore alla Pizzaiola

To serve 6

1 cauliflower weighing about 2¼lb

1 small onion

2 garlic cloves

¼ cup olive oil

¾-1 lb peeled tomatoes

a little sugar

oregano

4 fresh basil leaves

¼ cup butter

¼ lb Mozzarella cheese

¼ cup grated Parmesan cheese

Preparation and cooking time: about 1 hour

Preheat the oven to 400°F. Bring 3 cups of salted water to boiling in a saucepan. Wash the cauliflower thoroughly and simmer in the uncovered pan for about 12 minutes. Meanwhile, finely chop the onion and garlic, removing the green centers. Sauté in the olive oil and, after a few minutes, add the tomatoes, rubbed through a sieve or put through a food processor with the finest disk. Add a pinch of sugar and a little salt and pepper. Stir, and cook for about 15 minutes, stirring from time to time. Then add a pinch of oregano and the finely chopped basil leaves.

When the cauliflower is cooked and tender, remove it carefully from the pan with a slotted spoon and place it on a dish covered with a double layer of paper towels to absorb the moisture. Then place it in a buttered ovenproof dish with high sides that just contains it. Dice the Mozzarella and scatter the pieces between the cauliflower flowerets. Melt 2 tablespoons of butter and pour over the cauliflower and sprinkle with the grated Parmesan cheese. Place the dish in the oven for about 10 minutes. Pour some of the tomato sauce over the cauliflower and serve immediately, with the remaining sauce served in a sauceboat.

Cauliflower "Ninette"

Cavolifiore "Ninette"

To serve 6

2½lb cauliflower

1 small onion

1 cup small mushrooms

6 tbsp butter

1 tbsp olive oil

½ bouillon cube

½ cup whipping cream

2 tbsp flour

1¼ cups milk

ground nutmeg

2 or 3 celery leaves for garnish

Preparation and cooking time: about 50 minutes

Boil a large saucepanful of salted water. Wash and drain the cauliflower and simmer for about 15 minutes in the uncovered saucepan. While the cauliflower is cooking, finely chop the onion and mushrooms and lightly fry them in 2 tablespoons of the butter and the olive oil, taking care not to let them brown. Crumble in the bouillon cube and add the cream. Simmer for 2 or 3 minutes, then liquidize in a blender.

Melt the remaining butter in a saucepan and combine with the flour, stirring with a small whisk to prevent lumps forming. Boil the milk and pour in gradually. Bring to the boil, stirring constantly, add salt and a little ground or freshly grated nutmeg. Remove from the heat and stir in the mushroom and onion cream, then pour into a buttered ovenproof dish. Drain the cauliflower thoroughly, divide it into flowerets and arrange in the dish. Place over the heat and simmer gently for a few seconds. Chop the celery leaves and sprinkle over the top before serving.

Cauliflower with tomato and garlic sauce (above left) and *lima beans with mustard*

Lima Beans with Mustard

Fagioli Bianchi alla Senape

To serve 4-6

1½lb canned Lima beans

1 tsp white wine vinegar

1 tbsp mustard

4 tbsp olive oil

1 tbsp stock

½ garlic clove

a few sprigs parsley

a celery leaf

Preparation time: about 30 minutes

Drain the beans thoroughly and rinse under running water. Then leave them to dry on paper towels. In a small bowl, combine a pinch of salt, a pinch of finely ground white pepper, teaspoon of white wine vinegar and a tablespoon of mustard. Mix with a fork until the salt has dissolved, then add the olive oil followed immediately by a tablespoon of boiling stock. Stir vigorously to obtain a smooth sauce. Put the beans in a serving bowl rubbed with garlic and pour the sauce over. Sprinkle with chopped parsley and celery leaf and mix at table.

Cauliflower Ninette

Fava Beans Lyonnaise
Fave alla Lionese

To serve 4

4½lb fresh fava beans

1 large onion

1 garlic clove

3 slices bacon

2 tbsp olive oil

2 tbsp butter

a little stock (or use bouillon cube)

ground thyme

Preparation and cooking time: about 1½ hours

Shell the beans and remove their skins too, dropping them into cold water as they are done. Boil them for 5 minutes in salted water, then drain well. Slice the onion very thinly, crush the garlic and cut the bacon into short narrow strips. Heat the oil and butter and brown the garlic, then remove and discard it. Put the onion and bacon in the hot fat and fry them gently without browning, then add the beans and stir them in for a few minutes with a wooden spoon. Ladle in a little hot stock and flavor with a pinch of thyme and some freshly ground pepper. Stew the beans until they are tender and have absorbed nearly all the liquid, then adjust the seasoning and serve in a hot dish.

Young raw fava beans go well with Pecorino cheese, sliced salami and hard-boiled egg to make a nourishing snack or attractive appetizer. This habit of eating beans raw was originally Roman, but is now widespread.

Fava beans Lyonnaise

Casserole of New Potatoes, Artichokes and Peas
Patatine, Carciofi e Piselli in Tegame

To serve 6

4 artichokes

juice of ½ lemon

1 small onion

1 small garlic clove

1 sprig fresh parsley

5 tbsp olive oil

3 tbsp dry white wine

⅝ cup stock (or use bouillon cube)

thyme

¾-1 lb new potatoes

¼ cup butter

2 leaves sage

2¾ cups frozen tiny peas

2-3 slices bacon

dried mint

Preparation and cooking time: about 2 hours

Trim the artichokes, remove the tough outer leaves and put them in a bowl of water, together with the lemon juice. Chop half the onion finely with the garlic and a handful of parsley and place this in a pan that will hold the artichokes. Add 3 tablespoons each of olive oil, and white wine, and ¼ cup stock. Place the artichokes in the pan stalks upwards and season with salt, pepper and a pinch of thyme. Put the lid on and place on a low heat over a wire mesh or fireproof mat. Cook gently until the artichokes are tender and have absorbed most of the liquid.

Meanwhile, scrape the potatoes and boil them in salted water for 3-4 minutes, then drain well and place in a large casserole with the melted butter, 2 tablespoons of olive oil and the sage. Continue cooking over a very low heat until they are tender and slightly browned.

Boil the peas for 3-4 minutes. Chop the remaining onion finely with the bacon and sauté the mixture in the remaining butter, taking care that it does not brown. Add the peas and the remaining boiling stock, and season with a pinch of dried mint. Simmer until the peas have absorbed most of the liquid. Remove the sage, and add the peas to the potatoes. Cut the artichokes into 6 and add them too, with their cooking juices. Simmer for a further 5 minutes and serve.

Mushroom Soufflé
Soufflé di Funghi

To serve 4

2½ cups milk

¾ cup flour

8 tbsp butter

2 eggs plus 1 egg yolk

4 tbsp grated Parmesan cheese

nutmeg

2oz Fontina cheese

¾-1lb mushrooms

2-3 sprigs fresh parsley

1 medium onion

1 garlic clove

olive oil

½ bouillon cube

3 tbsp breadcrumbs

Preparation and cooking time: about 1½ hours

Prepare a thick Béchamel sauce with the milk, flour and 4 tablespoons of the butter. Take it off the heat and add the 3 egg yolks one at a time and the grated Parmesan. Season with pepper and nutmeg. Let it cool, stirring frequently

Wash the mushrooms quickly under running water, dry them and slice them thinly. Finely chop the parsley with the onion and garlic and sauté them in the remaining butter with 1 tablespoon of olive oil. Add the mushrooms and cook for about 15 minutes. Season with the crumbled half bouillon cube, remove from the heat and allow to cool. Whisk the 2 egg whites until stiff, add a pinch of salt and fold them very gently into the tepid Béchamel sauce.

Preheat the oven to 400°F. Turn a third of the Béchamel sauce mixture into a buttered 6-cup soufflé dish. Arrange half the mushrooms and a tablespoon of breadcrumbs on top, and cover these with half the remaining mixture, then the remaining mushrooms and another tablespoon of breadcrumbs. Cover the top with the sliced Fontina cheese and a last tablespoon of breadcrumbs. Cook in the oven for about 30 minutes and serve

Roulades with Cabbage and Spinach
Involtini di Verza con Spinaci

To serve 4

8 large savoy cabbage leaves, together weighing about 1 lb

½lb spinach, boiled and drained

6 tbsp butter

¾ cup grated Parmesan cheese

1 small egg

ground nutmeg

Preparation and cooking time: about 1 hour and 40 minutes

Bring to the boil a large saucepanful of salted water. Wash the cabbage leaves thoroughly, drain them and boil for about 15 minutes; do not overcook or the leaves may break. Drain, spread them on paper towels and leave to cool. Preheat the oven to 350°F.

Meanwhile prepare the stuffing: Sauté the spinach in 5 teaspsoons of the butter then chop finely and place in a bowl, add ½ cup of the grated Parmesan cheese, the egg, a pinch of salt, pepper and nutmeg. Mix together well. Divide each cabbage leaf in two, removing the central hard rib. On to each half place a tablespoon of the stuffing, then roll up the leaf enclosing the stuffing inside. Tie each package with thread and arrange the roulades in a buttered ovenproof dish. Sprinkle with the remaining grated Parmesan cheese and moisten with the rest of the butter, melting it first.

Bake for about 30 minutes. Serve the roulades, after removing the threads, from the dish in which they were cooked.

Roulades with cabbage and spinach

Baby Onions and Mushrooms in Marsala Wine

Cipollette e Funghi all'Antica

To serve 4-6

1 garlic clove, lightly crushed

4 tsp butter

2 tbsp olive oil

1¼lb baby onions

¾lb medium-sized mushrooms

½ tsp cornstarch

¼ cup dry Marsala wine

a little ground thyme

a little stock (or use bouillon cube)

Worcestershire sauce

1 tbsp chopped parsley

Preparation and cooking time: about 1¼ hours

Sauté a lightly crushed garlic clove in the butter and olive oil. Add the baby onions and cook for a few minutes.

Wash and slice the mushrooms and add them to the pan. Dissolve the cornstarch in the Marsala wine and pour it into the pan. Stir and season with a little salt, pepper and thyme. Cover and simmer gently for about 40 minutes, stirring occasionally and adding a little boiling stock if necessary.

When the vegetables are tender and a thick sauce has formed, remove the pan from the heat. Test and adjust seasoning according to taste, adding a splash of Worcestershire sauce. Sprinkle with the chopped parsley and serve.

Vegetable Medley

Tris Vegetariano

To serve 4

¾lb small tender French beans

2 firm cucumbers

¼lb onions

2 tbsp butter

olive oil

½ cup beef stock

1 tbsp dry sherry

marjoram

Preparation and cooking time: about 1¼ hours

Trim the French beans, wash them carefully, then boil them in salted water for about 15 minutes. Meanwhile peel the cucumbers, divide them in half lengthwise and scoop out the seeds. Next cut them in small sticks about 2-2½ inches long, drop them in salted boiling water, and boil them for 5 minutes. Drain both vegetables and put them on a tray covered with a double sheet of paper towels, to cool and drain.

Slice the onion very thinly and soften it slowly in a skillet, in the butter melted with 2 tablespoons of olive oil. Make sure the onion doesn't brown. Then add the French beans and cucumbers, leave them to brown and absorb flavor for about 10 minutes on a very low heat. Moisten them with the stock and sherry, and season with a pinch of marjoram. Cover the skillet and let the liquid reduce almost completely. Transfer the vegetables to a heated serving dish and serve at once.

Baby onions and mushrooms in Marsala

Peas with Mortadella

Pisellini con Petitella

To serve 6

3 shallots, finely chopped

butter

olive oil

1lb frozen peas

¼lb mortadella sausage

½ bouillon cube

ground nutmeg

Preparation and cooking time: about 30 minutes

Sauté the shallots in a large knob of butter and 2 tablespoons of olive oil. Cook the peas in salted boiling water for about 4 minutes. Skin the mortadella, cut it in half lengthwise and slice it thinly into crescent shapes. Drain the peas and add them to the shallots. Stir and season with half a crumbled bouillon cube, a pinch of pepper and a little ground nutmeg.

Pour on ½ cup of water, stir and cover the pan. Allow the peas to absorb all the liquid. Two minutes before removing from the heat, stir in the crescents of mortadella, replace the lid on the pan and finish cooking. Serve in a warmed dish.

Baby Onions with Tarragon

Cipollette al Dragoncello

To serve 4

2lb baby onions

butter

2 tbsp dripping

1 tbsp sugar

2 tbsp red wine vinegar

tarragon

Preparation and cooking time: about 1¼ hours

Heat plenty of water in a saucepan and salt it as soon as it comes to the boil. Peel and trim the onions and cook them in the water for 15 minutes. Drain them and leave them to dry on paper towels.

Preheat the oven to 350°F. Melt a large knob of butter and dripping in an ovenproof dish. As soon as the fats are hot, add the sugar and wine vinegar. Once the vinegar has evaporated to form a thick syrupy sauce, add the onions and cook briskly for a few minutes. Season with a little salt and pepper and a generous pinch of tarragon. Place in the oven and cook for about 40 minutes, turning the onions after 20 minutes. Remove from the oven and serve.

Zucchini with Scrambled Eggs

Zucchine con la "Stracciatella"

To serve 6

1¼lb fresh zucchini

3 slices bacon

5 tsp butter

1 tbsp olive oil

1 small onion

3 eggs

⅜ cup grated Pecorino cheese

1 tbsp fresh breadcrumbs

Preparation and cooking time: about 30 minutes

Wash, and trim the zucchini and cut them into slices about ¼ inch thick. Cut the bacon into very small pieces or thin strips and fry gently in the butter and olive oil. Add the finely chopped onion and cook gently until transparent, stirring frequently.

Add the slices of zucchini, stir and season with salt and pepper. Cover the pan and cook on a very low heat for about 10 minutes or until the zucchini are tender. Add a little hot water or stock during cooking if the mixture becomes too dry.

When the zucchini are almost cooked, beat the eggs in a bowl with the Pecorino cheese, breadcrumbs and a large pinch of salt. Pour the mixture over the zucchini, stir gently and keep the pan on the heat until the eggs have set slightly. Serve immediately.

Zucchini with scrambled eggs

Ham and Endive Rolls
Involtini di Indivia

To serve 4

4 large heads Belgian endive, together weighing about 1¼lb

3 tbsp butter

a little dry white wine

8 bacon slices, sliced lengthwise

1 slice Emmental cheese

Preparation and cooking time: about 1½ hours

Trim and wash the endive and cut them in half lengthwise. Cook in salted boiling water for about 10 minutes. Drain and leave to dry on paper towels.

Melt 2 tablespoons of butter in a large skillet. Cut the endives in half again lengthwise and fry briskly in the butter until golden brown. Pour on a little white wine and remove the pan from the heat as soon as the wine has evaporated. Drain the endive and leave to cool.

Preheat the oven to 350°F. Wrap each piece of endive in a bacon strip, leaving the tip free. Arrange the rolls tip to tail in a buttered ovenproof pan. Dot with strips of Emmental cheese and bake for about 20 minutes or until the bacon is lightly crisped. Serve.

Ham and endive rolls (top)

Mushrooms à la Grecque

Funghi di Coltura Ateniesi

To serve 6

¾-1 lb small fresh mushrooms

5 tbsp strained lemon juice

5 tbsp olive oil

1 bay leaf

2 garlic cloves

large bunch of parsley

1 small rib celery

4-5 black peppercorns

1 red onion

Preparation and cooking time: about 50 minutes plus cooling

Trim the stems of the mushrooms and peel or wipe the caps. Rinse them well. Place on the heat a saucepan with 2¼ cups of water, the lemon juice, the olive oil, bay leaf, 2 halved garlic cloves, 3-4 chopped parsley sprigs, the chopped celery, 4-5 peppercorns and a good pinch of salt; bring to the boil then simmer for a couple of minutes, half-covered.

Meanwhile, quarter the mushrooms then plunge them into the liquid and simmer for about 15 minutes. Meanwhile, chop a small handful of parsley and cut 6 thin rings from the onion. When the mushrooms are ready pour them into a bowl with the hot cooking liquid, removing the garlic and bay leaf. Leave to cool at room temperature, then sprinkle with the chopped parsley, garnish with the onion rings and serve. These mushrooms, kept in the liquid and covered with plastic wrap will keep for 3-4 days in the refrigerator.

Stuffed Tomatoes au Gratin

Pomodori all'Uovo, Gratinati

To serve 6

3 very large tomatoes

3 eggs

6oz canned tuna in oil

1½ cups fresh breadcrumbs

¼ cup grated Parmesan cheese

1 large sprig parsley, finely chopped

1 garlic clove, finely chopped

a little oil

Preparation and cooking time: about 1 hour 20 minutes

Cut the tomatoes in half using a sharp knife and discard the seeds. Sprinkle the insides with a little salt and place the tomatoes upside down on paper towels to drain.

Hard-boil the eggs, cool under running water and shell them. Crumble the egg yolks and mix them with the drained tuna, the breadcrumbs, the grated Parmesan cheese and the chopped parsley and garlic. Season with a pinch of salt and blend thoroughly.

Preheat the oven to 375°F. Stuff the tomatoes with the prepared mixture and arrange them in a lightly oiled baking tray. Pour on a little oil, cover with foil and cook in the oven for 20 minutes. Remove the foil and cook for a further 15 minutes or until the stuffed tomatoes are golden brown on top.

Arrange on a warmed dish and serve immediately while still piping hot. This dish is excellent as an appetizer or as an accompanying vegetable for a main course.

Mushrooms à la Grecque

Snow Pea Pie
Sfogliata di Taccole

To serve 6

½ lb puff pastry

5 tbsp butter

¾-1 lb small, tender snow peas

1 small onion

1 garlic clove

1 bouillon cube

ground nutmeg

½ cup grated Parmesan cheese

2 eggs

1 tbsp breadcrumbs

½lb Mozzarella cheese, sliced

Preparation and cooking time: about 1¼ hours plus any thawing time

Defrost the pastry if using frozen. Lightly butter a 9-inch round ovenproof pie dish.

Trim and wash the snow peas and cook them in salted boiling water for 3-5 minutes. Drain thoroughly.

Finely chop the onion and garlic and fry gently in 3 tablespoons of the butter until transparent. Add the snow peas and cook over a moderate heat for about 10 minutes, stirring occasionally. Season with the crumbled bouillon cube, a little pepper and a generous pinch of ground nutmeg.

Turn the mixture out on to a chopping board and chop all the ingredients quite finely. Place in a bowl, mix in the grated Parmesan cheese and the eggs, one at a time. Preheat the oven to 375°F.

Roll out the pastry to a thickness of about ⅛ inch and line the pie dish with it. Sprinkle the base with about a tablespoon of breadcrumbs and pour in the snow pea and egg mixture. Top with slices of Mozzarella cheese.

Bake in the lower part of the oven for about 35 minutes. Remove from the oven and leave to stand for about 10 minutes before serving.

Braised Celery and Fennel
Sedano e Ginocchio

To serve 4

¾lb celery heart

1 small leek, white part only

¼lb fennel bulb

butter

olive oil

pepper

ground nutmeg

2 tbsp grated Emmental cheese

Preparation and cooking time: about 1 hour

Bring to the boil a large pan of salted water. Cut the celery into pencil-thick pieces 2 inches long, removing any strings. Wash thoroughly and boil for about 15 minutes. Meanwhile wash the leek and fennel, and cut the leek into very fine slices and the fennel into wedges. Place them in a pan with a large knob of butter and 2 tablespoons of olive oil and brown them gently, uncovered. Remove the celery from the pan with a slotted spoon and add it to the other vegetables. Stir and continue cooking, still uncovered, adding a little of the celery water from time to time.

Preheat the oven to 350°F. When the vegetables are tender and there is no liquid left, season to taste with salt, pepper and ground nutmeg. Place in an ovenproof dish, sprinkle with the cheese and cook in the oven for about 10 minutes. Garnish, if you like, with a few fine fennel leaves and serve immediately.

Snow pea pie

Mixed Vegetables with Bacon

Ortaggi del Norcino

To serve 4-6

¾lb young carrots

1lb fresh asparagus

¼lb baby onions

2oz bacon

½ garlic clove

---

1 sprig fresh parsley

---

4 tbsp butter

---

olive oil

½lb fresh shelled peas

---

1 cup meat stock (or use bouillon cube)

---

1 sprig fresh chervil

Preparation and cooking time: about 1½ hours

Peel the carrots, cut them in half lengthwise and chop them into 1-inch pieces. Round the edges with a curved knife. Cook the pieces of carrot in salted boiling water for about 15 minutes or until tender. Drain and dry on paper towels.

Meanwhile peel and trim the asparagus and tie it in a bundle with kitchen twine. Stand the bundle upright in a saucepan containing enough salted boiling water to come halfway up the bundle and cook for about 15 minutes or until tender. Remove the twine and spread the asparagus out to dry on paper towels.

Finely chop the onions, bacon, half a garlic clove and a sprig of parsley and fry in 2 tablespoons of the butter and 1 tablespoon of olive oil. Add the peas and cook for a few minutes. Pour on the boiling stock, cover the pan and cook gently for about 20 minutes, adding a little hot water if necessary.

Cut the asparagus into 1½-inch pieces and sauté with the carrots and a few leaves of chervil in the remaining butter. Add all the ingredients to the pea mixture, stir and cook for a few more minutes. Taste and adjust the seasoning. Serve.

Vegetable and Ham Strudel

Strudel Vegetale

To serve 6

½lb carrots

2-3 stalks celery

---

2 medium zucchini

---

1 red bell pepper

---

3 eggs

---

about 1½ cups flour

---

1 tbsp olive oil

½lb finely sliced ham

2-3 dill pickle, cut into matchsticks

---

1 pickled onion, sliced

---

2 cups fresh mushrooms, trimmed, washed and finely sliced

---

about ½ cup butter

Preparation and cooking time: about 2 hours

Preheat the oven to 350°F. Clean and wash the carrots, celery, zucchini and bell pepper then cut up into matchstick-sized pieces. Parboil each vegetable separately for about 2 minutes then drain and lay them out on a tea-towel to dry, without mixing them. Hard-boil 2 of the eggs, cool them under running water and shell them. Cut into slices using an egg slicer.

Put 1⅓ cups of the flour on a pastry-board, add a pinch of salt and mix, then make a well in the center. Pour in 1 cup of warm water and a tablespoon of olive oil. Quickly mix into a smooth, soft dough. Roll out immediately on a large floured tea towel until the pastry is paper thin. Arrange two thirds of the ham slices down the center of the pastry and then, working outwards from the center, arrange the vegetable sticks in parallel lines alternating with sticks of dill pickle, slices of onion, mushroom and egg. Sprinkle with salt and freshly ground pepper then cover with the rest of the ham.

Lift up one side of the tea towel and carefully roll up the pastry. Melt ⅜ cup of the butter and brush a baking tray with it. Roll the strudel on to the tray and bake for about 40 minutes. Baste the pastry every 5 minutes with the rest of the butter. Remove the strudel from the oven and leave to cool before cutting it into fairly thick slices and serving.

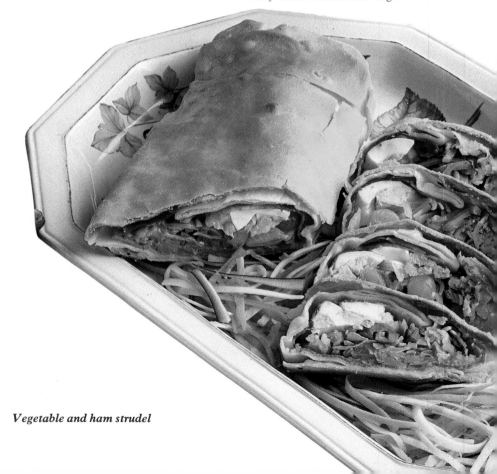

Vegetable and ham strudel

Vegetable Dome
Cupola di Verdure

To serve 8

2 large potatoes

1 cup frozen young peas

1 small chicken breast

flour

about ¼ cup butter

olive oil

2 slices white bread soaked in milk

1lb boiled spinach, well squeezed

½lb fat ham

4 eggs

⅜ cup grated Parmesan cheese

3 tbsp breadcrumbs

1 bouillon cube

ground nutmeg

2 small zucchini

ready-made tomato sauce for garnish

Preparation and cooking time: about 2½ hours

Wash the potatoes, boil and peel them and, while they are still hot, mash and place in a bowl. Boil the peas, then drain them and spread them to dry on a plate covered with paper towels. Lightly pound the chicken breast, roll it in flour and brown it lightly in 3 tablespoons of butter in a small saucepan with 1 tablespoon of oil, salt and pepper.

Squeeze the slices of white bread in milk, then grind them twice in the meat grinder using the fine disk together with the chicken breast, the spinach, the peas and the fat ham. Add the mixture to the potatoes. Mix everything well then bind with the eggs, the Parmesan cheese and 2 tablespoons of breadcrumbs. Salt lightly and add the bouillon cube dissolved in 3 tablespoons of hot water, pepper and ground nutmeg.

Heat a small saucepan with 5 cups of water adding salt when it boils. Meanwhile, trim off the ends of the zucchini, wash and cut in thin slices.

Plunge them into the boiling water and parboil for not more than 40 seconds. Drain with a slotted spoon and lay them to dry and cool on a plate covered with paper towels. Preheat the oven to 400°F.

Butter a semispherical mold about 8 inches in diameter or 3½ pints in capacity, line it with 3 or 4 aluminum strips, pressing them to adhere well, and buttering them; finally sprinkle with the remaining breadcrumbs. Start to fill the bottom of the mold with the zucchini slices, then as they rise up the sides tilt the mold slightly and place 4 or 5 slices in at a time, slightly overlapping them and fixing them with a small amount of the prepared mixture. Continue until you have completed the "dome". Fill the mold with the remaining vegetable mixture, pushing it down and leveling it at the surface. If you have a few zucchini slices left, spread them over the surface and sprinkle them with a tablespoon of breadcrumbs.

Place the mold in the oven for about 1 hour. During the last 15-20 minutes protect the surface with aluminum foil. Remove from the oven and leave to rest for about 15 minutes before unmolding and serving with tomato sauce.

Vegetables in Puff Pastry

Sfogliata di Verdure

To serve 6

1 lb puff pastry

1 small onion

2 zucchini

1 large tomato

1 red pepper

1 egg

dried oregano

plain flour

olive oil

knob of butter

Preparation and cooking time: 1 hour plus any defrosting time

Preheat the oven to 375°F.

1) Defrost the pastry if necessary and roll out thinly to ⅛ inch thickness on a floured pastry board. Cut out two 5 × 12 inch rectangles.

2) From one of the rectangles cut out a frame ¾ inch wide, and discard the center. Brush the edge of the other rectangle with beaten egg yolk.

3) Lay the frame over the rectangle to form a border and brush it with the egg yolk. Put it on a baking tray and cook in the oven for 20 minutes.

4) Wash and dry the pepper. You can remove the outer skin by holding it carefully over a gas flame (or it can be placed for a little while in the oven). Remove the seeds, peel and chop it. Clean, wash and dice tomato and zucchini.

5) Finely chop the onion and fry it until brown in a pan with 3 tablespoons of olive oil. Add the zucchini, cook for 10

minutes, then add the tomatoes and pepper.

6) Season with salt, pepper, oregano and cook for 15 minutes. Transfer the cooked pastry to a serving dish and spoon in the cooked vegetable mixture.

Serve hot or warm.

1

2

3

4

5

6

A delicious accompaniment to this veal and tongue salad are thinly sliced baby carrots, radishes, and raw fennel dressed with olive oil, salt, pepper and lemon juice.

SALADS

A side salad is a common accompaniment to a pasta or main course dish in Italy. Here are recipes for a wide range of salads from the simple to exotic, using such Mediterranean delights as olives and artichokes. Serve a salad as a side dish to a substantial main course, as a separate course or as a light meal on a hot day. Dress with olive oil and lemon juice or wine vinegar and present with Italian style.

Cold Pasta Twists with Salmon and Asparagus

Fusilli al Salmone e Asparagi

To serve 8

½ lb smoked salmon, cut in thin strips

3 tbsp pistachio nuts

½lb canned asparagus

1 lb pasta twists

large lemon

⅜ cup olive oil

Preparation and cooking time: about 30 minutes

Preheat the oven to 425°F. Parboil the pistachio nuts in a little salted water and then rub off their skins. Place the nuts on a baking tray and toast them lightly in the oven for 3-4 minutes. Drain the canned asparagus, trim the ends and cut the asparagus into ½-inch lengths.

Cook the pasta until *al dente* in salted boiling water. Drain thoroughly and spread on a tray to cool.

Strain the juice of a large lemon into a bowl and add a pinch of salt and pepper. Stir in the olive oil, beating vigorously with a fork.

Place the cold pasta in a salad bowl, add the strips of salmon, the pieces of asparagus and the chopped pistachio nuts. Pour on the prepared dressing, stir well and serve.

Pasta Salad "in evening dress"

Gramigna in Abito da Sera

To serve 8

1 egg

5 tbsp olive paste

about 2oz lumpfish roe

1lb gramigna pasta

a little oil

olive oil

Preparation and cooking time: about 20 minutes

Hard-boil the egg and cool it under running water. Shell the egg and take out the yolk. Place the black olive paste and the lumpfish roe in a salad bowl.

Cook the pasta in plenty of salted boiling water until slightly *al dente*. Drain well and spread out on a tray. Sprinkle with a little oil and leave to cool.

Pour the cold pasta into a salad bowl and stir in the olive paste and lumpfish roe. Dress with 5 tablespoons of olive oil and stir well. Finely crumble the egg yolk on to the pasta and top with a little lumpfish roe. Stir in the crumbled yolk and lumpfish roe at the table just before serving the pasta.

Ploughman's Salad

Insalata del Carrettière

To serve 4

1 head celery

1 fennel bulb

5 or 6 radishes

1 small onion

3 heads radicchio

2 heads Belgian endive

4-5 slices bacon

1 tbsp olive oil

2 slices white bread

½ cup fresh Quartirolo cheese

1 apple

6 large walnuts

vinaigrette dressing

Preparation and cooking time: about 45 minutes

Wash and slice the celery, fennel, radishes, onion, radicchio and Belgian endive.

Gently fry the diced bacon in the olive oil until crisp and golden. Dice the bread, discarding the crusts, and sauté in the oil until golden. Keep the bacon and bread hot.

Chop the Quartirolo cheese into ½-inch cubes and place in a bowl with the prepared salad vegetables. Peel, core and dice the apple, shell and chop the walnuts and stir into the salad.

Just before serving, dress the salad with a light *vinaigrette* dressing (prepared with oil, vinegar, salt, a generous pinch of paprika and a teaspoon of mustard). Top with the pieces of bacon and the *croûtons* of bread. Toss the salad, taste and adjust the seasoning if necessary. Serve immediately.

Cold pasta twists with salmon and asparagus

Bean Salad with Salmon

Insalata di Fagiolini al Salmone

To serve 4-6

¾lb frozen French beans

juice of 1 lemon

1 tbsp mustard

⅜ cup olive oil

3oz canned salmon

1 tbsp sliced pimiento

about 10 pickled onions

Preparation and cooking time: about 20 minutes

Bean salad with salmon

Cook the beans in salted boiling water until slightly *al dente*. Drain and leave to cool.

Prepare the dressing: Mix the lemon juice, mustard and a pinch of salt in a bowl. Gradually blend in the olive oil to form a smooth sauce.

Drain the salmon and break it up with a fork, discarding any bones and skin. Drain the sliced pimiento and the pickled onions. Cut the pickled onions in half.

Place the beans in a salad bowl and sprinkle on the pieces of pickled onion and pimiento. Top with the salmon. Serve with the prepared dressing. This salad is an excellent accompaniment for meat or fish.

Caper Salad

Insalata Capperina

To serve 4

2 tender lettuce hearts

2 large eggs

¼ lb Emmental cheese

3 tbsp capers in vinegar

½ garlic clove

Worcestershire sauce

anchovy paste

1 tbsp vinegar

4 tbsp olive oil

Preparation and cooking time: about 30 minutes

Separate and wash the leaves of the lettuce thoroughly and place them to dry on a tea-towel. Hard-boil the eggs, cool them under running water, shell and cut them in slices lengthwise. Slice the Emmental cheese thinly, drain the capers well and cut the lettuce leaves into wide strips. Place these 4 ingredients in 4 separate dishes, cover them with plastic wrap and leave in a cool place.

Now prepare the dressing: Brush half a garlic clove over the inside of a small bowl, add a pinch of salt, a dash of Worcestershire sauce, 2½ inches of anchovy paste and a tablespoon of vinegar. Stir with a fork until the salt is thoroughly dissolved, then dilute with 4 tablespoons of olive oil, continuing to stir with care. Combine the lettuce, eggs, cheese and capers in a salad bowl, season with the dressing and toss carefully. This excellent and inviting mixed salad can also be served as a light main course.

Caper salad

Celery, Mushroom and Endive Salad

Insalata di Sedano, Funghi e Belga

To serve 4

¼lb mushrooms, peeled and trimmed

juice of 1 lemon

1 garlic clove

2oz soft Gorgonzola cheese

Worcestershire sauce

1 tsp Dijon mustard

5 tbsp olive oil

a few tender celery stalks

2 small heads Belgian endive

Preparation time: about 40 minutes

Place the mushrooms in a bowl with water and half the lemon juice to cover. Set aside. Halve the garlic clove and rub it around the inside of a serving bowl. Place the Gorgonzola cheese, a pinch of salt, a generous splash of Worcestershire sauce and the remaining half of the lemon juice in the bowl. Stir in the mustard and beat with a fork to a smooth, creamy paste. Add the olive oil and beat until thoroughly blended.

Drain the mushrooms and slice them. Cut the celery and endive into thin strips. Mix the mushrooms, celery and endive and toss them in the bowl with the prepared sauce. Serve.

■ SALADS ■ SALADS ■ SALADS ■

Mixed Salad

Insalata Vigorosa

To serve 4

1 large yellow bell pepper

2 skinless frankfurter sausages, cooked

3 slices ham

¼ lb tuna in oil

1 tbsp chopped parsley

1 pimiento

2 tbsp tomato ketchup

1 tbsp mustard

Worcestershire sauce

½ cup mayonnaise

Preparation time: about 40 minutes

Wash the bell pepper and cut it into strips, discarding the stalk and seeds. Place in a bowl. Thinly slice the frankfurter sausages and cut the ham into wide strips. Mix with the bell pepper. Add the well-drained and coarsely flaked tuna and stir carefully. Transfer to a serving dish and sprinkle with a tablespoon of chopped parsley.

Prepare the dressing: Place the pimiento, ketchup, mustard and a generous dash of Worcestershire sauce in the blender and blend vigorously until smooth. Mix with the mayonnaise, test and adjust the seasoning according to taste. Serve the salad with the prepared dressing.

■ SALADS ■ SALADS ■ SALADS ■

August Delight

Delizia d'Agosto

To serve 4

1 tender heart Boston lettuce

1 tender heart Romaine lettuce

⅜ cup dry white wine

½ bay leaf

1 garlic clove

2-3 sprigs parsley

2-3 whole black peppercorns

½lb shrimp

1 cup canned yellow corn

4 radishes

2 anchovy fillets in oil

2 green olives in brine, pitted

1 artichoke heart in oil

4 tbsp plain full-cream yogurt

½ cup mayonnaise

Preparation and cooking time: about 1 hour

Pull the leaves off both lettuces, wash and drain and spread out to dry on a tea-towel.

Place on the heat a saucepan containing 2¼ cups of water, the dry white wine, half a bay leaf, a garlic clove and 2-3 sprigs of parsley. Season with a very little salt and 2-3 whole black peppercorns and bring slowly to the boil. Add the shrimp and cook for 2-3 minutes. Remove from the heat, cover the pan and leave to stand for about 10 minutes. Drain and peel the shrimp, keeping a little of the cooking liquid.

Rinse the corn under running water and spread out to dry on absorbent paper towels. Cut or break the lettuce leaves into pieces and thinly slice the radishes. Mix the corn, lettuce, radishes and shrimp in a salad bowl.

Place in the blender the anchovy fillets, olives, artichoke heart, a few leaves of parsley and the yogurt. Blend to form a smooth mixture and mix with the mayonnaise and a tablespoon of the strained cooking liquid from the shrimp. Check and adjust the seasoning to taste. Serve the salad with the dressing.

Celery, mushroom and endive salad (left); **August delight** (top right) and **mixed salad**

Summer Salad

Insalata Leggera

To serve 4-6

1 fresh Boston lettuce

3 slices ham

¼ cup chopped almonds

4 tbsp olive oil

1 tbsp wine vinegar

1 tbsp mustard

ground thyme

ground basil

Preparation time: about 30 minutes.

Pull the lettuce apart, reserving the greenest leaves for another use. Chop the lettuce and place in a salad bowl. Cut the ham into strips, discarding any fat, and add it to the lettuce. Stir in the almonds.

Prepare the *vinaigrette* dressing: Pour the olive oil, vinegar and mustard into a bowl and season with a pinch of salt and pepper. Blend well to a smooth sauce. Stir in a pinch of thyme and basil and pour into a sauce jug. Dress the salad at the table just before serving.

Cheese and Apple Salad

Insalata Vigorosa

To serve 4

¼ lb Emmental cheese, rind removed

2oz Gorgonzola cheese, rind removed

2 frankfurter sausages

2 pieces red pimiento

1 medium-sized apple

juice of ½ lemon

2 tsp mustard

Worcestershire sauce

3 tbsp olive oil

a few young fennel leaves for garnish

Preparation and cooking time: about 30 minutes

Dice the Emmental and Gorgonzola cheeses and mix in a bowl. Boil the sausages in lightly salted water for a minute then cut into slices about ¼-inch thick. When the sausage is cold, add to the cheese. Drain the pimiento and dry. Cut into ¾-inch squares and mix with the other ingredients in the bowl. Peel, core and dice the apple and add to the other ingredients.

Now prepare the sauce: Put a pinch of salt and a little freshly ground pepper in a bowl and add 1 tablespoon of strained lemon juice, 2 teaspoons of mustard and a dash of Worcestershire sauce. Mix with a fork to dissolve the salt then dilute with the olive oil, mixing thoroughly. Pour the sauce over the ingredients in the bowl and mix very carefully. Serve garnished with young fresh fennel leaves. If you wish, you can present the salad in a round wholemeal loaf: Cut off the top to make a "lid" and hollow out the soft bread inside. Fill with the salad and serve.

Summer salad (above); *cheese and apple salad*

Salad with Olives
Insalata Olivetta

To serve 4-5

1 small head Belgian endive

1 heart Batavian endive

1 head radicchio

2 tbsp white wine vinegar

6 tbsp olive oil

¾oz capers

a little parsley

anchovy paste

⅓ cup small black olives in brine

a small piece of leek (optional)

Preparation time: about 20 minutes

Trim and wash the two sorts of endive and the radicchio. Drain and dry, keeping the different types separate. Break up the leaves and arrange in a salad bowl. Prepare the salad dressing: Mix the wine vinegar with a pinch of salt and pepper in a bowl, stirring until the salt is dissolved. Add, one tablespoon at a time, the olive oil, stirring vigorously to blend the ingredients. Chop the capers and a few leaves of parsley and add to the *vinaigrette* together with 1½-2 inches of anchovy paste. Blend thoroughly.

To serve, place the olives in the center of the salad bowl and arrange a few finely cut strips of leek on top of them. Pour over the dressing and toss the salad before serving.

Navy Beans with Tuna
Cannellini Tonnati

To serve 6-8

6oz canned tuna in oil

juice of 1 lemon

1 hard-boiled egg yolk

⅜ cup olive oil

2¼ cups canned navy or cannellini beans

1 sprig fresh parsley, coarsely chopped, for garnish

Preparation time: about 20 minutes.

Drain the tuna and process it in a blender. Mix the lemon juice and tuna in a bowl. Mash the egg yolk and blend with the tuna. Gradually stir in 3 tablespoons of hot water and the olive oil to form a smooth, creamy sauce.

Thoroughly drain the beans, place in a serving dish and sprinkle with the chopped parsley. Serve cold with the tuna sauce.

Navy beans with tuna

Salad with olives

Cheese and Fennel Salad

Insalata di Finochi, Composta

To serve 4-5

2 fennel bulbs

a few drops lemon juice

½ garlic clove

3oz Emmental cheese

1 tsp mustard

1 tsp white wine vinegar

olive oil

1 chive

Preparation and cooking time: about 40 minutes

Clean the fennel bulbs, removing the green leaves, small shoots and the first layer, then cut them in half and place them in cold water with a few drops of lemon juice added.

Meanwhile rub the inside of a salad bowl with half a garlic clove. Cut the cheese into very thin slices and place in the salad bowl. Put a pinch of salt, a grinding of white pepper, a teaspoon of mustard and a tablespoon of white wine vinegar into a small bowl: stir with a fork until the salt has dissolved, then dilute with 4 tablespoons of olive oil and mix the ingredients well.

Drain the pieces of fennel well, dry them, cut them in thin slices and add to the cheese, also add the chopped chive, and toss gently. Pour over the prepared dressing and toss again.

Cheese and fennel salad

Country Salad

Insalata Rustica

To serve 4

¾lb fresh fennel bulb

6oz small fresh mushrooms

juice of ½ lemon

¼lb ham

3oz Emmental cheese

1 tbsp black olive paste

1 tbsp mustard

anchovy paste

Worcestershire sauce

1 tbsp red wine vinegar

olive oil

Preparation time: about 40 minutes

Wash and dry the fennel, keeping the best leaves. Peel the mushrooms and remove the earthy bases of the stalks. As you clean them, drop them into a bowl of cold water into which the juice of half a lemon has been squeezed. Cut the ham into short strips and the Emmental into thin slices.

Put the olive paste in a bowl and add the mustard, anchovy paste and a generous dash of Worcestershire sauce. Dilute with the vinegar and 6 tablespoons of olive oil, and stir carefully. Cut the fennel into thin slices, likewise the mushrooms, which have been well drained. Mix all the ingredients together in a salad bowl, pour over the sauce and toss carefully. Use the fennel leaves for garnish.

Vegetarian Pasta Salad

Conchiglie Vegetariane

To serve 8

1 cup fresh peas

2 baby carrots

1 lb fluted pasta shells

1 cup canned yellow corn

2 tbsp mustard

juice of ½ lemon

⅜ cup olive oil

Preparation and cooking time: about 45 minutes

Heat 2 saucepans of water (one large one and one slightly smaller) and salt them both when they come to the boil. Cook the fresh shelled peas in the smaller pan, boiling them for about 15 minutes. Drain well, reserving the water, and leave to dry on paper towels. Trim and dice the carrots and cook them in the same water for about 12 minutes. Drain and mix with the peas.

Cook the fluted pasta shells in the larger saucepan of boiling water. Drain the pasta when it is cooked *al dente* spread it out on a tray to cool.

Drain the canned corn and mix it in a salad bowl with the cold peas and carrots. Prepare the dressing: Place the mustard, the juice of half a lemon and a pinch of salt and pepper in a bowl. Beat the mixture with a fork and blend in the olive oil.

Mix the pasta with the vegetables in the salad bowl and dress with the prepared sauce. Stir well and serve.

Vegetarian pasta salad

Turkey Salad

Insalata di Tacchino

To serve 4

½lb cold roast turkey

½ garlic clove

3 gherkins

2oz Emmental cheese

1 small tomato

1 egg

anchovy paste

Worcestershire sauce

2 tbsp white wine vinegar

olive oil

Preparation and cooking time: about 30 minutes

Rub the inside of a salad bowl with half a garlic clove. Cut the turkey into thin strips, discarding any skin and bone, and place it in a bowl.

Slice the gherkins finely lengthwise and add to the turkey. Add the Emmental cheese, cut into matchsticks. Cut the tomato in half and discard the seeds. Cut the flesh into strips, and add to the turkey and cheese. Stir well, cover the bowl with plastic wrap and leave on one side for a few minutes.

Hard-boil the egg, cool it under running water and shell it. Crumble the yolk. In a bowl put a pinch of salt, 2-2½ inches of anchovy paste, a dash of Worcestershire sauce and 2 tablespoons of white wine vinegar. Stir in 5 tablespoons of olive oil to form a smooth sauce. Dress the salad with the prepared sauce, toss and serve topped with the finely crumbled egg yolk.

Rice Salad

Insalata di Riso

To serve 6

¾lb rice

olive oil

2 eggs

4 black olives in brine

¼lb peas

¼lb pimiento

¼lb cooked frankfurter sausage, skinned

¼lb ham

2oz tuna in oil

3 anchovy fillets in oil

Worcestershire sauce

juice of 1 lemon

Preparation and cooking time: about 1 hour

Cook the rice in plenty of salted water until it is tender but still firm. Drain well and spread out on a large plate. Pour over a fine trickle of olive oil and mash with a fork. Leave to cool.

Hard-boil the eggs and then cool under cold running water. Shell and slice them. Remove the pits from the olives, cut them into pieces and place in a bowl. Drain the peas and add them to the olives. Dice the pimiento into ½-inch squares and dice the sausage and ham into squares just a little larger. Mash the tuna and anchovies and add all these to the other ingredients.

Add the cooled rice and mix gently. Season with a pinch of salt, a generous dash of Worcestershire sauce, the strained lemon juice and 4 tablespoons of olive oil. Adjust the seasoning to taste. Arrange the salad on a serving dish and decorate with the slices of hard-boiled egg. Garnish as you please, then serve.

Potato and French Bean Salad

Insalata di Patate e Fagioli

To serve 4

1lb potatoes

½lb French beans

¾ cup mayonnaise

2 tsp mustard

2 tsp tomato ketchup

Worcestershire sauce

Preparation and cooking time: about 30 minutes

Heat two large saucepanfuls of water and when they begin to boil, add salt. Peel and wash the potatoes, then cut them into sticks of equal size, about 2 inches long. Rinse again and put into one of the saucepans of boiling water. Into the other put the beans. Bring both to the boil again and simmer for about 12 minutes, taking care that the beans remain whole. Remove from the water with a slotted spoon, drain and leave to dry and cool on a tray covered with a double layer of paper towels.

When the beans have cooled a little, cut them into lengths the same size as the potato sticks. Now make the dressing: Put the mayonnaise into a bowl and add the mustard, ketchup, and a few drops of Worcestershire sauce. Mix carefully so as not to "flatten" the mayonnaise. Taste, and adjust the seasoning. Put the beans and the potatoes in a salad bowl, pour in the dressing, mix with care then serve.

Veal and tongue salad

Veal and Tongue Salad

Insalata di Vitello e Lingua

To serve 4

½lb roast veal

½lb boiled ox-tongue

1 leek, green part only, for garnish

1 slice fresh white bread

white wine vinegar

1 tbsp capers

1 dill pickle

2 anchovy fillets in oil

few sprigs parsley

⅜ cup olive oil

Worcestershire sauce

1 tsp mustard

Preparation time: about 30 minutes

Cut the veal and ox-tongue into thin
strips and mix. Place in a serving dish.
Wash, drain and thinly slice the leek and
reserve it for garnish.

Prepare the dressing: Soak the bread in
wine vinegar and then place it in the
blender with the capers, pickle, drained
anchovy fillets, parsley and olive oil. Add
a generous dash of Worcestershire sauce,
a teaspoon of mustard and a little salt and
blend for just over a minute. Test and
adjust the seasoning according to taste.

Serve the veal and ox-tongue salad
garnished with the leek slices and with
the prepared dressing. Good
accompaniments for this dish are raw
baby carrots cut into long, thin strips and
thinly sliced raw fennel dressed with
olive oil, salt and pepper and, if desired,
a little lemon juice.

Snow Pea Salad

Insalata di Taccole

To serve 4

1-1¼lb small, tender snow
peas

3 slices lean ham

1 small onion or 2-3 scallions

½ garlic clove

¼ tsp mustard

1 tsp chopped parsley

Worcestershire sauce

1 tbsp aromatic vinegar

3 tbsp olive oil

Preparation and cooking time: about 30
minutes

Heat plenty of salted water in a saucepan.
Trim and wash the snow peas and cook
them in the salted boiling water for 3-5
minutes. Drain and spread out to dry and
cool on absorbent paper towels.

Cut the ham into short, thin strips and
slice the onions. Combine the ham and
onion with the cold peas and place in a
salad bowl.

Prepare the dressing: Rub the bottom
of a bowl with half a garlic clove and
place in it the mustard, a pinch of salt,
the chopped parsley, a generous dash of
Worcestershire sauce and the vinegar.
Stir with a fork until the salt has
completely dissolved and then add the
olive oil.

Pour the prepared dressing over the
peas and serve, mixing the salad at table.

Snow pea salad

Rustic Tomatoes

Pomodori alla Rustica

To serve 4

2 tbsp capers

1 onion

4 anchovy fillets

oregano

5 tbsp olive oil

¾lb tomatoes

Preparation time: about 40 minutes

Rinse the capers, peel the onion, cut it into as thin rings as possible, then keep them in cold water for about 30 minutes. Finely chop the anchovy fillets and place them in a bowl. Add a pinch of oregano, a grinding of pepper and a pinch of salt, then dilute with 5 tablespoons of olive oil, mixing vigorously with the tines of a fork. Set aside the dressing for a few minutes and prepare the tomatoes.

Remove the stems, wash and dry the tomatoes, and cut them in rather thin slices. Drain the onion rings and squeeze the capers; dry them, separately, on paper towels. Place the tomato slices in a bowl, alternating them with the capers and onion rings, then pour over the prepared dressing and serve immediately, tossing very gently.

Salad of Mussels, Bread and Beans

Insalata di Cozze, Pane e Fagioli

To serve 4-5

2¼lb fresh mussels

9 tbsp olive oil

2 large garlic cloves

a little lemon juice

1¾ cups canned navy beans

2 slices white bread

2 anchovy fillets in oil

1 tsp mustard

Worcestershire sauce

2 tbsp white wine vinegar

fresh chervil or parsley for garnish

Preparation and cooking time: about 45 minutes

Scrape the mussels under cold running water then put them into a saucepan with a tablespoon of olive oil, a lightly crushed garlic clove and a few drops of lemon juice. Cover and place the pan over a high heat. After a few minutes' cooking and when the mussels have opened, remove them from their shells and leave them to cool in a bowl.

Drain and rinse the canned beans then lay them out to dry on a tray covered with a double layer of paper towels. Add them to the mussels. Heat 3 tablespoons of oil and the other garlic clove in a skillet. Fry the bread until it is lightly toasted then cut it into ¾-inch squares. Mix these with the mussels and beans.

Now prepare the dressing: Crush the anchovy fillets with a fork in a bowl, then, still mixing with the fork, add the mustard and a dash of Worcestershire sauce, a little salt, 2 tablespoons of vinegar and 5 tablespoons of olive oil. Pour the dressing over the salad, mix once more and garnish with chervil or parsley. Serve immediately.

*Rustic tomatoes (left); **mussels, bread and bean salad (right)***

Shrimp and Tomato Salad

Terra-Mare Saporoso

To serve 4-6

⅝ cup dry white wine

1 bay leaf

2 peppercorns

¾lb very fresh shrimp, unpeeled

2 firm medium tomatoes

2 tbsp mustard

anchovy paste

juice of ½ lemon

⅜ cup olive oil

a few leaves fresh parsley

Preparation and cooking time: about 30 minutes

Heat a saucepan containing about 3½ cups water and pour in the wine. Add the

Shrimp and tomato salad

bay leaf, peppercorns and salt. Bring gradually to the boil and simmer for about 10 minutes. Meanwhile, rinse the shrimp thoroughly under cold running water and peel them. Simmer the shrimp in the boiling liquid for 5 minutes. Remove with a slotted spoon and lay them to cool on a tray covered with paper towels.

Wash the tomatoes and remove the stalks. Cut them in half horizontally and remove the seeds. Cut the flesh into fairly thin strips. Place the tomatoes and the shrimp in a salad bowl and prepare the dressing: Put 2 tablespoons of mustard in a small bowl together with 4 inches of anchovy paste and the strained lemon juice. Mix with a wooden spoon, gradually stirring in the olive oil. You should obtain a smooth, creamy sauce. Garnish the salad with parsley and serve the sauce in a sauceboat from which all can help themselves.

MAIN COURSES

Piatto di mezzo (middle dish) is the Italian term for the central course of a full meal. Italian cooking is noted for its many ways with veal, but here also are recipes for beef, lamb (traditionally eaten at Easter and as it is rather expensive in Italy, treated as a special-occasion dish), pork, poultry and game, a northern speciality. These dishes range from simple roasts to elaborate recipes with sumptuous sauces suitable for the grandest occasion.

Loin of Veal in Wine
Bianco Costato al Vino

To serve 6

2½lb loin of veal in one piece

flour

⅜ cup oil

2 medium-sized onions, finely chopped

4 garlic cloves

3 bay leaves

3 bouillon cubes

2 small tomatoes, peeled and chopped

4½ cups dry white wine

1 tsp cornstarch

Preparation and cooking time: about 4½ hours

Preheat the oven to 400°F. Tightly bind the loin of veal with kitchen string and coat in flour. Heat the oil in a roasting pan and add the veal, browning it on all sides. Add the onions, the whole garlic cloves, bay leaves, the crumbled bouillon cubes and the tomatoes. Pour on the white wine, cover and cook in the oven for about 2 hours.

Turn the meat every 30 minutes during cooking. After 2 hours, pour enough water into the pan to cover the meat. Re-cover the pan and cook for a further 2 hours, still turning the meat every 30 minutes.

Remove the meat from the pan and discard the kitchen twine. Place on a serving dish and keep warm. Strain the cooking juices into a saucepan and add a teaspoon of cornstarch dissolved in 3 tablespoons of cold water, stirring constantly. Simmer gently to form a smooth gravy. Test and adjust the seasoning according to taste.

Pour some of the gravy over the meat and the rest into a gravy-boat. Serve with fresh vegetables and follow with a green salad.

Blanquette of Veal with Broad Beans and Sausage

"Bianchetto" di Vitello con Fave e Salsiccia

To serve 4-5

1¼lb cubed stewing veal

flour

olive oil

1 medium onion

2 tbsp butter

1 garlic clove

1 fresh sage leaf

½ sprig rosemary

½ cup dry white wine

1¼ cups meat stock (or use bouillon cube)

½lb shelled fresh broad beans

½lb sausages

Preparation and cooking time: about 2 hours

Lightly coat the veal pieces in flour and brown in 3 tablespoons of olive oil. Drain. Thinly slice the onion and fry gently in the butter and 2 tablespoons of olive oil. Finely chop a garlic clove, a large sage leaf and the leaves of half a sprig of rosemary and add to the pan. Cook for a few seconds and then add the veal. Pour over the white wine and allow it to evaporate rapidly.

Season with salt and pepper and add the hot stock. Stir, and cook over a moderate heat for about 1½ hours, stirring occasionally and adding a little more stock if necessary.

Meanwhile parboil the beans in salted water for 5 minutes. Drain thoroughly. Skin the sausages, cut into small pieces (about 1¼ inches) and brown in a tablespoon of olive oil.

About 15 minutes before removing the veal from the heat, stir in the beans and sausage pieces and cover the pan. Check and adjust the seasoning according to taste before serving.

Veal Braised in the Oven

Ossibuchi in Forno

To serve 4

2lb knuckle or shin of veal in pieces

flour

4 tbsp olive oil

1 sage leaf

½ garlic clove

1 medium onion

½ celery heart, trimmed

5 tsp butter

½lb peeled tomatoes

2 fresh basil leaves

½ bay leaf

about 3 cups good meat stock

a little chopped parsley for garnish

Preparation and cooking time: about 2¼ hours

Preheat the oven to 375-400°F. Nick the meat around the bones with the point of a sharp knife, then flour the veal pieces and shake off any excess flour. Heat the olive oil in a large skillet with the sage and garlic and put in the veal pieces. As soon as they are slightly brown, arrange them in an ovenproof dish which is large enough to hold the meat in a single layer. Leave them to one side covered with a sheet of aluminum foil.

Finely chop the onion and celery and fry in the butter in the skillet used for the meat. Put the tomatoes through a food processor using the finest disk and add to the other ingredients in the skillet. Mix, and put in the basil and the bay leaf, a little salt and freshly ground pepper. Simmer for about 10 minutes over a moderate heat. Then remove the garlic, basil and bay leaf and pour the sauce over the meat. Bring the stock to the boil and pour that in too.

Cover the dish with the aluminum foil and put in the oven for about 1½ hours. From time to time check that the sauce has not all evaporated and add a little boiling water if necessary. Also make sure the meat is not sticking to the bottom of the dish. Turn the meat over once halfway through cooking. The sauce should be fairly thick by the end. Heat a serving dish and arrange the meat on it. Pour over the sauce, sprinkle with parsley and serve.

Veal braised in the oven

Valdostana Cutlets

Costolette alla Valdostana

To serve 4

4 thick veal cutlets, each weighing ½lb

¼lb Fontina cheese

flour

2 eggs, beaten

breadcrumbs

butter for frying

Preparation and cooking time: about 30 minutes

Using a sharp knife, cut the cutlets almost right through horizontally, leaving them joined at the bone side. Insert thin slices of the cheese into the cutlets and beat them lightly together again with a meat mallet. Coat them first with flour, then with beaten egg mixed with a little salt, then with breadcrumbs. Fry them in plenty of butter until they are golden on both sides. Drain thoroughly and serve at once on a warm dish.

■ MAIN COURSES VEAL ■

Meat Morsels with Mushrooms

"Bocconcini" di Carne ai Porcini

To serve 5

18oz veal

14oz pork

flour

olive oil

1 medium onion

1 medium carrot

1 celery heart

1 fresh sage leaf

1 sprig rosemary

4 tbsp butter

¾ cup dry white wine

2½ cups light stock (or use bouillon cube)

1 tbsp tomato paste

nutmeg

½lb small firm mushrooms (preferably ceps)

1 garlic clove

a little chopped parsley

Preparation and cooking time: about 2¼ hours

Cut the veal and pork into small cubes of about 1¼ inches and roll them in flour, shaking off the excess. Lightly brown them in 4 tablespoons of olive oil, then remove them from the pan and drain well.

Grind together, rather finely, the onion, carrot and celery heart, 1 sage leaf and 10 rosemary leaves. Soften the ground mixture in 2 tablespoons of the butter and 2 tablespoons of olive oil, in a pan, without browning. Add the morsels of meat and sauté gently for a few minutes, stirring with a wooden spoon. Moisten with the white wine and, when it has evaporated almost entirely, add the boiling stock, in which you have dissolved a tablespoon of tomato paste. Stir, salt lightly and season with a pinch each of pepper and nutmeg. Cover the pan, lower the heat to the minimum and cook for about 1½ hours, moistening if necessary with a little hot water so that nothing sticks to the bottom and there is always plenty of liquid.

While the meat cooks, clean the mushrooms, wipe them with a damp cloth and slice thinly. In a saucepan melt the remaining butter with a tablespoon of olive oil, add a slightly crushed garlic clove and then the slices of mushroom. Cook very slowly for 5 minutes, stirring with a wooden spoon; season lightly with salt and pepper. Add the mushrooms to the meat 5 minutes before removing it from the heat and stir in gently. Serve sprinkled with a little chopped parsley.

Stuffed Roast Veal with Spinach

Arrosto Farcito agli Spinaci

To serve 8-10

¾lb frozen leaf spinach

¼lb beef

¼lb pork

2oz bacon, fairly lean

1 slice white bread, soaked in milk

2-3 sprigs fresh parsley

2 eggs

¾ cup grated Parmesan cheese

nutmeg

1 boned breast of veal

olive oil

2 stalks celery

1 medium carrot

1 small onion

3 garlic cloves

1 sprig fresh rosemary

1 sprig fresh sage

2 tbsp butter

⅜ cup dry white wine

⅜ cup stock (or use bouillon cube)

½ tsp cornstarch

Preparation and cooking time: about 2½ hours

Cook the spinach in its own liquid, drain well and spread it out on a board to cool. Squeeze out the moisture thoroughly, chop the spinach and put it in a large bowl. Put the beef, pork, bacon and the drained and squeezed bread twice through the finest disk of a meat grinder, then add the mixture to the spinach. Chop the parsley very finely and add it to the rest. Bind to a smooth mixture with the eggs and the Parmesan cheese, and season with salt, pepper and nutmeg.

Preheat the oven to 400°F. Sprinkle a little salt on the breast of veal, then spread the prepared stuffing uniformly over it, stopping about ½ inch from the edges. Roll the meat up, enclosing the stuffing completely, then sew up the opening with kitchen thread. Tie the rolled meat with string, brush it all over with olive oil and put it in a roasting pan just large enough to hold it. Surround it with the chopped celery, carrot and onion, lightly crushed garlic, rosemary and 3 or 4 sage leaves. Dot with butter and roast for about 1½ hours, turning the meat 4 or 5 times, basting often and from time to time moistening with a little of the white wine. When the meat is cooked, remove it from the roasting pan and take off the string. Skim off some of the fat from the cooking juices, dilute with the cold stock in which you have dissolved the cornstarch, and simmer gently for a few minutes. Strain through a fine sieve into a warmed sauceboat. Serve this sauce with the roast, which should preferably be carved at the table.

Veal Galantine
Galantina di Vitello

To serve 12-14

3 tbsp pistachio nuts

¼lb lean bacon

½lb ham

1 large canned black truffle

¼lb calves' brains

½lb lean pork

¼lb veal

2oz fat bacon

¼lb Continental sausage

2 slices white bread, soaked in a little dry Marsala wine

2 eggs

½ cup grated Parmesan cheese

nutmeg

2lb bonded breast of veal

olive oil

1 small carrot

1 small onion

1 young rib celery

1 garlic clove

1 bay leaf

1 sprig fresh rosemary

2 fresh sage leaves

4 tbsp butter

1¼ cups dry white wine

a few young celery leaves and 1 canned black truffle for garnish

Preparation and cooking time: about 3¼ hours, plus overnight cooling

Blanch the pistachio nuts in salted water for a few moments, then remove the skins. Cut the lean bacon into slivers, dice the ham into 1-inch cubes and slice the truffle. Skin the brains under running water, then dry them well and divide into large pieces. Finely mince the pork, veal, fat bacon, sausage and drained bread. Add the eggs, the Parmesan cheese, freshly ground pepper and a generous pinch of ground nutmeg; add salt to taste.

Beat the breast of veal out thinly, taking care not to break it. Place the prepared mixture down the middle, then add a layer of the pistachios, strips of bacon, slices of truffle, cubes of ham and pieces of brain. Repeat the layers until the ingredients are used up.

Preheat the oven to 400°F. Fold the two sides of meat over the filling and stitch them together to make the shape of a meat loaf. Brush the galantine all over with olive oil, sprinkle with salt and place in a baking pan surrounded by the chopped carrot, onion and celery, the whole garlic clove and the bay leaf, the rosemary and sage. Dot with butter and place in the oven. Cook for about 2 hours, pouring a little white wine over it at intervals and turning every 30 minutes so that it is evenly browned on all sides. Take it out of the oven and allow to cool, then place it on a clean dish and cover it entirely with a sheet of foil. Place a weighted board on top and leave it overnight in a cool place.

Next day, remove the stitching. Remove and discard the jelly if desired and serve in fairly thick slices garnished, if you like, with young celery leaves and black truffle.

Veal Sweetbreads with Mushroom Sauce
Animelle di Vitello ai Funghi

To serve 4

2-3 dried cep mushrooms

1 lb calves' sweetbreads

juice of 1 lemon

4 tbsp butter

breadcrumbs

¼lb fresh mushrooms

½ small onion

1 garlic clove

a little parsley

4 tbsp olive oil

4 tbsp dry Marsala wine

a piece of bouillon cube

powdered thyme

¼ cup fresh cream

½ tsp cornstarch

Preparation and cooking time: about 1½ hours

Soak the dried mushrooms in cold water for about 1 hour. Wash the sweetbreads and simmer them for about 20 minutes in a saucepan of 4 pints lightly salted boiling water to which 2 tablespoons of strained lemon juice have been added. Remove from the water with a slotted spoon and place in a bowl of cold water. When they are cool enough to handle remove the membrane, veins and any nerves. When the sweetbreads are completely cold, remove from the water and drain well. Dry, and cut into fairly thick slices. Melt half the butter and brush the slices of sweetbread with this. Then coat them evenly with breadcrumbs.

Trim and wash the fresh mushrooms. Finely chop the onion with the garlic, removing the green shoot if there is one, and a few parsley leaves. Heat 3 tablespoons of olive oil in a skillet and gently fry this mixture. Then drain the dried mushrooms thoroughly, setting aside the water in which they soaked, and finely chop before adding these to the skillet too. Finely slice the fresh mushrooms and add them to the other ingredients after a short time. Fry for a few minutes then pour in 4 tablespoons of the water from the dried mushrooms and the Marsala. Crumble in a piece of bouillon cube and add a pinch of thyme. Simmer until the liquid has reduced by at least two-thirds before dissolving the cornstarch in the cream and adding this to the sauce. Stir in and simmer gently for a few minutes.

Meanwhile, heat a skillet with the rest of the butter and 1 tablespoon of olive oil and fry the slices of sweetbread in the skillet until golden brown on both sides. Sprinkle with salt when they are cooked. Arrange on a preheated serving dish and pour over the mushroom sauce. Sprinkle with a little chopped parsley and serve. The dish can be accompanied by polenta made with half stock and half milk.

Very Smooth Rissoles

Polpettine Vellutate

To make 16 rissoles

¾lb lean pork

¼lb veal

¼lb sausage

2oz mortadella sausage

3 slices white bread soaked in stock

a handful of parsley

1 garlic clove

lemon rind

1 large egg or 2 small ones

½ cup grated Parmesan cheese

ground nutmeg

olive oil

breadcrumbs

5 tbsp butter

1 small onion

2 small pieces dried mushroom

3 tbsp flour

2¼ cups light stock

celery leaves for garnish

Preparation and cooking time: about 1½ hours

Grind the pork, veal, sausage, mortadella and the well-squeezed slices of bread twice in the meat grinder, using the fine disk.

Chop a handful of parsley with half a garlic clove and a 1¼-inch piece of lemon rind, then add the chopped flavorings to the meats, mix thoroughly with the egg and the Parmesan cheese, salt lightly and season with pepper and ground nutmeg. Form into 16 patties or rissoles, moistening your hands with a little olive oil. Press the rissoles in breadcrumbs, then arrange them in a buttered casserole and sprinkle with 5 teaspoons of melted butter. Leave them in a cool place for about 10 minutes. Preheat the oven to 400°F.

Chop the onion and soften it in the remaining butter in a small pan. Add the pieces of dried mushroom and, after a few seconds, the sifted flour, stirring to prevent lumps forming. Add the hot stock, pouring it in a trickle and, still stirring, bring the sauce to the boil. Lower the heat and let it simmer for 15 minutes. Put the rissoles in the hot oven and cook them for about 15 minutes. Cover the rissoles with the strained sauce, sprinkle with the finely chopped celery leaves and serve immediately.

■ MAIN COURSES BEEF ■

Beef Rolls with Peas

"Braciole" di Manzo ai Piselli

To serve 8

about 1½lb lean beef in 8 slices

about 10oz ham, in 16 slices

4oz mild Provolone cheese, rind removed

8 fresh basil leaves

1 garlic clove

flour

4 tbsp butter

olive oil

1 sprig fresh sage

5oz onion

½ cup dry white wine

¾lb tomatoes

1 bouillon cube

sugar

½lb shelled peas

Preparation and cooking time: about 2¾ hours

Lightly beat the slices of beef, taking care not to split them. Sprinkle with salt and pepper, then lay 2 slices of ham on each beef slice – they should not overlap the edges of the beef. Cut the Provolone cheese into 8 small sticks and arrange them on the ham. Beside each one place a small basil leaf and a thin sliver of garlic.

Roll up the beef slices and tie them with kitchen twine. Roll them one at a time in flour, shaking them well to remove the excess.

In a saucepan, heat the butter, 2 tablespoons of olive oil and 2 sage leaves. When the fats are melted and thoroughly hot, put the beef rolls in the pan, and brown them lightly on each side. Then add the onion sliced very thinly; cover, and sauté gently for about 10 minutes. Moisten with the white wine and let it reduce by about two thirds. Add the peeled and puréed tomatoes.

Shake the pan to make sure nothing sticks to the bottom, then season with the crumbled bouillon cube, a grinding of pepper and a pinch of sugar. Replace the lid and simmer gently for about 1½ hours, adding a little boiling water from time to time if required.

Cook the peas in boiling salted water for 3-4 minutes, drain and add to the beef rolls. Add a little boiling water and continue cooking for another 30 minutes.

Finally remove the sage leaves from the pan, and cut the twine away from each beef roll. Serve on a warmed serving dish. If any of the tomato and pea sauce remains, it may be used to accompany pasta.

■ MAIN COURSES BEEF ■

Roast Beef with Tomato and Garlic Sauce

Filetto alla Pizzaiola

To serve 4

1 large ripe tomato

olive oil

1 garlic clove

a few fresh basil leaves

4 tbsp Mozzarella cheese

butter

¾lb fillet of beef, finely sliced by machine

Preparation and cooking time: about 20 minutes

Preheat the oven to 375°F. Cut the tomato in half horizontally, remove the seeds and then dice. Heat 2 tablespoons of olive oil and fry the garlic. Add the tomato, basil leaves and a pinch of salt.

Fry over a high heat without overcooking. Dice the Mozzarella cheese. Liberally butter a baking tray and place the slices of beef on it, setting them well apart. Pour over a trickle of olive oil and place in the oven for about 2 minutes. The meat should remain almost pink.

Remove from the oven and sprinkle with the cubes of Mozzarella cheese and tomato. Re-heat in the oven just long enough for the cheese to melt a little. Arrange the beef on individual, warmed plates.

■ MAIN COURSES BEEF ■

Mixed Meat Patties with Artichokes

Medaglioni di Carne con i Carciofi

To serve 4

2 fresh artichokes

a little lemon juice

1 small onion

1 small garlic clove

1 sprig fresh parsley

5 tbsp olive oil

¾ cup dry white wine

⅜ cup meat stock (or use bouillon cube)

ground thyme

3 tbsp butter

½ bouillon cube

2 slices white bread, soaked in milk

¼ lb ground beef

¼ lb ground veal

¼ lb ham

¼ cup grated Parmesan cheese

1 egg

ground nutmeg

flour

1 sprig fresh sage

Preparation and cooking time: about 1 hour

Top and tail the artichokes and remove the tough outer leaves. Cut them in half lengthwise, scoop out and discard the chokes. Place the artichokes in a bowl of water with a little lemon juice.

Finely chop about one-third of the onion, the garlic and the parsley and sauté in 3 tablespoons of olive oil. Drain the artichokes, cut them into small pieces and add to the pan. Cook gently for a few minutes and then pour on half the white wine. When the wine has been absorbed, add the boiling stock. Season with a pinch of salt and pepper and a little thyme. Cover the pan, lower the heat and cook for about 15 minutes, adding a little boiling water if necessary.

Meanwhile, prepare the steaks: Finely chop the remaining onion and sauté in 1 tablespoon of butter. Blend in half a crumbled bouillon cube. Thoroughly drain the bread and process it in a

blender with the beef, veal and ham. Place in a bowl and add the sautéed onions, the grated Parmesan cheese, the egg and a little pepper and ground nutmeg. Blend thoroughly and divide the mixture into 4 patties. Coat in flour.

Heat the remaining butter, 2 tablespoons of olive oil and 2 sage leaves in a skillet and fry the patties on a low heat, turning them once, until browned on both sides. Pour on the remaining wine and cook until the liquid has reduced by about two-thirds. Serve topped with the cooked artichokes.

Fillet Steak with Piquant Sauce

Controfiletto con Salsa Piccante

To serve 4

¼ cup shortening

1 small onion

2 tbsp butter

1½ tbsp flour

1 cup light beef stock

1-2 shallots

¼ cup white wine vinegar

3-4 dill pickles gherkins

olive oil

4 fillet steaks, each weighing 6oz

Worcestershire sauce

Preparation and cooking time: about 45 minutes

Cut the shortening into small cubes and finely chop the onion. Melt the butter in a small saucepan, then add the shortening and the chopped onion. Mix with a wooden spoon and brown gently for a few minutes, then sprinkle with the sifted flour, stir, and moisten with the hot stock, poured in a trickle; stir continuously with a small whisk until the sauce is well blended. Simmer gently for at least 15 minutes, then sieve the sauce.

Meanwhile, finely chop the shallots and put in a small saucepan, add the vinegar then simmer very slowly for about 10 minutes. Sieve into the sauce, stirring well with a small whisk; add the thinly sliced dill pickle and, still stirring, simmer for a few more minutes, then keep it warm in a *bain-marie*.

Brush the fillet steaks with olive oil and broil them briefly on both sides under a very hot broiler so that they are rather rare. Salt the steaks, season them with a dash of Worcestershire sauce, then serve with the prepared sauce.

Broiled Meatballs with Onion

"Delizie" Cipollate, alla Griglia

To serve 4

1 small onion

1 garlic clove

5 tsp butter

1 sprig fresh rosemary

1 sage leaf

a few young, fresh fennel leaves

cold stock (or use bouillon cube)

2 slices fresh white bread

¾lb ground beef

olive oil

breadcrumbs

Preparation and cooking time: about 1¼ hours

Preheat the oven to 400°F. Finely chop the onion and garlic and fry gently in the butter, taking care not to let them brown. Remove from the heat and place in a bowl to cool. Meanwhile, chop the rosemary leaves together with the sage and a little fennel. Add the herbs to the cold onion. Soak the bread in the stock then squeeze well and add to the bowl together with the ground beef, salt and pepper.

Combine all the ingredients together until smooth and make 16 equal-sized meatballs. Brush them all over with olive oil, then coat evenly with breadcrumbs. Heat the broiler and place the meatballs under it. Cook quickly, turning them over once only. Arrange them in an oiled ovenproof dish, pour over a trickle of olive oil, then bake for 10-12 minutes and serve on a bed of vegetables cooked in butter. Garnish with fennel leaves.

Baked Meat-loaf
Polpettone al Forno

To serve 8

1¼lb lean beef

¼lb ham

2 slices white bread soaked in milk

¼lb Emmental cheese

2in piece lemon rind

½ cup pistachio nuts

¼ cup fresh Mascarpone cheese

⅝ cup grated Parmesan cheese

2 eggs

ground nutmeg

oil

breadcrumbs

1 tsp cornstarch

½ cup dry white wine

5 tsp butter

a little parsley for garnish

home-made tomato sauce for accompaniment

Preparation and cooking time: about 1 hour 40 minutes

Finely grind the beef, ham and drained bread and place in a bowl. Finely chop the Emmental cheese with a 2-inch piece of lemon rind and add to the meat mixture. Preheat the oven to 400°F.

Wipe the pistachio nuts with a damp cloth and grind to a fine powder, without removing the shells. Add to the other ingredients together with the Mascarpone cheese, grated Parmesan cheese and eggs. Season with a little ground nutmeg and a generous pinch of salt and pepper.

Mix thoroughly and form into a smooth roll about 3 inches in diameter. Oil a sheet of aluminum foil, sprinkle it with breadcrumbs and wrap it tightly around the meat loaf. Cook in a baking pan for about 1¼ hours, turning 2-3 times during cooking.

When the loaf has been cooking for about 1 hour, carefully remove the aluminum foil, replace the loaf in the baking pan and pour over any cooking juices remaining in the foil wrapper. Add a teaspoon of cornstarch dissolved in the white wine and dot with pieces of butter.

Replace in the oven and complete cooking, basting occasionally with the cooking juices. Garnish with a few leaves of parsley and serve with hot tomato sauce.

Fillet of Beef with Mushrooms and Parmesan
Filetto con Funghi e Grana

To serve 1

¼lb lean fillet of beef, cut into very thin slices

1 medium-sized mushroom (preferably cep)

1oz young Parmesan cheese, flaked

celery leaves

½ garlic clove

anchovy paste

mild mustard

herb vinegar

olive oil

Preparation and cooking time: about 20 minutes

Baked meat-loaf

Arrange the fillet slices in a ring on a plate which you have chilled in the refrigerator. Trim the mushroom and wipe it with a damp cloth. Cut into slices and arrange the best ones on the slices of meat, the others in the center of the plate. Pile the flaked cheese on top and surround with the celery leaves.

Rub the bottom of a bowl lightly with half a garlic clove, put in ¾ inch of anchovy paste, a little mustard on the end of a teaspoon, 3-4 drops of vinegar and a pinch each of salt and pepper. Combine the ingredients with a fork then dilute with a tablespoon of olive oil. Pour this dressing over the slices of meat and serve.

■ MAIN COURSES BEEF ■

Meat-loaf with Olives
Polpettoncino alle Olive

To serve 4-6

2 slices white bread

milk

1lb ground beef

½ cup grated Parmesan cheese

1 egg

nutmeg

4 stuffed olives

breadcrumbs

olive oil

chicory

Preparation and cooking time: about 1 hour

Soak the 2 slices of bread in a little milk. Preheat the oven to 375°F. Squeeze the bread well then add it to the meat and grind both together. Place the mixture in a bowl, add the Parmesan cheese, the egg, a pinch of salt, a grinding of pepper and one of nutmeg. Mix well with a wooden spoon. The mixture should be rather firm. Shape it into a loaf about 7 inches long, pressing the olives into the mixture.

Roll the meat-loaf gently in the breadcrumbs to coat it, then place in a lightly oiled rectangular baking pan, sprinkle with a little olive oil and bake for about 35 minutes until the surface is

lightly browned. Remove the meat-loaf from the oven and let it rest for about 10 minutes before cutting it into slices. Arrange on a serving dish and garnish with tender leaves of chicory.

■ MAIN COURSES BEEF ■

Painter's Steak Tartare
Tartare del Pittore

To serve 4

1-1¼lb fillet beef

4 very fresh egg yolks

12 round slices lemon

32 capers in oil

1 pickled carrot

6 stuffed olives

4 anchovy fillets in oil

a handful of chopped parsley and a few sprigs

2 baby artichokes in oil

olive oil

a little lemon juice, strained

tomato ketchup

mustard

Worcestershire sauce

Preparation time: about 40 minutes

Chill a meat grinder in the refrigerator. Remove any gristle from the beef. Cut into pieces and put through the grinder twice using the medium disk. Collect the meat as it comes out of the grinder in long threads and form 4 individual heaps on separate dinner plates. These too should be very cold. Make a well in the center of the meat. Place an egg yolk, in half an eggshell, in the center of each well. Surround each "tartare" with 6 half-slices of lemon and on these arrange 8 capers, well drained from their oil, 3 slices of carrot, 3 half-olives, an anchovy fillet, well dried, 1 teaspoon of chopped parsley, and half an artichoke, divided into 2 again. Garnish with sprigs of parsley and serve with salt, freshly ground pepper, olive oil and lemon juice, ketchup, mustard and Worcestershire sauce for each guest to help themselves as they choose.

Painter's steak tartare

Broiled Fillet Steak with Danish Blue Cheese

Filetti Grigliati, con Danablu

To serve 6

6 thin ¼lb slices of fillet steak

1 garlic clove, thinly sliced

1 sprig fresh sage

1 bay leaf

4 black peppercorns

olive oil

5 tsp very fresh butter

¼lb Danish blue cheese

a little lemon juice

Worcestershire sauce

1 sprig fresh parsley

a few leaves fresh tarragon

1 small bunch fresh chives

lemon segments

a few tender lettuce leaves

Preparation and cooking time: about 45 minutes

Trim the steaks, then arrange them in a single layer on a fairly wide, deep dish. Scatter with the slices of garlic, 2 sage leaves and the bay leaf in small pieces, and the peppercorns pounded coarsely in a mortar. Moisten the meat with a little oil and let it rest in a cool place for at least 30 minutes, covering the dish with plastic wrap.

Meanwhile, mix the softened butter, cut in small pieces, with the cheese. Add a few drops of lemon juice, a generous dash of Worcestershire sauce and a finely chopped mixture of fresh parsley, tarragon and chives. Add a little salt, and beat well to obtain a creamy, smooth mixture. Turn into a serving bowl.

Heat the broiler, carefully brush the flavorings from the steaks and coat them on both sides with a little of the oil left over in the dish. Broil them quickly, turning them once. Lay the steaks on a serving dish, add a little salt and moisten them with a little olive oil. Garnish them with lemon segments and small lettuce leaves, and serve the cheese sauce separately.

■ MAIN COURSES BEEF ■

Roast Beef with Vegetable Sauce

Roast-beef con Salsa Vegetale

To serve 8

3½lb joint of beef

olive oil

2 tbsp butter

brandy

Worcestershire sauce

½lb potatoes

2 new medium-sized carrots

2 tbsp capers

6 yellow pimientos

2oz creamy Gorgonzola cheese

6 dill pickles/gherkins

2 tbsp white wine vinegar

2 tbsp mustard

2 egg yolks

a few slices zucchini

Preparation and cooking time: about 1 hour plus cooling

Preheat the oven to 400°F. Tie the joint in several places with kitchen string so that it retains its shape while cooking. Place it in a roasting pan, season with salt and pepper, pour over a few tablespoons of olive oil and dot with the butter. Roast it in the oven for about 1 hour. During cooking, pour over a few tablespoons of brandy, 3 or 4 dashes of Worcestershire sauce, and baste with the gravy which will have formed. Turn the joint at least three times, taking care not to pierce it with a fork or other implement. When cooked, remove from the oven and leave it to cool at room temperature.

Meanwhile, prepare the sauce: Boil the potatoes and the carrots separately; drain them and allow to cool. Cut them into slices and put them in a blender. Add the capers, the diced pimientos, the Gorgonzola, the sliced dill pickles, 8 tablespoons of olive oil, the vinegar and mustard, a generous dash of Worcestershire sauce, the egg yolks, 2 teaspoons of brandy, salt to taste and a little pepper. Process at maximum speed for 5 minutes until you obtain a creamy, smooth sauce, then blend in 2 tablespoons of boiling water.

Pour the sauce into a large sauceboat and serve as an accompaniment to the roast beef garnished, if you wish, with thin slices of zucchini.

Stuffed Cold Beef

Controfiletto Freddo, Farcito

To serve 6

⅔ cup canned sliced celery

1 small pimiento

1 tbsp capers

1 small canned artichoke in oil

¼ cup thick mayonnaise

1 tsp mustard

Worcestershire sauce

24 thin slices cold roast beef

olive oil

Preparation time: about 30 minutes

Drain the celery, dry it carefully on kitchen paper and place it in a bowl. Drain and dry the pimiento in the same way, cut it into short, thin strips and mix it with the celery. Add the finely chopped capers and artichoke.

Bind the mixture with the mayonnaise and fold in the mustard and a dash of Worcestershire sauce. Test and adjust the seasoning according to taste.

Spread the slices of meat on a work surface and place some of the prepared mixture on each slice. Roll the meat up and arrange the rolls on a plate. Brush each roll with a very little olive oil and garnish as desired. Serve with a fresh mixed salad and a simple *vinaigrette* dressing.

Autumn Stew

"Fusello" d'Autunno

To serve 4

2 large carrots

1 stalk celery, trimmed

1 small onion

1 large garlic clove

olive oil

3 tbsp butter

1½lb stewing beef

flour

½ cup dry Marsala wine

3½ cups good meat stock

2 tbsp concentrated tomato paste

1 bay leaf

2 red chilies

2 juniper berries

1 clove

1 small piece cinnamon stick

½lb baby onions

¼ bouillon cube

nutmeg

Preparation and cooking time: about 3 hours

Peel the carrots, cut them in half lengthwise and cut them into lengths of about 1½ inches. Then, using a small knife with a curved blade, pare the edges and chop the pieces trimmed off together with the celery, onion and garlic. Heat this mixture in a shallow saucepan in 4 tablespoons of olive oil and 5 teaspoons of butter. Fry gently without browning over a moderate heat. Cut the beef into large cubes, flour and brown them in the pan, stirring occasionally with a wooden spoon. Pour in the Marsala and let it evaporate, keeping the heat moderate and the pan uncovered.

Meanwhile, boil the stock. When nearly all the Marsala has been absorbed in the other pan, add the tomato paste

and stir, then pour in the boiling stock. Turn the heat down to simmer. Put the bay leaf, chilies, lightly crushed juniper berries, the clove and the cinnamon in a small cheesecloth bag, and put this into the pan. Cover and simmer for about 2 hours, stirring from time to time and adding a little boiling water towards the end of cooking if necessary.

When the meat is half-cooked, heat a skillet containing the rest of the butter and 1 teaspoon of olive oil. Put in the carrots and the onions and fry gently for a few minutes. Pour in ½ cup of boiling water and crumble in the quarter bouillon cube. Add a little grated nutmeg. Cover and cook over a moderate heat until all the liquid has disappeared and the vegetables are tender. Add this to the stew 10 minutes before the end of cooking, stirring carefully. Serve the stew with a steaming polenta.

Fillet Steak with Bearnaise Sauce
"Tagliata" di Manzo con Salsa Bearnaise

To serve 4

2 tbsp white wine vinegar

¼ cup white wine

1 fresh shallot

a few sprigs fresh tarragon

a few sprigs fresh chervil

a few sprigs fresh thyme

1 bay leaf

1 bouillon cube

2 egg yolks

⅞ cup butter

a few sprigs fresh parsley

2 large beef fillet steaks, each weighing ¾lb

olive oil

1 sprig rosemary

Preparation and cooking time: about 45 minutes

Pour 2 tablespoons of white wine vinegar and ¼ cup of dry white wine into a small pan; add a teaspoon each of finely chopped shallot and tarragon, half a teaspoon of chopped chervil and thyme together, a small piece of bay leaf and a quarter of cumbled bouillon cube. Simmer until the liquid is reduced to a third, then strain and cool. Place the saucepan in a *bain-marie*, add the 2 egg yolks and beat with a small whisk until creamy.

Remove from the *bain-marie* and, proceeding as for mayonnaise, add the butter, (first melted in a *bain-marie* and still warm) little by little. Do not add more butter until the previous addition has been completely absorbed; halfway through add a tablespoon of lukewarm water. When you have used up all the butter, stir a teaspoon each of chopped fresh tarragon and chopped parsley into the sauce, which should be creamy, then pour the sauce into a sauceboat and keep it warm in a *bain-marie*. Slightly flatten the two fillet steaks, then brush them on both sides with olive oil and broil for about 6 minutes on each side, first at a high heat, then moderate, to allow the meat to cook through without burning on the outside. Brush them with a little oil using a sprig of rosemary during cooking.

Remove the meat from the broiler, season with pepper and salt and serve on a serving board. Slice the meat in front of the guests and accompany it with the hot Bearnaise sauce.

■ **MAIN COURSES BEEF** ■

Onion-flavored Patties
False "Svizzere" alla Fornaia

To serve 4

1lb onions

4 tbsp butter

olive oil

flour

2½ cups light stock (or use bouillon cube)

2 tbsp dry Marsala wine

dry white wine

¾lb ground beef

2 slices bread soaked in milk

2 small eggs

½ cup grated Parmesan cheese

½ garlic clove

1 very small piece lemon rind, pith removed

2-3 sprigs fresh parsley

grated nutmeg

breadcrumbs

Preparation and cooking time: about 1¼ hours

Slice very thinly all but one of the onions and sauté them gently in a large knob of butter and a tablespoon of olive oil. Then sprinkle in a tablespoon of flour, stir and add the boiling stock in a thin stream, the Marsala and half the white wine. Stir once more, bring to the boil, then lower the heat to the minimum, cover the pan and let the onions simmer gently until they have absorbed almost all the liquid. Purée about a third of them. Add them to the remaining onions, then keep the mixture hot in a *bain-marie*.

While the onions are cooking, put the minced beef into a bowl, mix in the 2 slices of bread, having first squeezed out the milk thoroughly, the 2 eggs, the grated Parmesan cheese and a very finely minced mixture of the remaining onion, half a garlic clove with the green shoot removed, the lemon rind and a small handful of parsley. Mix all the ingredients together thoroughly, season moderately with salt, pepper and nutmeg.

Shape the mixture into 4 equal patties, coat them with the breadcrumbs then cook them very gently in the remaining butter, melted in a skillet together with 2 tablespoons of olive oil. When they are almost cooked, pour over the remaining white wine and let it evaporate. Put the 4 patties in individual earthenware serving dishes, cover with the hot onion mixture and serve immediately.

Sweet-sour Calves' Liver
Fegato di Vitello all'Agrodolce

To serve 6

6 slices calves' liver

¼ cup butter

1 sprig fresh sage

1 tbsp pine-nuts

5 capers

1 macaroon

1 dry cookie

1 tsp white wine vinegar

juice of ½ lemon

4-5 tbsp stock (or use bouillon cube)

¼ tsp mild mustard

a little flour

3 tbsp olive oil

½ garlic clove

a little chopped parsley

Preparation and cooking time: about 40 minutes

Trim the slices of liver, removing membrane and tendons but reserving the scraps. Heat a small skillet with 5 teaspoons of butter and a small sage leaf. As soon as it is hot, add the scraps of liver, brown them lightly, then put them with the other contents of the pan into a mortar. Add a large pinch of salt, the pine-nuts, capers, the macaroon, the cookie and the vinegar. Pound to a pulp, adding the strained lemon juice a little at a time.

Put the mixture into a small saucepan, dilute with the boiling stock and flavor with the mustard. Bring to the boil over a low heat, stirring all the time, then taste and adjust the seasoning. Keep warm in a *bain-marie*.
Flour the liver slices, shaking to remove any excess. Melt the remaining butter and the oil, flavored with 2 sage leaves and half a garlic clove, in a skillet that will just hold the liver. Brown the liver slices lightly. Salt them after cooking, then arrange them in a serving dish. Pour over the sweet-sour sauce, sprinkle on the chopped parsley and serve.

Kidney with Mushrooms

Rognoncino ai Funghi

To serve 1

2 tbsp butter

1 large mushroom cap (preferably cep)

½ tbsp olive oil

½ garlic clove

¼lb calves' kidney, fat removed, thinly sliced

flour

¼ cup meat stock

1 tbsp whipping cream

Worcestershire sauce

1 slice bread and chopped parsley for garnish

Preparation and cooking time: about 20 minutes

Preheat the oven to 400°F. Remove the crust from the bread, brush with 2 teaspoons of melted butter, then brown it in the oven for 3-4 minutes. Divide it into 4 triangles, lay them on a plate and keep hot. Wipe the mushroom cap with a damp cloth and slice it. Heat a small skillet with 2 teaspoons of butter, half a tablespoon of oil and half a garlic clove (which you then throw away). Put the kidney and mushroom in the pan and brown them lightly over a high flame for a couple of minutes.

In another skillet melt the remaining butter, mix in a little flour, then moisten with the hot stock. Bring to the boil, stirring all the time, then add the kidney and the mushroom, a tablespoon of cream and a dash of Worcestershire sauce. Keep over a very low heat for 2-3 minutes, taste and, if necessary, adjust the seasoning; then spoon on to a warmed plate. Sprinkle with a pinch of chopped parsley, garnish with the 4 *croûton* triangles and serve.

Kidney with mushrooms (top left); sweet-sour calves' liver (left)

Liver with Herbs

Fegato agli Aromi

To serve 4

4 slices calves' liver, together weighing 1 lb

2 fresh sage leaves

½ sprig rosemary

a bunch of fresh parsley

a handful of fresh basil

2 slices fresh white bread

5 tsp butter

3 tbsp olive oil

Preparation and cooking time: about 30 minutes

Remove the thin membrane and any nerves from the slices of liver. Finely chop together 2 sage leaves, half a rosemary sprig, a small bunch of parsley and 4 basil leaves; put the chopped mixture in a bowl and add a generous grinding of pepper. Crumble finely the 2 slices of bread and mix with the herbs. Spread the mixture over a plate and roll the slices of liver in it one by one, coating them as evenly as possible.

Heat the butter and oil in a large skillet and when hot put in the liver slices; brown and cook them on both sides, adding salt only when the meat is cooked. While they are cooking, do not prick the slices of liver but turn them with a spatula. Finally arrange them on a serving dish and serve immediately, garnishing them with a few parsley sprigs and more fresh basil leaves.

Liver with herbs

Venison Alpine Style
Cosciotto di Capriolo "Alpestre"

To serve 6

1 haunch or leg venison, perfectly hung

1 carrot

1 rib tender celery

1 sprig fresh rosemary

3-4 fresh sage leaves

1 bay leaf

2 garlic cloves

½ cup white wine vinegar

2 large onions

about ½ cup butter

2 tbsp flour

at least 1½ cups good meat stock

1 tsp sugar

olive oil

Preparation and cooking time: about 2 hours plus 24 hours' marination

Wash and thoroughly dry the haunch of venison then remove the bone from the meatiest part. Sew the meat up and arrange in a dish, preferably earthenware, just large enough to hold it. Slice the carrot and celery finely and place all round the meat, together with the chopped rosemary and sage leaves. Put in a bay leaf and lightly crush the garlic before adding them too. Pour in the vinegar and cover the dish. Leave in a cool place to marinate for 24 hours, during which time the haunch should be turned over 3 or 4 times.

The following day, finely slice the onions and lightly fry in ¼ cup of butter in a saucepan. Mix 2 tablespoons of butter with the same amount of flour and, when the onions begin to brown, stir this in. Mix and fry for a few seconds, then stir in 1 cup of boiling stock. Mix well and add the sugar. Cook the gravy for a few minutes.

Heat the remaining butter with 3 tablespoons of olive oil in a skillet. Remove the venison from the marinade, dry and flour it all over and sear it in the hot fat. Then carefully drain the oil from

it, and place it in the onion sauce. Add salt and pepper and pour in ½ cup of boiling stock. Cover and cook over a low heat for about 1½ hours, adding more boiling stock if the sauce becomes too dry.

Remove the meat from the saucepan. Blend the juices and pass them through a fine strainer. Serve the meat hot with the sauce.

■ MAIN COURSES GAME ■

Venison Stew
Lombo di Capriolo in Umido

To serve 6

3-4 shallots

1 sprig fresh rosemary

¼lb steaky raw ham

6 tbsp butter

12 venison loin chops

4 tbsp red wine vinegar

½ cup robust red wine

3½ cups good meat stock

2-3 juniper berries

1 clove

1 piece cinnamon stick

1 bay leaf

½ tsp meat extract

2 tbsp flour

2 tbsp dry Marsala wine

Preparation and cooking time: about 1¾ hours

Finely chop the shallots together with the rosemary leaves and the ham and put in a saucepan. Add about half the butter and fry gently for a few seconds without browning. Add the venison chops and brown gently. Turn them over carefully with a fork, without pricking the surface. Then pour over the vinegar and allow it to evaporate almost entirely before pouring in the wine. When that in turn has completely evaporated, pour in 2¼ cups of boiling stock. Add the juniper

berries, clove, cinnamon, bay leaf and meat extract. Cover the pan and simmer for about 1 hour, diluting with more stock if necessary.

Meanwhile, prepare a sauce by heating the rest of the butter and incorporating the flour with a wooden spoon. Pour in 1¼ cups of boiling stock gradually, as if for a Béchamel sauce. Remove the juniper berries, clove, bay leaf and cinnamon from the stew and pour the sauce into the stew. Shake the pan so that the sauce blends with the meat juices, then put in the Marsala and simmer for a further 20 minutes. Serve hot.

Venison Alpine style (upper right) and venison stew (lower left)

Baked Rabbit with Vegetables

Coniglio al Forno, con Verdure

To serve 4

hindquarters of 1 rabbit, weighing about 1¾lb

olive oil

1 bay leaf

1 small onion

1 small carrot

1 small stalk celery plus a few leaves for garnish

2oz butter

2 large garlic cloves

1 sprig fresh sage

1 bouillon cube

1¼ cups dry white wine

2 tsp cornstarch

parsley

Preparation and cooking time: about 1¾ hours

Cut the rabbit into even pieces and put them in a large skillet greased with oil, and add half a bay leaf. Cover the pan, put it on a low heat and draw out some of the moisture from the meat. Then drain well and leave to dry on a plate covered with a double sheet of paper towels. Preheat the oven to 400°F.

Slice the onion very thinly and cut the carrot and the celery into thin rounds. Mix these vegetables together and put them in the bottom of a small buttered baking pan just large enough to contain the rabbit. Add 2 large garlic cloves, lightly crushed, and 2 or 3 sage leaves.

Pack the pieces of rabbit closely on top of the vegetables and season with the crumbled bouillon cube and a generous grinding of pepper. Moisten with the white wine in which you have dissolved the cornstarch, then dot with the remaining butter cut into small pieces.

Seal the pan with aluminum foil, and bake in the oven for 1 hour or a little longer, until the rabbit is tender and the gravy reduced. Serve sprinkled with chopped parsley and garnish with a few celery leaves.

Rabbit Fricassee
Cibreo di Coniglio

To serve 2

2oz young peas

1 medium onion

butter

olive oil

2 fresh sage leaves

½ garlic clove

2 rabbit loins, boned, each weighing about ¼lb

¼lb rabbit's liver, cleaned

¼ bouillon cube

Worcestershire sauce

2 tbsp dry sherry

cornstarch

Preparation and cooking time: about 30 minutes

Boil the peas, in salted boiling water, then drain them and lay them to dry and cool on a plate covered with kitchen paper. Finely slice the onion and soften it gently in a large knob of butter and a tablespoon of olive oil, flavored with 2 leaves of sage and half a garlic clove. Meanwhile slice the 2 rabbit loins and cut the liver into roughly rectangular slices. Add both to the sautéed onion, at the same time discarding the sage and garlic.

Fry and lightly brown the meats, seasoning with the crumbled quarter bouillon cube and a dash of Worcestershire sauce, then moisten with 2 tablespoons of dry sherry in which you have dissolved a little cornstarch on the tip of a teaspoon. Now simmer over a vigorous heat so that the liquid reduces rapidly to form a thick sauce. Add the peas, stir and keep on the heat for a few moments more, then serve.

Golden Lamb Cutlets with Piquant Sauce
Costolettine di Agnello Dorate, con Salsa

To serve 4

8 lamb cutlets

a little flour

1 egg, beaten with a pinch of salt

breadcrumbs

2 tbsp finely chopped onion

1 sprig fresh parsley

1 tbsp capers

1 anchovy fillet

½ cup mayonnaise

Worcestershire sauce

a little mustard powder

2 tsp butter

2 tbsp corn oil

2 fresh sage leaves

Preparation and cooking time: about 40 minutes

Lightly beat the cutlets with a meat mallet. Dip them first in the flour, then in the beaten egg and finally in the breadcrumbs.

Put the onion, the chopped parsley, the capers and the anchovy fillet in a bowl. Fold in the mayonnaise and season with a dash of Worcestershire sauce and a pinch of mustard. Stir well and pour into a sauceboat.

Heat the butter and 2 tablespoons of oil in a skillet and add 2 sage leaves. Fry the cutlets until golden brown on both sides. Drain on paper towels and sprinkle with salt. Arrange the cutlets on a plate, garnish as desired and serve with the prepared sauce.

Golden lamb cutlets with piquant sauce

Grilled Lamb Cutlets

Costolettine D'Agnello Grigliate

To serve 4

16 lamb cutlets

1 small onion

1 large garlic clove

1 sprig fresh sage

1 small tender rib celery

8 tbsp olive oil

juice of 1 large lemon

Worcestershire sauce

1 tsp mustard

oregano

Preparation and cooking time: about 1 hour

Remove the fat from the cutlets, and any tendons or membrane, but leave the bony part at the base of each one. Arrange them in a large, deep dish which can hold them in a single closely packed layer. Slice the onion very thinly, and chop very finely the garlic, 2 sage leaves and the celery rib. Sprinkle these ingredients over the cutlets and season with a grinding of pepper. Pour over half the olive oil mixed with 1 tablespoon of lemon juice and a pinch of salt. Cover the dish with plastic wrap and leave to stand in a cool place (not the refrigerator) for about 30 minutes.

Meanwhile, put a large pinch of black pepper and a pinch of salt into a deep dish. Add the strained juice of half a lemon, the remaining olive oil, a light dash of Worcestershire sauce, the mustard and a small pinch of oregano and beat until smooth.

Heat the broiler. Clean the cutlets one at a time with a small brush, then broil them to taste turning them once only.

Arrange them on a warmed serving dish and dress them with the prepared sauce. Garnish according to taste, then serve.

Lamb and Artichoke Stew

Agnello e Carciofi in Umido

To serve 6

1¾lb boned leg of lamb

1 medium onion

2 garlic cloves

1 sprig fresh sage

2 tbsp butter

4 tbsp olive oil

⅜ cup dry Marsala wine

½lb tomatoes, peeled and finely chopped

⅝ cup meat stock (or use bouillon cube)

1 tsp cornstarch

1 lemon

Worcestershire sauce

3 medium-sized artichokes

a few sprigs fresh parsley

ground thyme

Preparation and cooking time: about 2 hours

Cut the lamb into pieces the size of a small egg. Finely chop two-thirds of the onion, a garlic clove and 2 sage leaves and fry them in 5 teaspoons of butter and 2 tablespoons of olive oil. Add the pieces of lamb and cook for at least 5 minutes, stirring frequently.

Pour on the Marsala and cook until the wine has been absorbed, moving the pan occasionally to prevent sticking. Stir in the tomatoes and the cold stock in which a teaspoon of cornstarch has been dissolved. Add a small piece of lemon rind (about 2 inches), a pinch of salt and

a dash of Worcestershire sauce. Cover the pan and cook for about 1¼ hours, adding a little more stock if necessary.

Meanwhile, cut off the stalks and tips of the artichokes, remove the tough outer leaves and place the artichokes in a bowl of water with the juice of half a lemon. Thinly slice the remaining onions, finely chop a garlic clove and a small handful of parsley and sauté them in the remaining butter and 2 tablespoons of oil.

Discard the chokes from the artichokes, and cut each one into 6 pieces. Add them to the pan. Cook for a few minutes and then stir in ½ cup of boiling water, a little salt and a pinch of thyme. Cover the pan and cook the artichokes on a moderate heat until slightly al dente.

When the meat has been cooking for about 1 hour, add the artichokes to it and complete cooking. Pour into a serving dish and garnish with a few sprigs of parsley. Serve. Plain or rice pilaf is an excellent accompaniment for this dish.

Roast Leg of Lamb with Mint Sauce

Cosciotto di Castrato Arrosto, con Salsa alla Menta

To serve 8

1 leg of lamb, weighing about 5½lb

2 garlic cloves

1 slice bacon, diced

1 sprig rosemary

2 tbsp shortening

about 1¼ cups dry white wine

1 tbsp sugar

few sprigs fresh mint, finely chopped

⅜ cup cider or white wine vinegar

Preparation and cooking time: about 2¾ hours.

Bone the leg of lamb, leaving only the shin bone. Lightly salt the inside of the meat and season with 2 crushed garlic cloves and bacon. Stitch up the opening and bind with kitchen twine. Preheat the oven to 400°F.

Finely chop the leaves of a large sprig of rosemary and place in a bowl. Add a generous pinch of pepper and a teaspoon of salt and stir in 2 heaping teaspoons of shortening. Spread the mixture over the lamb.

Roast for about 2 hours, turning occasionally. Baste the meat frequently with the juices during cooking and now and again sprinkle with a little of the white wine.

Meanwhile, prepare the mint sauce. Dissolve a tablespoon of sugar in ¼ cup of hot water and stir in the finely chopped mint and the vinegar. Leave to stand at room temperature for a couple of hours. Then stir well and serve with the roast leg of lamb. If desired, garnish the meat with fresh vegetables and a sprig of parsley.

Lamb Stew with Flowers

Spezzatino di Agnello, Fiorito

To serve 4-6

1¾lb boned leg or shoulder of lamb

¾ cup dry white wine

2 large sage leaves

1 sprig rosemary

2 garlic cloves

2 tbsp butter

2 tbsp olive oil

1 small onion

⅜ cup dry Marsala wine

petals of 7-8 white daisies (optional)

1 piece lemon rind

⅝ cup meat stock

½lb peeled tomatoes

1 tsp cornstarch

extra fresh daisy petals for garnish (optional)

Preparation and cooking time: 1½ hours plus overnight marination

Dice the lamb into 1½-inch cubes. Put the meat in a bowl and pour over the wine. Add the sage leaves, rosemary and 1 lightly crushed garlic clove. Cover the bowl with plastic wrap and marinate overnight in a cool place or in the least cold part of the refrigerator.

The following day, remove the lamb from the marinade and dry it. Heat the butter and oil in a large skillet and finely chop the onion together with 1 garlic clove, removing the green shoot. Fry these without browning them, put in the meat cubes and lightly brown them. Pour over the Marsala and let it reduce almost completely. Then put in the daisy petals and a 2-inch piece of lemon rind, which should later be discarded.

After a few minutes, pour over the boiling stock and put the tomatoes through a food processor, using the finest disk, before adding these too. Stir and season with salt and pepper. Dissolve the cornstarch in 3 tablespoons of cold water and stir into the pan. Simmer the stew for about 1 hour, adding more boiling stock if necessary. Serve on a warm dish, garnished with fresh daisy petals.

Lamb stew with flowers

Pork Rolls with Rhubarb
Bauletti al Rabarbaro

To serve 6

¼lb rhubarb, trimmed

12 slices of wide pork sausage, weighing about 1 lb in all

¼lb ham

¼ cup grated Parmesan cheese

1 egg

ground nutmeg

2 tbsp butter

2 tbsp olive oil

2 fresh sage leaves

½ garlic clove

a little flour

⅜ cup dry white wine

⅜ cup meat stock (or use bouillon cube)

Preparation and cooking time: about 1 hour

Cut the rhubarb into 2-inch lengths and simmer in salted boiling water for a few minutes. Drain and dry on paper towels.

Beat the slices of sausage, flattening them as much as possible, and season with salt and pepper. Finely grind the ham and mix it thoroughly with the grated Parmesan cheese, the egg, a pinch of salt and pepper and a little ground nutmeg. Spread the mixture on the slices of sausage. Place a piece of rhubarb on one half of each slice and roll up the meat, binding each roll with kitchen string.

Heat the butter and olive oil in a skillet. Add 2 sage leaves and half a garlic clove – discard the garlic once it is golden brown. Coat the pork rolls in flour and brown them gently.

Pour on the white wine and stock. Move the pan gently to make sure that nothing is sticking, cover it and allow the liquid to reduce by three-quarters before removing the string from the rolls and serving them. Garnish as desired.

Pork Cutlets with Oregano

Costolette di Maiale all'Origano

To serve 4

4 pork cutlets, each weighing 6oz

flour

2 tbsp olive oil

5 tsp butter

1 garlic clove

1 sprig fresh basil

1 tbsp spiced white wine vinegar

¼ cup dry white wine

1 cup canned tomatoes, puréed

½ bouillon cube

oregano

2 tbsp capers

Preparation and cooking time: about 40 minutes

Remove any tendons and sinews from the cutlets, then beat them lightly. Coat them one at a time in the flour, shaking them well to remove any excess. Put 2 tablespoons of oil and the butter in a skillet wide enough to contain the cutlets in a single layer. Heat the fats, together with the lightly crushed garlic clove and the basil; remove the flavorings when they have browned. Arrange the cutlets in the pan and brown them over a vigorous heat. Moisten them with the vinegar, then add the white wine. Cook until the liquid is reduced by two-thirds.

Add the puréed tomatoes, season with the crumbled half bouillon cube and a grinding of pepper, flavor with a pinch of oregano and finally sprinkle over the well-drained capers. Shake the pan to prevent sticking and reduce the sauce, turning the cutlets once only. Finally, arrange on a hot serving dish, pour over the sauce and garnish according to taste. Serve immediately.

Pork with Grapes on Skewers

Delizie Settembrine

To serve 6

¼lb chicken breast

36 white grapes

¼lb rather thick sausage

½lb pork loin in one piece

12 thin slices smoked bacon

olive oil

1 tbsp lemon juice

1 tsp mustard

Worcestershire sauce

Preparation and cooking time: about 1¼ hours

Divide the chicken breast into 12 equal-sized pieces; cut the sausage into 12 identical round slices, and the pork loin into 24 small cubes. Cut the slices of bacon in half and wrap each one around a piece of pork loin. Thread tightly on each of 12 wooden skewers: first a piece of pork loin wrapped in bacon, then a grape, then a slice of sausage, then another grape, then a small piece of chicken breast, another grape and another piece of pork loin wrapped in bacon. Brush each skewer with olive oil.

Preheat the broiler (or barbecue), then arrange the skewers under (or over) it and brown them on each side, turning them with a large spatula. When they are cooked, remove them from the broiler, season with salt and pepper and serve with a sauce made from 2 tablespoons of olive oil, one of lemon juice, 1 teaspoon of mustard and a dash of Worcestershire sauce, mixed to an emulsion in a bowl.

Pork with grapes on skewers (above)

Sausage and Pepper Kebabs

Spiedini di Salsiccia e Peperone

To serve 4

¾lb spicy sausages

6 small bell peppers

mustard

flour

butter

olive oil

1 garlic clove

2 sage leaves

3 tbsp dry white wine

1 heart chicory

Preparation and cooking time: about 30 minutes

Cut the sausages into 32 equal-sized pieces, without removing the skin. Wash the peppers, discard the stalks and cut into 24 equal-sized pieces in all. Spread a little mustard on one side of each piece of sausage. Thread the pieces of sausage and pepper on to 8 thin wooden skewers, alternating 4 pieces of sausage and 3 pieces of pepper on each one. Each piece of pepper should be against the mustard side of the sausage and the kebabs should be compact.

Lightly coat the kebabs in the flour, shaking them gently to remove any excess. Heat the butter and 2 tablespoons of olive oil in a skillet and add the garlic and sage leaves. Place the kebabs in the skillet one at a time and cook over a moderate heat until browned on all sides. Just before removing the kebabs from the heat, sprinkle them with a little white wine. Allow the wine to evaporate quickly. Serve the kebabs on a bed of chicory.

Liver and Pork Roulades

Involtini di Fegato e Maiale

To serve 4

1 small onion

1 garlic clove

butter

6oz calves' liver

1 tbsp capers

1 tsp anchovy paste

1 tbsp breadcrumbs

16 thin slices of pork fillet, weighing about 1lb in all

flour

½ cup dry white wine

Preparation and cooking time: 45 minutes

Chop the onion finely together with the garlic and fry in a knob of butter. Chop the liver and place in a bowl. Add the fried onions, thoroughly drain and chop the capers and add these, mix in a heaping teaspoon of anchovy paste and a heaping tablespoon of breadcrumbs. Add salt and pepper and mix thoroughly.

Beat the slices of pork as thinly as possible and spread a little of the liver mixture on one side of each piece. Roll up the meat, sealing the stuffing well inside and tie up with kitchen twine like a small parcel. Flour the roulades and shake off any excess flour. Melt a knob of butter in a skillet and fry the roulades, browning them well on all sides. Add very little salt, then pour over the wine. Shake the pan vigorously to prevent the meat sticking to the bottom then cover the pan. The wine will evaporate leaving a delicious sauce. Serve.

Pork Cutlets with Grapes

Costolette di Maiale all'Uva

To serve 4

4 dozen perfectly ripe white grapes

4 pork or veal cutlets

a little flour

2 tbsp butter

1 tbsp olive oil

½ bay leaf

about ¼ cup dry white wine

a piece of bouillon cube

¼ cup brandy

Preparation and cooking time: about 1 hour

Using a short, sharp knife, peel and pip the grapes. Remove any sinews and membranes from the cutlets. Beat the cutlets lightly and flour them all over. Shake off any excess. Heat the butter and olive oil in a large skillet and flavor with the bay leaf. Put the cutlets into the hot fat and brown on both sides, turning them over without piercing. Splash over a little wine from time to time.

When the wine has almost entirely evaporated, put in the grapes. Turn up the heat, crumble in the piece of bouillon cube and shake the skillet from side to side frequently to allow all the cutlets to absorb the flavor. Then pour in the brandy and set it alight. Finally, arrange on a serving dish with the grapes on one side together with the sauce from the pan. Serve at once. Ideally, follow with a mixed salad.

Pork cutlets with grapes

Woodcutter's Roulades
Involtini Boscaoli

To serve 6

12 slices loin of pork, weighing about 1½lb in all

1 large cep mushroom

6 tbsp olive oil

1 garlic clove

½ cup dry Marsala wine

½ bouillon cube

1oz raw ham

¼ cup grated Parmesan cheese

a little flour

2 tbsp butter

⅝ cup dry white wine

1 tsp cornstarch

Preparation and cooking time: about 40 minutes

Lightly beat the slices of pork to flatten them and make them all the same size, then lay them out on a tray. Wipe the mushroom then slice it, including the stalk. Heat half the olive oil in a small saucepan, brown the lightly crushed garlic clove then remove it. Put in the slices of mushroom and heat over a high heat for a few minutes, then pour in the Marsala. Crumble in the half bouillon cube and cook over a high heat until the Marsala has evaporated.

Finely chop the ham together with the mushroom and put into a bowl. Add the grated Parmesan and mix thoroughly. Sprinkle the meat with salt and pepper and spread a tablespoon of stuffing on each slice keeping it well away from the edges. Roll the meat up tightly to seal the stuffing in. Secure with a toothpick and flour lightly.

Heat the butter with the remaining olive oil in a large skillet and put in the roulades. Brown them quickly over a high heat. Pour on the wine and cook until it has nearly all evaporated. Arrange the roulades on a hot serving dish. Dissolve the cornstarch in a little cold water and add to the juices in the pan to thicken the sauce. Pour this over the roulades and serve.

Pork Chops with Balsam Vinegar
Braciole di Maiale all'Aceto Balsamico

To serve 6

6 pork chops, each weighing 6oz

2 tbsp mild mustard

flour

1 sprig fresh sage

1 garlic clove

butter

olive oil

½ cup dry white wine

Worcestershire sauce

½ bouillon cube

1 tbsp balsam vinegar

a few sprigs fresh parsley for garnish

Preparation and cooking time: about 40 minutes

Remove excessive fat from the chops, then beat them lightly, taking care not to split the meat. Put the mustard in a bowl and coat the chops with it on both sides. Then coat them with flour, shaking them gently to remove the excess. Chop finely 2 sage leaves and the garlic. Melt 2 tablespoons of butter with 3 tablespoons of olive oil in a large skillet and soften the sage and garlic gently, taking care not to brown them.

Now put the chops in the pan and allow them to cook and brown. Moisten them with the white wine, and season with a dash of Worcestershire sauce and the crumbled half bouillon cube. When the meat has absorbed almost all the wine, moisten it with the balsam vinegar and keep the pan on the heat for a few moments more. Serve very hot, garnished with fresh parsley.

Sausages with Grapes
Salsicce all'Uva

To serve 4

12 large white grapes

4 poaching sausages

⅝ cup dry white wine

1 bay leaf

1 garlic clove

Preparation and cooking time: about 1 hour

Carefully peel and de-seed the grapes. Rinse the sausages, plunge them in boiling water and leave them for a few moments; remove them with a slotted spoon and prick them in several places with a trussing needle.

Arrange the sausages in a saucepan large enough to contain them in one layer, pour over the white wine and enough cold water to cover. Add a bay leaf and a crushed garlic clove, then simmer the sausages, over a moderate heat, until the liquid has almost entirely evaporated.

At this point, add the halved grapes and leave the sausages to brown lightly in their sauce. Then discard the bay leaf and the garlic. Halve the sausages lengthwise, using a very sharp knife, and arrange them on a serving dish. Pour over the grapes and the cooking sauce, then serve.

A good accompaniment to the sausages and grapes is to serve them on a bed of sauerkraut which has been braised for a long time in white wine with some finely chopped onion and slices of apple.

Woodcutter's roulades

Piquant Pork Escalopes
Scaloppe di Maiale Piccanti

To serve 4-6

12 slices pork loin weighing about 1¼lb in all

flour

2 tbsp butter

3 tbsp olive oil

1 sprig fresh sage

2 large garlic cloves

3 tbsp dry Marsala wine

2 tbsp mustard

Worcestershire sauce

½ bouillon cube

½ cup very fresh cream

a little parsley for garnish

Preparation and cooking time: about 30 minutes

Lightly beat the slices of meat, then dip them one at a time in the flour, shaking well to remove any excess. Heat a large skillet with the butter and oil, 3 sage leaves and the lightly crushed garlic. When the butter and oil are hot, remove the sage and garlic and put the slices of pork in the pan. Brown them on each side for a few moments, adding a little salt at the end of cooking.

Remove them from the pan and arrange on a heatproof dish just large enough to hold them. Keep them warm.

Pour the Marsala into the skillet and let it evaporate almost completely. To the remaining liquid add the mustard, a generous dash of Worcestershire sauce, and the half bouillon cube, crumbled. Stir with a wooden spoon and finally pour in the cream. Simmer for a few moments, shaking the pan almost continuously and stirring.

Pour the sauce over the escalopes and serve immediately, sprinkled, if you like, with a little finely-chopped parsley.

Pork Sausage Parcels

Involtini di Lonza

To serve 6

1 eggplant

12 slices wide pork sausage

¼lb Provola cheese

oil for frying

12 fresh basil leaves

2 anchovy fillets in oil, broken up

flour

olive oil

butter

1 small onion, sliced

3 tbsp dry Marsala wine

½ cup stock (or use bouillon cube)

Preparation and cooking time: about 1¼ hours

Peel the eggplant and cut it into 12 equal slices about ⅛ inch thick. Arrange the slices on a tilted plate, sprinkle with salt and leave for about 30 minutes for the juices to drain off.

Lightly beat the slices of sausage with a meat mallet. Cut the Provola cheese into 12 equal pieces. Rinse the slices of eggplant under running water, drain and dry them. Fry them in plenty of oil, then drain thoroughly on paper towels.

Arrange the slices of sausage on a tray, keeping them well apart from each other, and place a slice of eggplant on each slice of sausage. Place a leaf of fresh basil, a piece of Provola cheese and a small piece of anchovy fillet one on top of the other in the center of each piece of eggplant. Roll the meat tightly around the other ingredients and secure with kitchen twine. Coat the parcels in flour.

Heat 3 tablespoons of olive oil and a large knob of butter in a large skillet. Add the sliced onion, discarding it as soon as it has browned. Fry the parcels until golden brown. Pour in the Marsala wine and the boiling stock. Season with salt and pepper and cook until the liquid has reduced to form a thick sauce. Remove from the heat, discard the twine from the parcels and serve immediately.

Rissoles with Tomato Sauce

Polpettine al Pomodoro

To serve 6

2 slices white bread, soaked in milk

1lb sausage meat

¼lb ham, diced

¾ cup grated Parmesan cheese

2 eggs

ground nutmeg

olive oil

1 medium onion

1 garlic clove

1lb firm ripe tomatoes

5-6 fresh basil leaves

sugar

Preparation and cooking time: about 1¼ hours

Drain the bread and grind with the sausage meat and ham. Place the minced mixture in a bowl and stir in the grated Parmesan cheese, the eggs, a pinch of salt and pepper and a little ground nutmeg. Mix thoroughly to form a smooth paste. Make 24 rissoles from the mixture, shaping them with your hands, and place them on an oiled baking pan. Sprinkle with a little oil and leave to stand in a cool place for at least 15 minutes.

Meanwhile finely slice the onion and fry it gently with the lightly crushed garlic clove in 4 tablespoons of olive oil. Stir in the coarsely chopped tomatoes, a few basil leaves, a little salt and pepper and a pinch of sugar. Bring slowly to the boil and then lower the heat, half-cover the pan and cook for about 15 minutes, stirring occasionally.

Preheat the oven to 400°F. Process the sauce in a blender and pour it back into the pan. Test and adjust the seasoning according to taste. Bake the rissoles in the oven for 12-13 minutes, transfer to the sauce in the pan and cook gently for a further 4-5 minutes. Place in a warmed dish, garnish with fresh basil and serve.

Chicken and Pork with Port

Pollo e Maiale al Porto

To serve 4

½lb chicken breast

½lb loin of pork, sliced fairly thinly

1 slice of smoked bacon

butter

olive oil

1 garlic clove

1 sage leaf

3 tbsp port wine

cornstarch

½ cup skimmed chicken stock

Worcestershire sauce

Preparation and cooking time: about 30 minutes

Remove any gristle from the chicken and pork, then cut them both into thickish strips. Cut the bacon into short, thin strips and heat a skillet containing a knob of butter and 2 tablespoons of olive oil. Flavor with the garlic and sage leaf and fry lightly. Then add the bacon and brown for a few seconds. Remove the garlic and sage and put in the chicken and pork. Fry lightly, shaking the pan almost continuously.

Pour in the port and wait until it has almost entirely evaporated before dissolving a large pinch of cornstarch in the cold stock and pouring that in. Add a generous dash of Worcestershire sauce and continue shaking the pan to prevent the meats from sticking to the bottom. When the stock has reduced, remove the pan from the heat and add a little salt. Stir and serve immediately.

Stuffed Turkey Breast
Fesa di Tacchino Farcita

To serve 8

4 slices fresh bread

milk

handful of peas

1¾lb turkey breast, in one slice

6oz raw ham, in thin slices

2 eggs

1 cup grated Parmesan cheese

nutmeg

olive oil

1 medium onion

1 stick celery

1 carrot

1 sprig fresh sage

1 sprig fresh rosemary

2 garlic cloves

dry white wine

Preparation and cooking time: about 2 hours

Soak the slices of bread in the milk. Cook the peas in boiling salted water for a few minutes, then drain them and lay them on a cloth to dry. Flatten the slice of turkey breast, dipping the meat mallet in cold water from time to time and taking care not to break the meat. Place the ham in an even layer on top, stopping ½ inch from the edges. Squeeze the milk thoroughly from the slices of bread and break them into a bowl. Add the 2 whole eggs, the Parmesan cheese, salt, a grinding of white pepper and a little grated nutmeg. Stir and combine the ingredients perfectly to obtain a smooth, creamy mixture, then add the cooled peas. Spread this stuffing on top of the slices of ham.

Preheat the oven to 400°F. Roll up the slice of turkey, enclosing the stuffing, and sew it up so that the stuffing does not escape during cooking. Tie it in several places with kitchen twine, checking that there are no openings in the meat. Brush

all over with olive oil, sprinkle with salt and place in a roasting pan just large enough to hold it. Surround it with the onion, celery and carrot cut into small pieces, 2 sage leaves, the rosemary and lightly crushed garlic. Roast in the oven for about 1 hour, turning the meat from time to time, being careful not to pierce it. Moisten it frequently with the wine, a little at a time.

When the meat is cooked, remove the twine and thread and serve either hot or cold. If serving hot, accompany it with the cooking juices, strained and with the fat removed. If serving cold, serve it with a light mayonnaise to which you add a little liquid gelatin and a little lightly whipped cream.

Turkey Breast au Gratin with Asparagus
Petto di Tacchino Gratinato, agli Asparagi

To serve 6

3oz bacon

2½lb turkey breast, trimmed

rosemary

2 bay leaves

5 tbsp butter

1¼lb asparagus

¼ cup grated Parmesan cheese

Preparation and cooking time: about 1½ hours

Preheat the oven to 400°F. Cut the bacon into pieces and place it "inside" the turkey breast. Roll the meat up fairly tightly to enclose the bacon and bind with kitchen twine, pushing a little rosemary and 2 bay leaves beneath the twine. Sprinkle with salt and papper and spread with 3 tablespoons of the butter. Place in a baking pan and cook in the oven for about 1 hour. Turn and baste occasionally during cooking.

Meanwhile, trim and wash the asparagus and tie in a bundle with kitchen twine. Stand the asparagus upright in a saucepan of salted boiling water (the water should come halfway up

the asparagus) and cook for 15-18 minutes. Drain, discard the twine and spread the asparagus out to dry and cool on absorbent paper towels. Cut into pieces about 1¼ inches long and sauté in the remaining butter.

Remove the turkey from the oven and leave to rest for about 10 minutes. Increase the oven temperature to 425°F. Slice and arrange the turkey on an ovenproof plate which has been brushed with the cooking juices. Place the pieces of asparagus on top of the meat and sprinkle with the grated Parmesan cheese and remaining cooking juices. Cook in the oven for a further 3-4 minutes and serve.

Breast of Turkey with Orange
Fesa di Tacchino all'Arancia

To serve 6-8

2¼lb breast of turkey in one piece

olive oil

¼ cup butter

1 small celery stalk

1 small carrot

2 garlic cloves

1 bay leaf

2 sage leaves

1 sprig rosemary

⅜ cup dry sherry

4 slices bacon

2 tsp orange marmalade

juice of ½ orange

cornstarch

Worcestershire sauce

¼ cup stock (or use bouillon cube)

Preparation and cooking time: 1½ hours

Tie up the turkey with kitchen string as

you would for a normal joint. Brush with olive oil and sprinkle with salt and pepper. Preheat the oven to 400°F. Place the turkey in a buttered roasting pan, surrounded by the coarsely chopped onions, celery and carrot, the crushed garlic, 1 bay leaf, 2 sage leaves and a sprig of rosemary. Dot with the remaining butter and cook in the oven for about 1 hour. Baste the turkey regularly, turn occasionally and sprinkle with sherry.

Halfway through cooking, add the diced, parboiled bacon. When the meat is cooked, remove the string and place the turkey on a plate. Cover with a sheet of aluminum foil and keep warm in the oven. Add to the cooking juices the orange marmalade, the orange juice (with ½ teaspoon of cornstarch dissolved in it), a dash of Worcestershire sauce and the stock. Stir and simmer over a moderate heat until thickened. Strain and serve with the meat, which should be sliced thinly at the table.

Chicken Legs with Juniper
Cosce di Pollo al Ginepro

To serve 4

butter

1 large onion

4 chicken legs, together weighing about 2½lb

1 bay leaf

2 tbsp olive oil

4 juniper berries

¼ cup gin

1 cup dry white wine

1 tsp cornstarch

Preparation and cooking time: 50 minutes

Preheat the oven to 400°F. Butter the base of an oven dish capable of holding the 4 chicken legs in a single layer. Slice the onion very thinly and place half of it in the bottom of the dish. Season with salt and pepper and place the chicken legs on top, putting a bay leaf between them. Scatter the remaining onion over the top, moisten with the oil, and season with salt and pepper and the juniper berries, broken into small pieces.

Cook in the oven for about 40 minutes. After 15 minutes, pour over the gin, then the white wine in which you have dissolved the cornstarch. Finish cooking, basting often, but without turning.

■ MAIN COURSES CHICKEN ■

Country-style Chicken
Pollo alla Contadina

To serve 4

2 cups mushrooms

¼lb baby onions

1 chicken, weighing about 2½lb

flour

2 tbsp butter

2 tbsp olive oil

1 bay leaf

Worcestershire sauce

1 cup dry white wine

2 tbsp dry Marsala wine

1 tsp tomato paste

1 bouillon cube

Preparation and cooking time: about 45 minutes

Peel the mushrooms and wash them well; also wash the onions. Divide the chicken into 8 even pieces. Flour them, shaking off the excess flour, then brown them in a large skillet in the butter and olive oil. Add the onions and the quartered mushrooms, flavor with a bay leaf and a dash of Worcestershire sauce then fry them for a few moments. Pour in the white wine and Marsala, in which you have dissolved the tomato paste and the bouillon cube. Stir the pan, cover, and cook over a moderate heat for about 30 minutes.

Chicken legs with juniper (above left) and *country-style chicken; chicken and ham in aspic* (right)

Chicken and Ham in Aspic

Aspic di Pollo e Spalla

To serve 6-8

1 small onion

2 cloves

½ small carrot

½ celery stalk

2 garlic cloves

1 leek, white part only

4 sprigs parsley

1 bouillon cube

4 portions chicken, together weighing 1½lb

½ cup frozen tiny peas

2 tbsp gelatin

6oz boiled ham

¼lb ground lean beef

1 egg white

ground nutmeg

3 tbsp dry Marsala wine

1 lemon

Preparation and cooking time: about 2¼ hours plus at least 2 hours' refrigeration

Heat 4 pints of water in a large pan, with the onion cut in half and studded with the cloves, the carrot and the celery cut in small pieces, 2 slightly crushed garlic cloves, the leek and the parsley sprigs. When the water boils, salt it lightly, add the crumbled bouillon cube, then simmer for a few minutes. Next plunge in the 4 chicken portions and simmer them for about 40 minutes, uncovered and over a moderate heat.

Simmer the peas in salted boiling water in a small pan until cooked; drain them and spread them to dry on a plate covered with a double sheet of paper towels. Dissolve the gelatin in a little cold water.

Cut the ham into thin strips. When cooked, remove the chicken from the stock and leave on a plate to cool; strain the stock through a cloth (it should be about 3 cups). In a small saucepan mix

the ground beef with the egg white and the ground nutmeg then, still stirring, pour the hot stock over in a trickle. Place the pan on the heat and keep beating until the stock comes to the boil. Lower the heat and simmer the consommé for a few minutes, then strain it very carefully through a fine cloth. Fold in the gelatin and flavor it with 3 tablespoons of dry Marsala wine.

Remove the skin from the chicken portions, then bone them and chop the meat coarsely. Take a small oval mold, about 1¾ pints in capacity. Place the small peas at the bottom, sprinkle them with a little of the hot consommé and put the mold in the freezer for a few minutes to set the liquid without freezing it. Next arrange a layer of chicken meat in the mold, sprinkle it with more consommé and put it in the freezer for a few minutes. Then make a layer with the ham and consommé and continue in this way, alternating the chicken and ham layers, pouring some consommé over each one and setting it in the freezer. When all the ingredients are used up, leave the mold in the refrigerator for at least 2 hours. To serve, immerse the mold for a few seconds in a bowl of hot water, dry it and unmold on to a serving plate. Garnish with lemon slices, and accompany with mayonnaise.

Stuffed Chicken Breasts in Breadcrumbs

Petti di Pollo Farciti e Dorati

To serve 6

6 chicken breasts, weighing about 2lb in all

12 thin bacon slices

1 sprig fresh sage

1 garlic clove

¾ cup Parmesan cheese

2 eggs plus 2 yolks

breadcrumbs

butter

flour

½ cup milk

¼ bouillon cube

½ cup grated Emmental cheese

⅓ cup cream

nutmeg

olive oil

Preparation and cooking time: about 1 hour

Beat the chicken breasts lightly, taking care not to break them. Place on one side of each breast 2 slices of bacon, a small leaf of sage and a sliver of garlic, then close them up into their original shape. Roll them first in the grated Parmesan cheese, then in 2 of the beaten eggs, lightly salted, and finally in the breadcrumbs, making sure that they are thoroughly coated each time. Trim the edges using a large knife, then lay the chicken breasts on a tray.

Melt 2 tablespoons of butter in a small saucepan, add the flour and stir with a wooden spoon to stop lumps forming. Slowly pour in the cold milk, and bring the mixture to the boil, stirring continuously, and season with the crumbled piece of bouillon cube. Remove the sauce from the heat, mix in the grated Emmental, 2 egg yolks and the cream, mixing well after each addition. Season the sauce with a pinch of ground nutmeg and pepper, then keep it warm in a *bain-marie*.

Heat 2 skillets, and in each one put a knob of butter, 4 tablespoons of olive oil and 2 sage leaves. As soon as the fat is hot, fry the breaded chicken breasts. Remove them from the skillets and lay them on a plate covered with paper towels. Then transfer them to a warm serving dish, garnish to taste, pour the prepared sauce over them and serve.

■ MAIN COURSES CHICKEN ■

Chicken and Artichokes

Pollo con i Carciofi

To serve 4-6

1 chicken, weighing about 2½lb, cleaned, head, neck, feet and wing tips removed

flour

7-8 tbsp olive oil

1 large garlic clove

1 sprig fresh rosemary

¼ cup brandy

⅝ cup dry white wine

powdered thyme

powdered marjoram

¾ cup stock (or use bouillon cube)

4 large artichokes

juice of 1 lemon

1 shallot

a little fresh parsley

Preparation and cooking time: about 1¼ hours

Singe the chicken, then carefully wash and dry it. Cut it into 8 pieces, without breaking the bones. Flour the pieces and shake off any excess flour. Heat 4-5 tablespoons of olive oil in a skillet and put in the lightly crushed garlic and the rosemary. When the oil is hot, put in the chicken and sauté until the pieces are browned all over. Pour in the brandy and flambé. Then pour in the wine and shake the skillet to prevent sticking. Flavor with a pinch of thyme, a pinch of marjoram, salt and pepper. Turn the heat down, cover the skillet and simmer for about 40 minutes, adding a little boiling stock if necessary to prevent drying out.

In the meantime, trim the artichokes, and put them in a bowl of cold water to which a little strained lemon juice has been added. Finely chop the shallot together with a little parsley and gently fry in 3 tablespoons of olive oil. Drain the artichokes well, cut them in half and remove the chokes. Cut into fine slices. (Keep the stalks for another dish.) Add the artichokes to the fried shallot and parsley and cook for a few seconds, shaking the skillet from side to side. Pour in ½ cup of boiling stock, cover the pan and simmer for 5 minutes or a little longer, until the artichokes are tender. Then remove the garlic and rosemary from the skillet containing the chicken and replace with the artichokes. Continue cooking for a few seconds, taste and correct the seasoning and serve, preferably directly on to individual warmed plates.

Chicken and artichokes

Chicken with Ham au Gratin

Pollo alla Coppa, Gratinato

To serve 6

¼lb chicken meat, skinned and boned

flour

6 tbsp butter

⅝ cup dry white wine

2oz thinly sliced coppa or raw ham

1 tsp chopped parsley

3 tbsp grated Parmesan cheese

⅝ cup milk

nutmeg

Preparation and cooking time: about 1¼ hours

Cut the chicken (preferably leg and thigh meat) into regular pieces about 2½ inches long. Flour lightly and brown on all sides in 3 tablespoons of the butter, adding salt and pepper. Then pour in the wine and allow to evaporate over a high heat. Shake the pan to prevent sticking.

Cut the coppa into short thin strips. Remove from the heat and cut the chicken pieces into short but thicker strips and arrange, alternating with the coppa, in a large, buttered, ovenproof dish. Sprinkle chopped parsley and the Parmesan cheese over the meat.

Preheat the oven to 400°F. Make a Béchamel sauce by melting the remaining butter in a pan, stirring in just over 2 teaspoons of flour and adding the milk; season with salt and grated nutmeg. Pour the sauce over the meat and bake for about 20 minutes, until the surface is golden brown. Serve hot from the oven.

Chicken Legs with Onions

Cosce di Pollo Cipollate

To serve 6

6 fresh or frozen chicken legs

flour

3 tbsp cooking oil

1 garlic clove

2 sprigs fresh sage

2 tbsp butter

1 tbsp olive oil

2 small onions, finely sliced

⅝ cup dry white wine

1 bouillon cube

ground thyme

ground marjoram

Preparation and cooking time: about 45 minutes

Allow the legs to thaw if frozen, preferably by transferring them from the freezer to the refrigerator; then rinse and dry them carefully. Truss them at two points with kitchen string, so that they keep their shape well, then dip them in flour and shake them to remove any excess. Put the cooking oil in a skillet, flavour with the garlic and fresh sage and place on the heat. When the oil is hot, add the chicken legs and brown them gently.

Heat the butter and a tablespoon of olive oil in a pan and add the onions, without browning them. Add the chicken legs, allow them to absorb the flavor for a few minutes, then pour the white wine over them, adding the crumbled bouillon cube, a pinch of thyme and a pinch of marjoram. Keep the pan moving to prevent sticking, then cover, lower the heat and cook for about 30 minutes; moisten with a little boiling water if the food seems to be drying out too much. By the end of cooking the sauce should be thick. Now remove the string from the chicken legs and arrange them on a large dish, pour the cooking juices over them and serve.

Stuffed Chicken Drumsticks

Fusi di Pollo Farciti

To serve 6

6 fresh or frozen chicken drumsticks

3 sprigs fresh sage

1 garlic clove

3-4 slices smoked bacon

1 small onion

1 small carrot

1 small stalk celery

2 tbsp olive oil

2 tbsp butter

¼ cup dry white wine

½ cup stock (or use bouillon cube)

½ tbsp cornstarch

Preparation and cooking time: 1½ hours

Preheat the oven to 400°F. Allow frozen drumsticks to thaw, preferably in the refrigerator; rinse and dry them. Slit the skin, take out the bones and remove the sinews, turning the meat inside out, without cutting it up. Then push the meat back into shape and insert half a small sprig of fresh sage, a thin strip of garlic clove and a sliver of smoked bacon into each drumstick. Stitch up the opening on the drumstick. Cover the base of an ovenproof dish with the finely chopped onion, celery and carrot. Arrange the drumsticks on top. Add 2 tablespoons of oil, dot with butter and season lightly with salt and pepper.

Bake for about 45 minutes; turn the drumsticks a couple of times and, halfway through the cooking time, add the white wine. Remove the drumsticks from the dish, place the dish on top of the stove and add the stock, with half a tablespoon of cornstarch dissolved in it; allow to simmer for a few minutes, stirring constantly. Then strain the gravy over the drumsticks and serve. Arrange them, if you like, on top of buttered peas, with parsley for garnish.

Chicken with Herbs

Galletti Amburghesi, in Tegame

To serve 6

3 small chickens

4-5 tbsp olive oil

1 sprig rosemary

2 fresh sage leaves

½ garlic clove

⅜ cup dry white wine

Preparation and cooking time: about 1 hour

Wash, trim and gut the chickens. Cut them in half (preferably using poultry shears) along the backbone (to one side of it) and flatten the chickens gently with a meat mallet, taking care not to break or shatter the bones.

Place 4-5 tablespoons of olive oil, a sprig of rosemary, 2 sage leaves and half a garlic clove in a very large skillet and fry gently for a few minutes. Add the chickens, open side upwards. Sprinkle with salt and pepper, cover the pan and cook on a low heat for 10 minutes.

Turn the chickens, sprinkle with salt and pepper and pour over the white wine. Cover the pan and cook briskly for a further 20 minutes. Arrange on a warmed dish and serve immediately.

Chicken legs with onions (top left) and *stuffed chicken drumsticks* (below)

Chicken Breasts with Mushrooms in Marsala

Petti di Pollo al Marsala, con Funghi

To serve 6

¾-1 lb small mushrooms

1 small onion

6 small chicken breasts, each weighing ¼lb

¼ cup butter

2 tbsp olive oil

flour

9 tbsp dry Marsala wine

½ tsp tomato paste

1 garlic clove

meat extract

a little chopped parsley for garnish

Preparation and cooking time: about 50 minutes

Trim the mushrooms, wipe with a damp cloth and slice thinly. Chop the onion very finely and put it in a skillet large enough to hold the chicken breasts, add 2 tablespoons butter and a tablespoon of oil, then fry very gently until the onion is soft.

Remove any sinews from the chicken breasts and flatten them with a met mallet; flour them and shake them lightly to remove the excess. Brown them lightly in the pan with the fried onion; seasoning with salt and pepper and moistening them with 6 tablespoon of dry Marsala in which you have dissolved half a teaspoon of tomato paste.

When the Marsala has formed a creamy sauce and the chicken is cooked, remove the pan from the heat, arrange the chicken breasts on a serving dish, and pour over the boiling sauce, strained through a fine sieve. Cover the dish with a sheet of aluminium foil and keep it hot in the lit oven with the door open.

Put the remaining butter in the skillet you have already used together with a tablespoon of oil, and flavor with the lightly crushed garlic. Add the thinly sliced mushrooms and sauté them gently for a few minutes. Then pour over 3 tablespoons of dry Marsala in which you have dissolved a little meat extract on the end of a teaspoon. Add salt and pepper to taste and let the mushrooms absorb all the liquid, becoming tender and flavorful. Arrange them alongside the chicken breasts, sprinkle over some chopped parsley and serve.

■ MAIN COURSES CHICKEN ■

Chicken Pie
Teglia di Pollo

To serve 6-8

¾lb puff pastry

about ¼ cup butter

5 tbsp grated Parmesan cheese

1 tbsp breadcrumbs

1 small leek

1 garlic clove

a little parsley

2 tbsp olive oil

½lb chicken breast

1 tbsp flour

2 tbsp dry Marsala wine

⅝ cup milk

1 bouillon cube

2 eggs

2 slices bacon

Preparation and cooking time: 1¼ hours plus any thawing time

Defrost the pastry if using frozen. Preheat the oven to 400°F. Use the pastry to line a shallow, buttered 9 x 6 inch pie dish. Prick the base with a fork and sprinkle with 2½ tablespoons of Parmesan cheese, mixed with the breadrumbs. Chop the leek finely and soften with the garlic and a small bunch of chopped parsley in 2 tablespoons of melted butter and the oil. Add the diced chicken breast, and brown gently. Sprinkle with the flour, stir and add the dry Marsala, followed immediately by the boiling milk, pouring this in gradually and stirring all the time. Flavor

with the crumbled bouillon cube and allow to simmer for a few minutes, still stirring.

Remove from the stove and mix in the 2 beaten eggs, with the rest of the Parmesan cheese and the bacon cut into small strips. Pour everything into the dish and bake in the lower half of the oven for about 30 minutes.

■ MAIN COURSES CHICKEN ■

Chicken Breasts with Cheese and Artichokes
Petti di Pollo, Fondenti

To serve 4

2 chicken breasts

a little flour

5 tbsp butter

2 fresh artichokes

a little lemon juice

2 tbsp olive oil

1 garlic clove

a little parsley

½ bouillon cube

4 slices Provolone cheese

Preparation and cooking time: about 1 hour

Trim and debone the 2 chicken breasts, cut them in half and beat them with a meat mallet to form 4 "fillets". Coat lightly in flour. Briskly fry the fillets in 3 tablespoons of butter, cooking them for no longer than 3-4 minutes on each side. Remove from the pan, season with salt and pepper and keep warm.

Prepare the artichokes. Cut off the stalks and tips and remove the tough outer leaves. Quarter and slice finely, discarding the chokes. Place in a bowl of water to which lemon juice has been added. Drain and sauté in the olive oil. Add the crushed garlic, a little chopped parsley and the half bouillon cube dissolved in warm water. Cook for about 15 minutes, adding more water if necessary. Meanwhile, preheat the oven to 375°F.

Place the chicken fillets in a greased ovenproof pan, being careful that they do not overlap. Cover with the artichoke mixture and place a slice of Provolone cheese on top of each fillet. Dot with 5 teaspoons of butter and bake in the oven until the cheese has melted. Do not cook for too long or the cheese with harden. Serve immediately.

Chicken pie

Stuffed Chicken
Pollo Ripieno

To serve 6

1 chicken, weighing about 2½lb

6oz lean beef

3oz raw ham

2 slices bread soaked in milk

1 egg

¼ cup grated Parmesan cheese

nutmeg

ground thyme

1 small onion, coarsely chopped

1 small carrot

1 celery heart

2 garlic cloves

2 sprigs fresh sage

1 sprig fresh rosemary

olive oil

dry white wine

Preparation and cooking time: about 2 hours

Singe the chicken quickly over a high heat, wash it and dry it. Grind the lean beef and the ham finely twice, together with the slices of bread, well squeezed to remove the milk. Add the egg, the Parmesan cheese, salt, pepper, nutmeg and a pinch of thyme to the ground mixture and mix well together. Stuff the chicken with this mixture, then stitch up the opening under the tail and finally truss the bird with kitchen twine.

Preheat the oven to 400°F. Place the bird in a well-fitting oven dish, surround it with the chopped carrot and onion, celery heart and add the garlic, sage and rosemary. Baste all over with 4 tablespoons of olive oil, season with salt, then place in the oven for about 1¼ hours. Pour a little white wine over the bird from time to time, turning it and basting it frequently with its own juices.

When it is ready, remove the chicken from the dish and strain the juices into a heated sauceboat. Take immediately to the table, divide the bird into 6 equal portions and cut the stuffing into slices.

Chicken Breasts in Curry Sauce
Petti di Pollo al Curry

To serve 4

2 chicken breasts, together weighing about 1lb

1 small onion

1 garlic clove

4 tbsp butter

¼ cup flour

1 tsp curry powder

¾ cup chicken stock

1 tbsp white wine

½ cup cream

1 small piece lemon rind, pith removed

olive oil

sage

Preparation and cooking time: about 30 minutes

Divide the chicken breasts in half, removing the breastbones and any small particles of fat and sinews. Finely chop the onion with the garlic, then sauté gently in a knob of butter, taking care not to brown them. Sprinkle over the flour, stir to prevent lumps forming, then add the curry powder and moisten with the boiling chicken stock. Stir, bring the sauce to the boil and lower the heat to simmer. Add the white wine and cream to the mixture. Stir, add the lemon rind and simmer gently for at least 5 minutes.

Flour the chicken breasts, then brown them lightly on both sides in the remaining butter, melted in a skillet with a tablespoon of olive oil. At the end of cooking, salt them. Pour over the sauce, strained through a fine sieve, and simmer for a couple of minutes before serving. Garnish them, if you like, with *croûtons* of bread browned in butter and tender celery leaves.

Stuffed Spring Cockerels
Galetti di Primo Canto Ripieni

To serve 4

2 cleaned spring cockerels, together weighing 1¾lb

2oz ham

1 slice bacon

1 slice bread

1 egg

3 tbsp grated Parmesan cheese

sprig fresh sage

2½ garlic cloves

½ sprig fresh rosemary

grated nutmeg

2 tbsp olive oil

1 tbsp butter

¼ cup dry white wine

Preparation and cooking time: about 1 hour

Rinse and dry the cockerels. Grind the ham, the bacon and the bread together and put in a small bowl with the egg and the Parmesan cheese. Add 2 finely chopped sage leaves, half a garlic clove and the rosemary leaves, season with pepper, a little salt and grated nutmeg. Mix thoroughly.

Preheat the oven to 400°F. Stuff the cockerels with the mixture, sewing up the openings under the tails. Then tie them with kitchen string. Arrange them in an ovenproof dish, pour over the olive oil, sprinkle with salt and dot with the butter. Put in the 2 remaining garlic cloves, crushed, and 3 sage leaves. Roast for about 40 minutes. Halfway through cooking, moisten with the white wine; brush them often with the cooking juices and turn them three or four times so that they brown on all sides. Serve with roast new potatoes.

Chicken Stew with Olives and Anchovy

Spezzato di Pollo alle Olive

To serve 4

2¼lb spring chicken, cleaned, with feet, neck and wing tips removed

flour

butter

olive oil

4 tbsp dry white wine

small onion

1 garlic clove

1oz anchovy fillets in oil

¼lb peeled tomatoes

⅓ cup pitted green olives

Preparation and cooking time: about 1 hour

Singe any remaining down off the chicken, then rinse and dry it. Cut it into joints, roll them in flour and shake off the excess. Brown the pieces of chicken in a large knob of butter and 2 tablespoons of olive oil, season with salt and pepper. Pour in the white wine and let it evaporate almost completely, with the pan uncovered.

Meanwhile finely chop the onion with a clove of garlic and the drained anchovy fillets. When the white wine has almost completely evaporated, remove the pieces of chicken from the pan, arrange them on a dish and keep them warm by placing them inside a heated oven with the door open. Put the chopped mixture into the pan and let it fry for a few moments, then add the peeled and puréed tomatoes, and the olives. Simmer for a few minutes, then replace the pieces of chicken in the pan.

Cover and cook for about 40 minutes, adding, if necessary, a little hot water.

Arrange the chicken joints on a warmed serving dish, pour over the tomato and olive sauce and serve at once.

Chicken breasts in curry sauce (upper) *and* **stuffed spring cockerels**

Chicken Wings with Vegetables

Ali di Pollo alle Verdure

To serve 4

1¾lb chicken wings

flour

olive oil

1 garlic clove

1 small onion

1 celery heart

¼lb carrots

butter

½ cup dry white wine

1 cup thin stock (or use bouillon cube)

1 bay leaf

a little parsley

Preparation and cooking time: about 45 minutes

Singe the chicken wings briefly over a high heat, then wash and dry them. Dip them in flour and shake them well to remove any excess, then brown them lightly in 3 tablespoons of olive oil with a crushed garlic clove. As soon as they turn slightly brown, remove them and place them on a dish.

Slice the onion very finely and chop the celery heart and carrots finely. Place the vegetables in a pan with 2 tablespoons of butter and 2 tablespoons of olive oil and leave to cook for a few minutes; then add the chicken wings and after a few moments pour over the white wine. When the wine has almost all evaporated, add the boiling stock and a little salt, and flavor with half a bay leaf and a little ground pepper. Stir, then cover, lowering the heat to a simmer, and cook for about 20 minutes; add a little boiling water from time to time if necessary. By the end of the cooking time, the liquid should have turned into a thick sauce. Serve garnished with parsley.

Chicken with Walnuts and Olives

Sopracosce con Noci e Olive

To serve 6

6 chicken legs

a little flour

butter

3 fresh sage leaves

1 sprig fresh rosemary

½ cup dry white wine

⅔ cup stock (or use bouillon cube)

10 pitted green olives

10 walnuts

cornstarch

cream

a little chopped parsley

Preparation and cooking time: about 40 minutes

Tie each chicken leg in 3 places with kitchen twine and coat lightly in flour. Heat a large knob of butter in a large skillet with 3 leaves of sage and the sprig of rosemary. Fry the chicken pieces briskly until crisp and golden on all sides. Pour on the white wine and let the liquid evaporate before adding the stock. Cook on a moderate heat for about 20 minutes.

Meanwhile quarter the olives and break the walnuts up into fairly large pieces. As soon as the chicken is cooked and the liquid has reduced, remove the meat from the pan and discard the twine. Place the chicken on a plate and keep hot. Discard the sage and rosemary and add the olives and walnuts to the pan. Dissolve a teaspoon of cornstarch in a little cold water and stir it into the mixture, together with 5 tablespoons of cream. Blend thoroughly.

Replace the chicken in the pan and soak in the sauce for a few minutes. Transfer to a heated serving dish, coating the meat with the sauce. Sprinkle with a little chopped parsley if desired. Serve.

Flambéed Breast of Duck

Petto d'Anitra a Ventaglio

To serve 4

5 tsp butter

olive oil

1 garlic clove

2 sage leaves

1 shallot

2 slices bacon

2 breast fillets from a large duck weighing about 5½lb, skinned

Calvados apple brandy

⅜ cup good meat stock

Worcestershire sauce

3 tbsp juices from a roast

1 tsp mustard

½ tsp cornstarch

glazed carrot rounds for garnish

zucchini sticks, boiled and fried in butter, for garnish

a few onion rings, lightly boiled, for garnish

Preparation and cooking time: about 30 minutes

Heat a skillet containing the butter and ½ tablespoon of olive oil, a thin slice of garlic, the sage leaves, the shallot cut in half and the bacon cut into strips. Fry gently for a few seconds, shaking the skillet from time to time. Put in the fillets of duck breast, and lightly brown on both sides. Put a plate or lid on top of them and weight them down to keep them relatively flat while cooking. When a drop of pinkish juice appears when you prick them with a fine skewer, pour in a generous dash of Calvados. Sprinkle with salt, turn up the heat and flambé, rapidly reducing the brandy. Remove the duck breasts from the pan, place them on a serving dish, cover them with aluminum foil and keep them warm.

Pour the boiling stock into the skillet, add a dash of Worcestershire sauce, the juices from a roast if you have them, and the mustard, mixing well after each new ingredient is added. Dissolve the cornstarch in a little cold water and mix this in to thicken the gravy. Simmer for a few minutes until the gravy is smooth and creamy. Taste and adjust the seasoning, and strain into a sauceboat. Cut the duck into thin oblong slices and fan them out on a serving dish. Decorate the dish with the garnish, and pour some of the sauce in the center.

Flambéed breast of duck

Quail with Golden Raisins

Quaglie all'Uvetta

To serve 4

½ cup seedless golden raisins

8 quails, cleaned

4 slices bacon

4 fresh sage leaves

2 garlic cloves

1 juniper berry

½ sprig rosemary

flour

5 tsp butter

2 tbsp olive oil

¼ cup brandy

1 small onion

⅜ cup dry Marsala wine

¼ bouillon cube

Preparation and cooking time: about 45 minutes

Soak the raisins in warm water for about 15 minutes. Scorch any remaining feathers on the quail, then wash and dry them well. Place a small piece of bacon inside each bird, along with half a sage leaf and a quarter garlic clove. Chop a juniper berry with the leaves of half a sprig of rosemary, mix in a large pinch of salt, and sprinkle inside the quail.

Truss the birds with twine so that they keep their shape, then coat them with flour and shake well to remove the excess. Melt the butter with 2 tablespoons of oil in a large skillet; as soon as the butter and oil are hot, put the quail in the pan and let them brown slightly. Pour over the brandy, flambé it and allow to evaporate. Add the drained raisins and the finely chopped onion and cook them gently together for a few moments before pouring over the Marsala.

Season with the quarter bouillon cube and cook over a moderate heat, uncovered, for about 20 minutes, turning the quail two or three times so that they brown. If the dish becomes too dry during cooking, add a little hot water. Serve the quail in a warmed deep serving dish, pouring the cooking juices over them.

■ MAIN COURSES QUAIL ■

Stuffed Quail

Quaglie del Salumaio

To serve 4

1 slice bread

dry white wine

8 quail

2½ oz bacon

2½ oz Italian sausage, skinned

3-4 sprigs fresh parsley

2 garlic cloves

1 tbsp grated Parmesan cheese

1 egg

grated nutmeg

1 sprig fresh rosemary

1 sprig fresh sage

olive oil

Preparation and cooking time: about 1½ hours

Soften the slice of bread in a little white wine. Singe the quail and remove any remaining feathers, cut off the heads, then wash and dry them. Now prepare the stuffing: Chop the bacon, then grind it together with the sausage and the well-squeezed slice of bread. Chop the parsley with a small garlic clove and add to the sausage mixture, mix in the grated Parmesan cheese and an egg. Season with a pinch of salt, a little grated nutmeg and a good grinding of pepper, then mix until all the ingredients are well combined.

Preheat the oven to 400°F. Stuff the quail with the mixture, then sew up the openings with thread and place them in an ovenproof dish, together with a garlic clove, the rosemary and 3 small sage leaves. Pour over a little oil and roast in the oven for about 30 minutes, brushing the birds two or three times with the cooking juices. Shortly before taking them out of the oven, moisten them with a splash of white wine, letting it evaporate completely.

Before serving, remove the threads and lay the quail on a hot serving dish.

Chicken in Red Wine

Pollo al Vino Rosso

To serve 6

1 chicken weighing about 2½ lb

¼ cup red wine

⅓ cup butter

½ cup onion

3 tbsp cognac

⅛ cup dry Porcini mushrooms

plain flour

olive oil

Preparation and cooking time: 1¼ hours

Soak the mushrooms in warm water for 1 hour. Remove the head, neck, ends of legs and wings from the chicken.

1) Carefully wash and wipe the chicken.

2) Cut into equal portions avoiding breaking the bones.

Flour the portions and fry in 2 tablespoons of melted butter and a tablespoon of olive oil.

3) Lift out and drain, and put aside in a clean dish, and keep warm in a low oven.

4) Chop the onion finely, and fry it gently in 2 tablespoons of butter in the previously used frying pan. Drain, wash and squeeze the mushrooms, and slice them into strips, (like the bacon) and add to the onions with the bacon.

5) Fry for a few moments then add the chicken and stir.

6) After a few minutes sprinkle on the cognac.

7) Leave it to evaporate before adding the wine. Stir and lower the heat, and season with salt and pepper.

Cook gently for 30 minutes, half-covered, adding a little warm water if it looks too dry.

Meanwhile grease a 9-inch flat tin with

a loose bottom and a fluted edge and line with the pastry.

Prick with a fork, cover with wax paper and fill with dry beans.

Cook in a preheated oven at 430°F for 20 minutes, then remove beans and paper and leave it to cook for another 5 minutes.

8) Transfer to serving dish and arrange the chicken in the pastry base.

9) Pour the chicken and wine stock over it.

Serve hot with the same type of wine as used in the cooking.

1

2

3

4

5

6

7

8

9

Turkey Breast in Pastry

Fesa di Tacchino in Croste

To serve 6-8

2 lb turkey breast

½ lb puff pastry

1 small lettuce

¼ lb smoked bacon (in one piece)

¼ lb cooked ham

⅝ cup light cream

1 stick celery

1 carrot

1 onion

1 egg

¼ pint dry white wine

corn meal

mustard

sage

rosemary

olive oil

butter

all-purpose flour

Preparation and cooking time: 2 hours plus any defrosting time

Preheat the oven to 375°F.

1) Slice the bacon into strips and cover the turkey with shortening.

2) Cover the turkey with rosemary and sage, then tie up with kitchen string. Wash and chop the celery, carrot and onion.

3) Place the turkey in a roasting dish, add the vegetables, salt and pepper, ¼ pint of oil and brown for 10 minutes over a high flame. Cook in the oven for 30 minutes (after 15 minutes pour the wine over the turkey and turn the meat over).

Turn the oven up to 400°F.

4) Clean, wash and finely slice the lettuce. Roll out the puff pastry, defrosted if necessary, into a 12 × 15 inch rectangle.

5) Place on the pastry half the cooked ham, half the sliced lettuce, and then the turkey. Spread 4 tablespoons of mustard over the meat and then cover with the rest of the ham and lettuce. Enclose the turkey with the pastry, securing well.

Cut away the excess pastry and roll it out into strips.

6) Transfer to a greased and floured baking tray. Brush the top of the roll with beaten egg yolk. Arrange the pastry strips on it in a criss-cross design. Brush the strips with egg.

Cook in the oven for 20 minutes.

Complete by straining the stock into a small pan, reheat it, adding a teaspoon of corn meal and the cream. Strain again and serve with the roll.

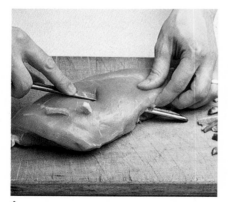

1

2

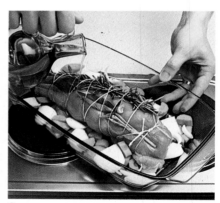

3

4

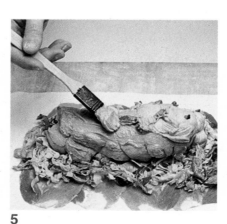

5

6

CHEESE, EGG & RICE DISHES

A selection of snack and supper dishes using cheese, eggs and rice with an Italian flavor. In northern Italy rice is widely eaten, particularly in risottos. Of the many Italian cheeses some such as Gorgonzola and Parmesan have become international household names. Use recommended equivalent soft, hard, blue cheeses if the Italian ones are hard to come by.

Savory Calzone
Calzone di Tropea

To serve 4

¾lb red onions, finely sliced

olive oil

12 pitted black olives in brine

2 tbsp capers

6 anchovy fillets in oil

a small handful of parsley

2 large fresh basil leaves

flour

¾-1 lb pizza dough

3 tbsp grated Pecorino cheese

1 tbsp breadcrumbs

2 tbsp ready-made tomato sauce

Preparation and cooking time: about 1 hour plus any defrosting time

Preheat the oven to 400°F. Gently fry the onions in 4 tablespoons of olive oil and lightly sprinkle with salt and pepper. Make sure they do not brown. Quarter the olives. Drain the capers and crush the anchovies. Finely chop the parsley and basil together.

Flour a pastry-board and roll the dough, defrosted if necessary, into a ball, then flatten it out to a 16-inch round. Lightly oil a baking tray and place the dough on it. With your fingertips, press down the dough just inside the edge to give it a raised edge. Brush half the surface with olive oil and sprinkle with 2 tablespoons of grated Pecorino cheese.

Add to the onions, which should have cooled by now, the capers, olives, parsley and basil, anchovies and the breadcrumbs. Mix well. Spread half this mixture on the part of the dough sprinkled with Pecorino to within 1¼ inches of the edge. Spoon on the tomato sauce and sprinkle with another tablespoon of grated Pecorino cheese.

Make another 2 layers with the rest of the ingredients (the aromatic mixture and the cheese) and fold the dough over into a semicircle to cover the filling. Seal the edges and bake on a greased baking tray for about 30 minutes. Remove and leave for a few minutes then serve.

Italic Cheese Tart
Crostata "Italica"

To serve 4

2 cups flour

1½ sticks butter

¾lb onions

a little butter and flour

1 tbsp fresh breadcrumbs

½lb Italic cheese

3 eggs

⅔ cup milk

Preparation and cooking time: about 1¼ hours

Sift the flour and a pinch of salt. Cut 8 tablespoons of the butter into small pieces and rub it into the flour until the mixture resembles fine breadcrumbs. Mix in enough water to make a soft, but not too sticky, dough. Roll the dough into a ball, wrap it in wax paper and place in the refrigerator for 30 minutes.

Meanwhile thinly slice the onions and fry them gently in 2 tablespoons of the butter. Season with a little salt and pepper. If necessary, add a little water to prevent browning. Preheat the oven to 350°F.

Roll out the pastry on a floured board. Grease and flour an 11-inch pie dish and line it with the pastry. Prick the base with a fork and sprinkle over the fresh breadcrumbs.

Grate the Italic cheese. Beat the eggs and milk in a bowl, season with salt and pepper and add the onions and cheese. Pour the mixture on to the pastry and bake in the lower part of the oven for 35-40 minutes. Serve hot.

Savory calzone

Omelet Cooked in the Oven

"Frittata" della Fornarina

To serve 4

1 small onion

¼ cup olive oil

1 very large ripe tomato

1 bunch fresh basil

½ bouillon cube

4 eggs

¼ cup grated Parmesan cheese

butter

Preparation and cooking time: about 50 minutes

Preheat the oven to 350°F. Finely slice the onions and fry gently in the olive oil. Dice the tomato and add it to the onion, together with 2 basil leaves and half a crumbled bouillon cube. Increase the heat and let the tomato dry out thoroughly. Remove from the heat and leave to cool. Discard the basil.

Beat the eggs in a bowl and season with a little salt and pepper. Add the grated Parmesan cheese and the cold tomato mixture.

Butter a 9½-inch round ovenproof dish. Cut out a circle of aluminum foil or wax paper the same size as the dish, butter it and place it in the bottom of the dish, making sure that it sticks well. Pour in the egg mixture and cook in the oven for about 20 minutes.

As soon as the top of the omelet is golden brown, remove the dish from the oven and turn it out on to a plate, discarding the foil or paper. Slice, garnish with fresh basil leaves and serve.

Eggs in Piquant Sauce

Uova Rosate

To serve 6

6 eggs

½ cup mayonnaise

2 tbsp mustard

2 tbsp tomato ketchup

Worcestershire sauce

1 tbsp whipping cream

6 small black olives

2 leaves radicchio, cut into strips

a few sprigs chicory

Preparation and cooking time: about 30 minutes

Hard-boil the eggs, shell them and halve them lengthwise. Sprinkle with salt and pepper. Arrange the eggs curved-side up on a dish, slightly apart from each other. Blend the mayonnaise in a bowl with 2 tablespoons each of mustard and tomato ketchup and a generous splash of Worcestershire sauce. Adjust seasoning to taste. Add a tablespoon of cream.

Pour the sauce over the eggs and sink half an olive into the sauce on the top of each egg. Garnish the center of the plate with radicchio and the edge with sprigs of chicory. Serve.

Eggs in piquant sauce (above); omelet cooked in the oven

Artichoke and Swiss Cheese Pie

Sfogliata Vallese

To serve 6

½ lb frozen puff pastry

a little butter

1 tbsp breadcrumbs

¼-½ lb rindless Appenzell cheese, thinly sliced

1lb frozen or canned artichoke hearts

½ cup grated Sbrinz cheese

3 large eggs

2-3 sprigs parsley

Preparation and cooking time: about 1 hour plus thawing

Defrost the puff pastry if using frozen, roll it out and line a 9-inch round buttered pie dish with it. Prick the base of the pastry with a fork, then sprinkle over a tablespoon of breadcrumbs and cover with the thin slices of Appenzell cheese. Preheat the oven to 375°F.

Following the instructions on the packages, cook the artichoke hearts in boiling salted water, then drain and leave them to dry for a few minutes on a plate covered with a tea-towel. Blend the artichokes to a pulp or put them through a food processor with a medium disk. Collect the pulp in a bowl. Add the grated Sbrinz, the 3 whole eggs, chopped

parsley, a little salt and a grinding of pepper. Mix thoroughly, then pour the mixture into the pie dish over the cheese.

Bake for 35 minutes in the lower part of the oven until the pastry is cooked through. Remove the pie from the oven, leave it to rest for a few minutes and then serve.

■ CHEESE, EGG & RICE DISHES ■

Endive Pie

Teglia di Scarola

To serve 6

6 tbsp butter

9 half-slices square white bread

1lb Batavian endive

1 medium onion

2 large garlic cloves

parsley

olive oil

½ bouillon cube

½ cup grated Parmesan cheese

½ cup grated Emmental cheese

1 large egg

¾ cup cream

Preparation and cooking time: about 1¼ hours

Preheat the oven to 375°F. Butter a rectangular 9 x 6 inch pie dish. Cover the bottom with the slices of bread, making sure they fit perfectly. Parboil, dry and finely shred the endive and slice the onion. Chop the 2 large garlic cloves finely, removing the green centers. Wash, dry and finely chop a handful of parsley. Melt the remaining butter in a skillet with the oil and sauté the onion, garlic and parsley. Then add the shredded endive and crumble in the bouillon cube. Fry gently for about 10 minutes, stirring from time to time with a wooden spoon.

Combine the Parmesan cheese with the Emmental cheese and spread half over the bread in the bottom of the dish. Then make an even layer of the endive mixture and sprinkle over the remaining cheese. Beat the egg with the cream, a little salt and grated nutmeg in a bowl, then pour the mixture over the rest. Bake for about 30 minutes until the surface is golden brown. Remove from the oven and set aside for a few minutes before serving.

Artichoke and Swiss cheese pie

Swiss Chard Pie

Sfogliata di Coste e Uova

To serve 8-10

1 lb puff pastry

½lb Swiss chard, green part only

½ small onion

4 tbsp butter

½ bouillon cube

ground nutmeg

6oz Ricotta cheese

¼ cup ground ham

8 eggs

2 tbsp grated Parmesan cheese

⅞ cup flour

1 cup milk

2 tbsp breadcrumbs

Preparation and cooking time: about 1 hour 40 minutes plus any thawing time

Defrost the pastry if necessary. Bring to the boil a little salted water in a large saucepan. Wash and drain the chard, plunge it into the boiling water and cook, covered, for 10 minutes. Drain and cool it under running water. Squeeze out excess moisture and chop finely.

Chop the onion and fry it gently in 2 tablespoons of the butter without browning it. Add the chard and cook gently together, stirring occasionally with a wooden spoon. Season with the crumbled half bouillon cube and a pinch of ground nutmeg. Remove from the heat and allow to cool.

Preheat the oven to 375°F. Sieve the Ricotta into a large bowl and add the ham, the cooked chard, 3 whole eggs and the grated Parmesan. Stir briskly until all the ingredients are thoroughly combined

and leave it to stand. Prepare a Béchamel sauce with 2 tablespoons of butter, the flour and the milk; season with salt and nutmeg and add it to the mixture in the bowl, stirring well.

Butter a 10-inch pie dish with fluted sides and line it with just over half the pastry rolled out very thinly. Trim the edges and sprinkle the breadcrumbs over the bottom. Fill it with the chard mixture, level it off and make 5 hollows in it with the back of a teaspoon. Fill each hollow with a raw egg yolk. Reserve the white of 1 egg. Roll out the rest of the pastry to make a lid and seal it well. Brush the top with the lightly beaten egg white and pierce the center with a fork. Cook the pie in the oven for about 40 minutes, on a low shelf so that the pastry base gets cooked through. Serve immediately from the cooking dish.

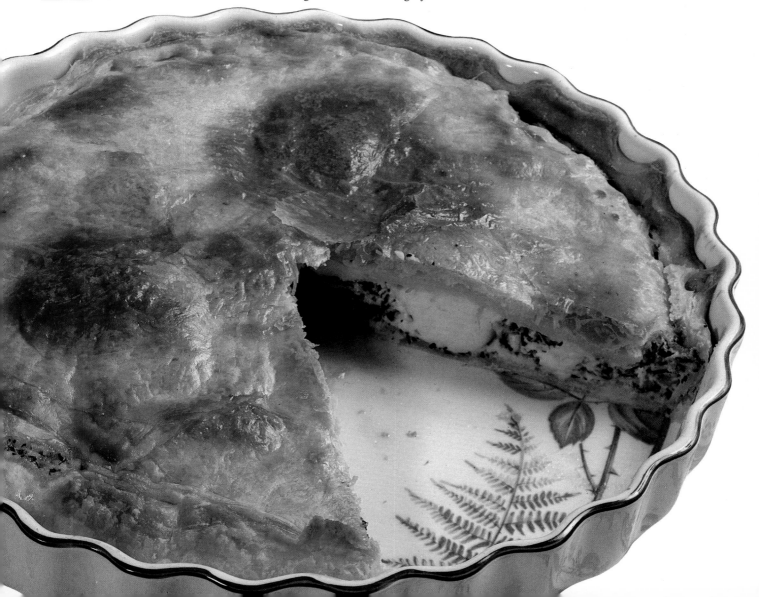

Endive Quiche
Sfogliata di Scarola

To serve 8

¾lb puff pastry

½lb onions

1 garlic clove

4 tbsp butter

olive oil

¼lb smoked bacon

1½lb Batavian endive, boiled and drained

1 bouillon cube

ground nutmeg

about 1 tbsp breadcrumbs

1½ cups grated Emmental cheese

3 eggs

3 tbsp grated Parmesan cheese

flour

⅔ cup milk

Preparation and cooking time: about 1½ hours plus any thawing

Defrost the pastry if necessary. Thinly slice the onions, finely chop a clove of garlic and fry gently in a knob of butter and 3 tablespoons of olive oil until transparent.

Cut the bacon into short, thin strips and coarsely chop the endive. Add first the bacon and then the endive to the onion and garlic. Cook for about 10 minutes, stirring frequently. Season with the crumbled bouillon cube and a little ground nutmeg and pepper.

Butter a 10-inch round, fluted pie dish and line it with the pastry. Pierce the base with a fork and sprinkle over a heaping tablespoon of breadcrumbs. Preheat the oven to 400°F.

Remove the endive mixture from the heat and blend in first the grated Emmental cheese and then 2 of the eggs, stirring vigorously. Pour the mixture into the pastry base and smooth the surface with the back of a spoon. Top with a tablespoon of grated Parmesan cheese.

Prepare a light Bechamel sauce by melting 2 teaspoons of butter, stirring in 3 tablespoons of flour and adding the milk. Season with salt and a little ground nutmeg. Blend in an egg yolk. Pour the boiling sauce into the pie shell and sprinkle on 2 tablespoons of grated Parmesan cheese. Cook in the oven for about 40 minutes or until the pie is cooked and golden brown on top. Remove from the oven and leave to stand for about 10 minutes before serving.

■ CHEESE, EGG & RICE DISHES ■

Shrimp and Salmon Omelet
Omelette di Gamberetti e Salmone

To serve 2

1 tbsp tomato paste

½ cup fish stock

¼ cup canned salmon

2 tbsp butter

cornstarch

5 tbsp dry white wine

Worcestershire sauce

12 fresh shrimp

flour

½ small onion

1 garlic clove

parsley

4 tbsp olive oil

4 eggs

1 large thin slice smoked salmon, cut in strips

1 celery heart, chopped

Preparation and cooking time: about 50 minutes

Dissolve the tomato paste in the fish stock and blend it with the salmon, being careful to remove any skin and bones. Sieve. Melt 2 teaspoons of the butter in a saucepan and add the blended mixture, together with a quarter teaspoon of cornstarch dissolved in a tablespoon of the white wine. Stir and season with a splash of Worcestershire sauce and simmer gently for a few minutes. Taste and adjust the seasoning if necessary. Keep the sauce hot in a *bain-marie*.

Shell the shrimp, cut into small pieces and then coat in the flour. Finely chop the onion, a quarter of a garlic clove and a few leaves of parsley and fry in 3 tablespoons of the olive oil until transparent. Add the pieces of shrimp and fry gently. Sprinkle with 4 tablespoons of white wine. Allow almost all the wine to evaporate and then remove the pan from the heat.

Beat two eggs in a bowl with a pinch of salt and pepper. Melt 2 teaspoons of butter and a tablespoon of oil in a skillet and pour in the eggs. Stir gently so that the eggs set smoothly. Lower the heat and shake the skillet gently to prevent sticking. Pour on half the shrimp mixture and fold the omelet with a spatula. Turn on to a heated dish and keep warm while you prepare the second omelet in the remaining butter. Arrange strips of smoked salmon on each omelet, sprinkle with chopped celery and surround with the hot sauce. Serve immediately.

Eggs in Rich Sauce

Uova alla Ricca

To serve 4

---

white wine vinegar

---

8 eggs and 1 egg yolk

¼ cup butter

---

flour

---

1 cup milk

---

nutmeg

¼ cup grated Emmental cheese

---

1 small black truffle, canned

---

tender celery leaves for garnish

Preparation and cooking time: about 40 minutes

Put a fairly wide, low-sided saucepan on to heat with plenty of water; when it comes to the boil, salt it and put in 1 tablespoon of vinegar for every 2 cups of water, then lower the heat so that the water just simmers. Break 8 eggs, one at a time, into a small plate or bowl, then slide them very carefully into the boiling water. With a spoon, try to collect the white above the yolks, then leave the eggs to poach uncovered for about 6 minutes.

Remove them one at a time with a slotted spoon and put them immediately into a bowl of lukewarm water. After a few minutes put them to dry on a plate covered with a double sheet of paper towels, and lay another sheet of paper gently on top. As soon as the eggs are dry, trim off any ragged fringes of egg white and arrange them on a buttered ovenproof serving dish. Preheat the oven to 425°F.

Melt 5 teaspoons of the butter in a small saucepan, add 2½ tablespoons of sieved flour and stir with a small whisk to prevent lumps forming. Pour the boiling milk in a thin stream on to this *roux*, then bring the sauce to the boil, stirring all the time. Salt moderately, add a little pepper and ground nutmeg, then remove from the heat, mix in the egg yolk and the cheese, stirring after each addition.

Pour the sauce over the eggs and place a thin slice of black truffle on each one. Pour over the remaining lukewarm melted butter and place in the oven for 2-3 minutes.

Pilaf with Cheese Sauce and Ham

Pilaf con Salsa di Formaggio

To serve 6

2½ bouillon cubes

1 large onion

5 tbsp butter

2 tbsp olive oil

2 cups white rice

2½ oz raw ham

1½ tbsp flour

1 cup milk

¼ lb Royale cheese

1 egg yolk

1 thick slice cooked ham

a few tender celery leaves

Preparation and cooking time: about 40 minutes

Preheat the oven to 400°F. Place a saucepan on the stove with 3 cups of water and 2 bouillon cubes, and bring the liquid gradually to the boil. In the meantime, finely chop half of the onion and sauté it very gently in 3 tablespoons of the butter and 2 tablespoons of oil, melted in a pan which can be put both on the stove and in the oven. Add the rice and seal for a few moments, stirring with a wooden spoon. Then pour over the boiling stock, stir again and place in the preheated oven for about 15 minutes, until the rice is cooked and dry.

Meanwhile, slice the remaining onion very finely and sauté it gently in the remaining butter. Then add the raw ham cut into thin strips and, after letting it fry for a few moments, sprinkle over the flour, stirring to avoid lumps forming. Pour in the boiling milk in a thin stream and season with the remaining crumbled half bouillon cube. As soon as the mixture comes to the boil, remove the pan from the heat and mix in the diced cheese and the egg yolk, stirring well after each addition.

Take the rice out of the oven, separate the grains with a fork and arrange on a warmed serving dish. Pour over the cheese sauce, sprinkle over the diced ham and chopped celery leaves. Serve immediately, stirring at table.

Emmental Cheese "Cake"

Cake all 'Emmental

To serve 8-10

½ cup butter

3 eggs

ground nutmeg

1 tsp mustard

1 tsp chopped parsley

½ lb Emmental cheese

½ lb sliced ham

1½ cups all-purpose flour

1½ tsp baking powder

⅜ cup fresh light cream

a little butter and flour

Preparation and cooking time: 1½ hours

Use butter and eggs at room temperature. Beat the butter until soft and creamy. Mix in the eggs one at a time, beating well to form a smooth paste. Season with a pinch of salt and pepper and plenty of ground nutmeg. Fold in one heaping teaspoon each of mustard and chopped parsley. Preheat the oven to 350°F.

Dice the Emmental cheese and the ham, discarding the fat.

Stir the pieces of ham and cheese into the prepared mixture and then add the sifted flour and the baking powder. Mix thoroughly and then stir in the cream.

Pour the mixture into a greased and floured cake pan and bake for about 50 minutes. Before removing from the oven, check that it is cooked by pushing a wooden skewer into the center. If the skewer comes out clean, the cake is ready.

Allow to cool and then turn out on to a plate. Slice and serve while still warm.

Pilaf with cheese sauce and ham

Spicy Pastries

Calcioni Piccanti

To serve 4

½ lb pizza dough

flour

2oz Mozzarella cheese

2½oz mortadella sausage

tomato paste

16 baby mushrooms in oil

a little oregano

a little paprika

1 egg yolk

a little olive oil

Preparation and cooking time: about 45 minutes plus any defrosting time

Preheat the oven to 375°F. Roll out the dough, defrosted if necessary, on a floured pastry-board to a thickness of ⅛ inch. Cut out 16 circles with a 3 inch diameter cookie cutter. Dice the Mozzarella cheese and mortadella sausage very small and place a few cubes in the center of each of 8 of the dough rounds. Also add a small teaspoon of tomato paste, 2 well-drained baby mushrooms, a pinch of oregano, a tiny pinch each of paprika and salt. Take care to leave space around the edges.

Brush the edges of each round with egg yolk and cover with the other 8 rounds. Press down firmly to seal in the filling. Grease a baking tray with olive oil and place the pastries on the tray well apart from each other. Brush the surfaces with egg yolk and cook for 15-20 minutes, until they are golden brown. Remove from the oven and place on a serving dish. Serve at once while they are hot from the oven. They make an excellent first course or snack but can also be served as a light main course.

Individual Rice Timbales

Piccoli Timballi "Segreto"

To serve 6

3 cups stock (or use bouillon cube)

1 small onion

3 tbsp butter

olive oil

2 cups white rice

1 envelope saffron

2oz Emmental cheese

1 frankfurter sausage

a few tender celery leaves

Preparation and cooking time: about 40 minutes

Put the stock on to heat. Preheat the oven to 400°F. Chop the onion finely and sauté it gently in half the butter and a tablespoon of oil, melted in an ovenproof dish, taking care not to let it brown. Add the rice and fry gently for a few moments, stirring with a wooden spoon. Then add the saffron and, after stirring, pour on the boiling stock. Bring back to the boil, then place the pan in the oven for about 15 minutes.

Meanwhile, oil generously 6 individual molds. Dice the Emmental cheese and the frankfurter sausage. When the rice is ready, remove it from the oven and fluff it up with a fork, adding the remaining butter in small pieces. Place a little rice in each mold, put in a few cubes of Emmental and frankfurter and pile the rest of the rice on top, pressing down well with a spoon.

Place the molds in the oven for 3-4 minutes, then turn the rice timbales out on to a suitable plate. Garnish them with a few tender celery leaves and serve immediately.

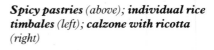

Spicy pastries (above); *individual rice timbales* (left); *calzone with ricotta* (right)

Cod and Mushroom Pie

"Pie" Marinara

To serve 8

1½lb fresh cod fillets

3⅛ cups milk, at room temperature

½lb small mushrooms

about 6 tbsp butter

1 garlic clove

⅜ cup flour

nutmeg

1 slice crustless, slightly dry, bread, finely crumbled

3 eggs

2-3 sprigs fresh parsley

½lb puff pastry

Preparation and cooking time: about 1 hour 20 minutes

Preheat the oven to 375-400°F. Hard-boil 2 of the eggs, cool them under running water and shell them. Arrange the cod fillets in a pan that just holds them so that there are no gaps. Season with salt and freshly ground white pepper, then pour over the milk, covering the fish. Cover the pan and put on a low heat. Gradually bring to the boil and as soon as it begins to boil, leave it on the heat for a minute, then remove from the heat but leave covered for about 5 minutes.

Remove the lid. Drain the milk from the fish and cut it into large chunks. Make sure there are no scales left anywhere. Put 2¼ cups of the milk in which the cod was cooked through a fine strainer and reserve it. Trim the mushrooms, rinse under running water and cut into thickish slices. Melt ¼ cup butter in a saucepan and fry the lightly crushed garlic. When it is brown, remove and discard it. Put in the mushrooms and sauté for a few minutes until they begin to brown. Sift on ⅜ cup flour and mix in at once to prevent lumps forming. Then gradually pour in the milk reserved from the fish and, stirring constantly, bring to the boil. Taste and correct the seasoning and add a pinch of grated nutmet.

Butter a 7-inch soufflé dish, not too deep, and sprinkle with the crumbled bread. Cut the hard-boiled eggs into thin slices. Make a layer of fish in the dish, followed by a little sauce, a few slices of hard-boiled egg and a little parsley. Pour over a little more sauce and repeat until the ingredients have all been used up, finishing with a thin layer of sauce. Melt a teaspoon of butter and pour this on top.

Roll out the pastry on a lightly floured pastry-board until it is about ⅛ inch thick and cover the soufflé dish with this, letting about ¾ inch hang over the edge all round. Beat the remaining egg in a bowl and use it to glaze the surface of the pastry. Bake the pie in the oven for about 30 minutes and then serve.

■ CHEESE, EGG & RICE DISHES ■

Calzone with Ricotta

Calzone con la Ricotta

To serve 4-5

1¼ cups very fresh Ricotta

3oz spicy salami

¼ cup Mozzarella cheese

2 thick slices ham

2 eggs

¼ cup grated Parmesan cheese

¼ cup grated Pecorino cheese

1 lb pizza dough

flour

olive oil

Preparation and cooking time: about 1 hour

Preheat the oven to 400°F. Sieve the Ricotta into a bowl. Cut the salami into small cubes and the Mozzarella cheese into larger cubes. Coarsely chop the ham, then add all these ingredients to the Ricotta. Bind with the 2 whole eggs, the Parmesan and Pecorino cheeses, salt and pepper and mix thoroughly. Taste and, if necessary, adjust the seasoning.

Roll out the bread dough on a lightly floured pastry-board to an 11-12 inch diameter circle. Place the Ricotta mixture over half the circle to within about ¾ inch of the edge. Fold the other half of the dough over the filling sealing the two edges by pinching them together. Place the calzone on an oiled baking sheet and brush it with olive oil; put it in the oven for about 25 minutes, or until the dough is baked and crisp both top and bottom. Serve immediately.

Rice and Artichoke Timbale

Timballo di Riso ai Carciofi

To serve 4

1 small onion

1 sprig fresh sage

1 garlic clove

3 tbsp butter

olive oil for frying

1 slice smoked bacon

¼lb boned breast of chicken

flour

1 tbsp brandy

4 tbsp dry white wine

⅝ cup milk

¼ bouillon cube, crumbled

ground nutmeg

1 sprig fresh parsley

2 fresh artichokes

3 cups good meat stock

1 tbsp dry sherry

1¾ cups rice

½ envelope saffron

Preparation and cooking time: about 1¼ hours

Finely chop a third of the onion, one sage leaf and half a garlic clove and fry gently in 5 teaspoons of butter and a tablespoon of olive oil until transparent. Cut the bacon into short thin strips and the chicken into ¾-inch cubes. Coat the chicken cubes in flour and add the bacon and chicken to the pan. Fry gently for a few minutes, then pour on the brandy and wine. As soon as the wine has evaporated, pour on the boiling milk, blended with the crumbled quarter bouillon cube and a little ground nutmeg. Stir, cover and allow the liquid to reduce slowly to a smooth, creamy sauce. sauce.

Chop another third of the onion, half a garlic clove and the parsley and fry gently in 3 tablespoons of oil until transparent. Top and tail the artichokes and remove the tough outer leaves. Add them to the pan. Cook for a few minutes and then pour on ½ cup of boiling stock and the sherry. Stir, cover and cook on a very low heat for about 15 minutes or until the artichokes are tender. Preheat the oven to 400°F.

Meanwhile, bring the remaining stock to the boil. Finely chop the rest of the onion and sauté in 5 teaspoons of butter in a deep ovenproof pan. Add the rice, cook for a few minutes and then add the saffron. Pour on the stock, stir and bring back to the boil. Cover with aluminum foil and cook in the oven for about 15 minutes or until the rice has absorbed all the stock.

Remove from the oven and use three-quarters of the rice to line a 3-cup oiled baking pan. Pour in the chicken and bacon mixture and cover with the remaining rice. Replace in the oven and cook for a further 5 minutes. Turn the timbale out on to a warmed dish and arrange the artichokes around it. Serve immediately.

Fontina Cheese Parcels

Involtini di Fontina, in Crosta

To serve 4

¾ lb puff pastry

3 tbsp butter

4½ tbsp flour

1⅜ cups milk

ground nutmeg

¼ cup grated Parmesan cheese

¼lb Fontina cheese

1 egg and 1 egg yolk

8 thin slices raw ham

a pinch of aniseed (optional)

Preparation and cooking time: 1¼ hours plus any defrosting time

Defrost the pastry if using frozen. Prepare a béchamel sauce by melting 2 tablespoons of butter in a pan, stirring in 3 tablespoons of flour and adding the milk. Season with salt, pepper and a little ground nutmeg, then blend in the grated Parmesan cheese and the diced Fontina cheese. Allow the cheeses to melt, stirring constantly to form a smooth sauce. Whisk in 1 egg yolk. Remove from the heat and allow to cool.

Remove the fat from 8 thin slices of raw ham. Spread a heaping tablespoon of the cheese sauce on each slice of ham and roll up. Preheat the oven to 375°F.

Roll out the pastry on a floured board to a thickness of ⅛ inch. Cut the pastry into 8 rectangles the same length as the ham rolls. Place a roll of ham on each piece of pastry and brush the edges of the pastry with beaten egg. Fold up the parcels, making sure that they are tightly sealed.

Arrange on a greased baking tray and brush with beaten egg. Sprinkle with a pinch of aniseed and bake in the oven for about 20 minutes or until golden brown. Serve hot with a green salad or fresh vegetables.

Ligurian Pie

"Torta" Ligure

To serve 6-8

¾lb puff pastry

2 fresh artichokes

juice of ½ lemon

1 medium onion

1 garlic clove

a little parsley

about 6 tbsp butter

olive oil

½ cup stock (or use bouillon cube)

5oz parboiled, drained lettuce

½ mushroom-flavored bouillon cube

flour

⅔ cup milk

2 eggs

½ cup grated Parmesan cheese

1 tbsp breadcrumbs

Preparation and cooking time: 1½ hours plus any thawing

Defrost the puff pastry if necessary. Trim the artichokes and peel the stems, placing them in cold water with the juice of half a lemon. Chop the onion and soften it, together with a garlic clove and a small bunch of parsley, in a knob of the butter and 2 tablespoons of oil. Drain the artichokes well, slice them thinly and add to the mixture in the pan. Brown for a few minutes, then pour over the stock and cook in a covered pan until the artichokes are tender and have absorbed all the liquid. Preheat the oven to 400°F.

Chop the lettuce and sauté it in 2 tablespoons of butter, then sprinkle with the mushroom-flavored cube and the flour. Stir, and gradually pour in the boiling milk. Leave to simmer for a few minutes, then stir and pour into a bowl. Stir the artichokes, then add them to the lettuce mixture, mixing well. Add the beaten eggs, the Parmesan cheese and a little salt.

Line a buttered oval pie dish measuring about 12 x 8 inches with the puff pastry, prick the base and sprinkle with about 1 tablespoon of breadcrumbs. Pour in the prepared mixture and bake in the oven for about 30 minutes.

Ligurian pie

Cheese and Walnut Pie

Torta di Formaggio e Noci

To serve 4

¾ lb puff pastry

a little flour

a little butter

¼lb Emmental cheese

¾ cup walnuts

2 eggs plus 1 egg white

1 tbsp Calvados liqueur

ground nutmeg

Preparation and cooking time: about 50 minutes plus any defrosting time

Defrost the pastry, if using frozen, and roll out on a floured surface to a thickness of ⅛ inch. Grease a 9-inch ovenproof pie dish with a little butter and line it with the pastry.

Cut the Emmental cheese into small pieces and grate in a blender, together with the walnuts. Place in a bowl and stir in 2 eggs, a tablespoon of Calvados, a pinch of salt and pepper and a little ground nutmeg. Pour this mixture into the pie shell.

Preheat the oven to 375°F. Roll out the remaining pastry and cover the pie with it. Brush the edges with the lightly beaten egg white and seal the lid to the sides of the pastry. Bake in the lower part of the oven for about 30 minutes or until golden brown. Serve hot.

Valdostana Fondue

"Fondua" Valdostana

To serve 3

¾lb Fontina cheese

⅝ cup milk at room temperature

1 tbsp butter

3 egg yolks

3 slices white bread

Preparation and cooking time: about 20 minutes plus 2 hours' soaking

Cut the rind off the cheese, slice it into a bowl and cover it with the milk. Leave it to soak for a couple of hours, stirring occasionally.

Melt the butter in a fondue pan, add the cheese and place over a simmering *bain-marie*. Stir continuously until the cheese melts, then raise the heat and stir more briskly, adding the egg yolks one by one, making sure each is perfectly incorporated before adding the next. Continue stirring until the cheese is completely melted and dissolved. Pour the fondue into warmed individual dishes and serve with slices of bread toasted in the oven.

Broccoli with Scrambled Eggs

Broccoletti con le Uova Strapazzate

To serve 4

2lb green broccoli

7 tbsp olive oil

1 garlic clove

1 small piece red chili pepper

2 large eggs

2 tbsp grated Pecorino cheese

Preparation and cooking time: about 1 hour

Trim the broccoli and cut it into pieces, including the tender stalks of the larger pieces. Break the larger heads into flowerets. Put into lightly salted cold water for 30 minutes then rinse well. Boil a large saucepanful of water and add salt. Put in the broccoli and cook for 5 minutes. When the broccoli is tender, remove with a slotted spoon, drain carefully and place on a large sloping dish for a few minutes.

In the meantime, heat a skillet with 4 tablespoons of olive oil, put in the lightly crushed garlic and the chili. Discard the garlic and chili and replace with the broccoli. Shake the pan to ensure it does not stick to the bottom. Beat the eggs and the Pecorino cheese in a bowl and season with a little salt and pepper. Heat 3 tablespoons of olive oil in a small skillet and, when it is hot, pour in the eggs. Continue stirring with a fork until they take on a creamy consistency. Arrange the broccoli on a hot serving dish and top with the scrambled eggs. Serve immediately.

Cheese and walnut pie (left); broccoli with scrambled eggs (right)

Rice with Tomatoes and Mushrooms

Riso al Pomodoro con Funghi

To serve 4

¾lb mushrooms (preferably ceps)

2 tbsp butter

3 tbsp olive oil

1 garlic clove

2-3 sprigs fresh parsley

1¾ cups rice

⅞ cup tomato sauce

grated Parmesan cheese

Preparation and cooking time: about 1 hour 10 minutes

Clean the mushrooms carefully, scraping any earth from the stalks and wiping the caps. Rinse quickly, dry carefully and then slice them. Melt the butter with the oil and the crushed garlic clove. Add the mushrooms and cook for about 10 minutes, then add some pepper and the chopped parsley.

Meanwhile bring to the boil a pan of water, add salt and cook the rice in it until barely soft. Drain, turn on to a heated deep serving dish and coat with the boiling tomato sauce. Add the mushrooms, which should also be very hot.

Serve immediately with grated Parmesan cheese.

Eggs Stuffed with Artichokes

Uova Ripiene ai Carciofini

To serve 6

6 large eggs

½ small jar canned artichoke hearts in oil

2 heaping tbsp thick mayonnaise

heaping tbsp mustard

anchovy paste

Worcestershire sauce

1 large slice red pimiento

a few tender chicory leaves

Preparation and cooking time: about 35 minutes

Boil the eggs, which should not have been in the refrigerator. Cool them under running water, shell them and cut them in half lengthwise. Scoop out the yolks and sieve them in to a bowl. Reserve the half-whites. Squeeze the oil from the artichokes thoroughly, chop them as finely as possible, then add them to the sieved yolks. Add the mayonnaise, mustard, about 1 inch anchovy paste and a dash of Worcestershire sauce. Mix the ingredients thoroughly, then taste and adjust the seasoning.

Using a small tear-shaped cookie cutter, press out 9 shapes from the slice of pimiento. Put the prepared mixture in a pastry bag with a round, pointed nozzle and fill the 12 egg white halves. Arrange them on a round serving dish. Garnish with the pimiento "tears" and the chicory leaves and serve immediately.

Ricotta Cheese Pie
"Cassetta" alla Ricotta

To serve 6-8

¾lb puff pastry

1 medium onion

about ¼ cup butter

3 tbsp olive oil

½lb very small fresh mushrooms

small piece dried cep mushroom

ground thyme

½ mushroom-flavored bouillon cube

? tbsp dry Marsala wine

⅜ cup whipping cream

¼lb long sausage

⅝ cup very fresh Ricotta cheese

½ cup grated Parmesan cheese

3 eggs

1 tbsp breadcrumbs

Preparation and cooking time: 1½ hours plus any thawing time

Defrost the puff pastry if using frozen. Slice the onion finely and soften in 2 tablespoons of melted butter with 2 tablespoons of olive oil. Peel the mushrooms, wash them well, then slice finely and add to the mixture. Allow to cook, flavoring with the crumbled piece of dried mushroom, a pinch of thyme and the mushroom-flavored cube crumbled into small pieces. Then pour the dry Marsala wine over the mixture followed by the cream, and allow to reduce almost completely.

Preheat the oven to 375°F. Skin the sausage and brown gently in a small skillet in 1 tablespoon of heated oil, then chop finely and put into a bowl. Stir the mushrooms and add to the sausage, then add the sieved Ricotta, the Parmesan cheese and the eggs. Stir well after the addition of each ingredient and finally taste and adjust the salt if necessary.

Roll out the puff pastry on a floured surface and line a buttered rectangular pie dish, measuring about 10 x 4 inches, with it, prick the base and sprinkle the breadcrumbs over, then pour in the prepared mixture evenly. Shake the dish gently to remove any pockets of air, then bake in the oven for about 40 minutes. Turn out the pie and serve 10 minutes later.

Poor Man's Steak
"Bistecche" del Taxista

To serve 4

4 thick slices mortadella sausage

½ cup goat's milk cheese

mustard

1 egg

fresh breadcrumbs

olive oil for frying

Preparation and cooking time: 30 minutes

Remove the rind from 4 fairly thick slices of mortadella sausage. Place the goat's milk cheese in a bowl and season with a pinch of salt and plenty of pepper. Beat lightly until smooth and creamy, and spread on to one half of each slice of mortadella, leaving about ¼ inch around the edges. Spread the other half of each slice with a heaping teaspoon of mustard. Fold the slices in half and fix with wooden toothpicks.

Beat an egg and season it with salt. Dip the slices of mortadella in the egg and coat them with breadcrumbs. Fry the "steaks" in plenty of olive oil and place them on absorbent paper towels to drain off the excess oil. Serve with fresh vegetables or a salad.

Ricotta cheese pie

Country-style Risotto
Risotto Alla Rusticana

To serve 4

6 leaves savoy cabbage

3½ pints stock

3-4 shallots

¼ cup butter

1 tbsp olive oil

1¾ cups rice

3 tbsp dry white wine

2oz Italian sausage

¼ cup canned chick peas

¼ cup canned borlotti beans

5 tbsp grated Parmesan cheese

Preparation and cooking time: about 40 minutes

Remove the central rib from the cabbage leaves, wash the leaves, and cook in boiling salted water for about 10 minutes. Remove them from the water with a slotted spoon and lay them on a sloping plate to drain. Heat the stock. Finely chop the shallots and sauté them in 5 teaspoons of the butter and a tablespoon of oil. Add the rice, stir and seal for a few moments, then moisten with 3 tablespoons of white wine and let it evaporate. Start to add the stock, pouring in a ladleful at a time and waiting until it is absorbed before adding more.

When the rice is half-cooked, mix in the coarsely chopped cabbage leaves, the skinned sliced sausage, the drained chick peas and beans, a third of them passed through the food processor. Taste, and add salt if necessary. Once the rice is cooked but still a little firm, remove the pan from the heat and mix the remaining butter, softened and cut in pieces, and the grated Parmesan cheese, into the risotto. Then serve.

Pilau with Eggs and Creamed Asparagus

Pilaf con Uova e Crema d'Asparagi

To serve 5

3 cups light stock (or use bouillon cube)

1 medium onion

8 tbsp butter

¾lb rice

½lb boiled green asparagus tips

flour

⅔ cup milk

½ bouillon cube

nutmeg

3 eggs

¼ cup grated Parmesan cheese

4 tbsp cream

olive oil

Preparation and cooking time: about 40 minutes

Put the stock on to heat slowly. Preheat the oven to 400°F. Finely chop half the onion and soften it in a large knob of butter, melted in an ovenproof pan. Add the rice and let it brown lightly for a few moments, stirring with a wooden spoon. Then moisten it with the boiling stock, bring back to the boil, and put in the oven for 15 minutes or a little longer, until the rice has absorbed almost all the liquid.

Meanwhile soften the remaining onion, sliced very thinly, in 2 tablespoons of butter, then add three-quarters of the asparagus tips, in small pieces, and let the flavors mingle for a few moments. Sprinkle in a heaping tablespoon of sifted flour, stir and immediately pour on the boiling milk in a thin stream. Stirring continuously, bring the sauce to the boil, flavoring it with the crumbled half bouillon cube, the pepper and nutmeg. Then, keeping it hot in a *bain-marie*, whisk it for a couple of minutes.

Beat the eggs with the grated Parmesan cheese, the cream and a little salt and pepper. In a large skillet melt a large knob of butter with 2 tablespoons of olive

oil. When the butter and oil are hot, pour in the beaten eggs and beat vigorously with a fork until they are very creamy.

Take the rice out of the oven, quickly stir in the remaining, softened butter, cut in pieces, and arrange the rice in individual serving dishes. Pour over the beaten eggs, then the boiling asparagus cream, and arrange the reserved asparagus tips on top. Serve immediately.

■ CHEESE, EGG & RICE DISHES ■

Polenta and Cheese Pudding

"Budino" di Polenta al Formaggio

To serve 6-8

1¾ cups milk

1½ bouillon cubes

2 cups quick-cooking polenta

5 tbsp butter

olive oil

¾ cup grated Parmesan cheese

1½ tbsp flour

2 egg yolks

¼lb Fontina cheese

celery leaves for garnish

Preparation and cooking time: about 40 minutes

Heat 6 cups of water and 1 of milk. Add a little salt and crumble in a bouillon cube. As soon as the mixture begins to boil, sprinkle in the polenta, stirring with a whisk and then a wooden spoon. Cook for about 20 minutes, then remove from the heat. Mix in 3 tablespoons of butter in small knobs and half the Parmesan cheese, stirring constantly. Put the polenta into a 3½-pint greased mold with fluted sides. Cover with a cloth and prepare the sauce.

Melt the remaining butter in a saucepan and incorporate the flour, mixing with a small whisk. Boil the remaining milk and combine it with the *roux* a little at a time. Stirring constantly, bring the sauce to the boil and flavor with half a bouillon cube. Remove from the heat and add the 2 egg yolks, the remaining Parmesan cheese and the Fontina cheese cut into small pieces. Mix well, then pour the boiling sauce over the polenta which has been turned out on to a deep dish. For garnish, place the chopped celery leaves in the center of the polenta pudding and serve immediately. This substantial hot appetizer can also be served as a first course.

Polenta and cheese pudding (above); *cauliflower quiche* (right)

Cauliflower Quiche
Quiche di Cavolfiore

To serve 8

1lb puff pastry

1lb cauliflower

1 tbsp breadcrumbs

¼lb smoked bacon, cut into thin slices

butter

olive oil

nutmeg

¼ cup grated Emmental cheese

1 tbsp chopped parsley

2oz sausage meat, skin removed

2oz rindless Fontina cheese

¼ cup flour

1½ cups milk

2 egg yolks

¼ cup grated Parmesan cheese

Preparation and cooking time: about 1½ hours plus any thawing

Defrost the pastry if necessary. Boil the cauliflower in salted water in an uncovered pan for about 10 minutes. Remove from the water with a large slotted spoon, drain well and leave to dry on a dish covered with a double thickness of paper towels. Preheat the oven to 375°F.

Roll out the pastry to a thickness of about ⅛ inch and line a round, buttered pie dish, 10 inches in diameter, with it.

Prick the bottom of the pastry with a fork, sprinkle with breadcrumbs and make an even layer of bacon slices.

Break up the cauliflower and sauté the flowerets gently in 2 tablespoons of butter and the olive oil. Add a little salt and grated nutmeg. Arrange the cauliflower on top of the bacon. Sprinkle with the grated Emmental and the parsley. Crumble the sausage meat and sprinkle it about the cauliflower. Cut the Fontina into small pieces and scatter them among the cauliflower pieces. Prepare a Béchamel sauce by melting a large knob of butter in a pan, stirring in the flour and then the milk. Season with salt and nutmeg. Remove from the heat and stir in the egg yolks and the Parmesan. Pour the sauce over the quiche.

Bake the pie for 40 minutes, in the lower part of the oven to ensure it is cooked all the way through. Remove the quiche carefully from the dish and place on a wooden serving board. Serve immediately, piping hot.

■ CHEESE, EGG & RICE DISHES ■

Cheese "Tear-drops"
Gocce Ovette

To serve 6

1 egg

6 slices fresh white bread

6 slices Pariser cheese

mayonnaise

1 sprig parsley

Preparation and cooking time: about 30 minutes

Hard-boil the egg and cool it under running cold water. Using a pastry-cutter, cut 12 tear-drop shapes out of the bread and cheese. Spread each piece of bread with a little mayonnaise and place the pieces of cheese on top, fitting the shapes carefully together.

Shell the egg and chop it coarsely, together with a sprig of parsley. Place a little of this mixture on each "tear-drop", leaving a border of about ¼ inch. Arrange on a tray or plate garnished with parsley and serve.

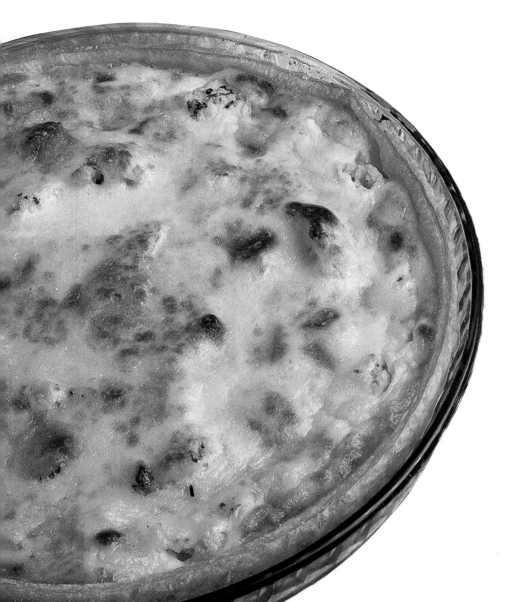

Vegetable Paella
Paella di Verdure

To serve 4

1 large turnip

¼lb whole small frozen French beans

2-3 frozen artichoke hearts

1 medium trimmed leek

1 small carrot

small piece celery heart

9 tbsp olive oil

½ cup frozen young peas

1 piece yellow pimiento

1¾ cups white rice

powdered saffron

2 cups best chicken stock

Preparation and cooking time: about 50 minutes

Preheat the oven to 400°F. Cut the turnip into small cubes and cook it in boiling salted water. Cook the frozen beans and artichoke hearts, then drain them all separately. Cut the leek, carrot and celery into thin round slices. Heat a large skillet or fireproof paella dish with 6 tablespoons of the oil and soften the raw vegetables in it. Add the peas, still frozen, and immediately afterwards the artichoke hearts (reserving 1) cut into thin wedges, the cubes of turnip and the slice of pimiento cut into small squares. Braise very gently for a few minutes, then add the rice. Sprinkle over a pinch of saffron and immediately afterwards pour on the boiling stock. Stir and simmer for 5 minutes over a moderate heat.

Cover the paella and cook in the oven for 10 minutes. Meanwhile, cut the French beans into small pieces and sauté them in 3 tablespoons of oil, together with the artichoke heart which you have kept in reserve. Let the paella rest for 5 minutes after cooking, then serve it garnished with the beans and the artichoke heart, opened out to a flower shape.

Seafood Paella
Paella Marina

To serve 4

5 tbsp olive oil

1 large garlic clove

2 frozen plaice or cod fillets

2 slices frozen dogfish

1 small onion

½ cup shelled frozen mussels

3-4 shelled frozen jumbo shrimp

1¾ cups white rice

3 pieces red pimiento

powdered saffron

2 cups fish stock

a few celery leaves

Preparation and cooking time: about 1 hour

Preheat the oven to 400°F. Heat a large skillet or fireproof paella dish with the oil and lightly crushed garlic, then fry from frozen the 2 fillets of plaice. Once cooked, remove them and keep them to one side. In the same oil, cook the frozen slices of dogfish and put them aside also. Finally remove the garlic and put the chopped onion in the pan and soften it. Add the shelled mussels and shrimp, still frozen. Cover and gently fry the shellfish, shaking the pan from time to time.

Cut the plaice fillets and the slices of dogfish into small pieces and add them to the pan with the rice. Stir carefully, mixing in 1 piece of red pimiento, cut into small squares, and a pinch of saffron. Pour on the boiling stock, stir and simmer for 5 minutes. Cover and cook the paella in the oven for another 10 minutes. Let it rest for 5 minutes before serving, garnished with the remaining pieces of pimiento, cut into strips, and a few chopped celery leaves.

Paella with Chicken and Peas
Paella con Pollo e Pisellini

To serve 4

1 small cleaned chicken weighing about 2lb

5 tbsp olive oil

1 small onion

1 small garlic clove

¾ cup frozen young peas

1¾ cups white rice

powdered saffron

3 cups chicken stock

1 slice yellow pimiento for garnish

6 tender leek leaves for garnish

Preparation and cooking time: about 1 hour

Preheat the oven to 400°F. Singe the chicken to remove any remaining feathers, wash it well, rinse and dry it. Then divide it into 8 pieces. Heat a large skillet or fireproof paella dish with the olive oil, lightly brown the pieces of chicken, adding a little salt and pepper. After 15 minutes of cooking, remove the chicken and put the onion in the pan, finely chopped with a small garlic clove. Let it fry for a few moments, then add the frozen peas. Stir and cook, covered, for 5 minutes.

Now add the rice and the 8 chicken pieces and fry for a few moments. Finally, color with a pinch of saffron and moisten with the boiling stock. Stir and simmer for 5 minutes, then cover the "paella" and cook it in the oven for about 10 minutes. Remove and leave for 5 minutes before serving, garnished with the slice of pimiento, cut in two, and the leek leaves, blanched and curled.

Seafood paella (top), *vegetable paella* (center left) and **paella with chicken and peas** (bottom)

Cheese and Potato Soufflé

Pasticcio di Patate Soufflé

To serve 4

2lb potatoes

⅔ cup cream

ground nutmeg

1 cup grated Gruyère cheese

4 eggs

butter

1 tbsp fresh breadcrumbs

Preparation and cooking time: 1¼ hours

Preheat the oven to 350°F. Boil the potatoes in salted water. Peel and mash. Stir in the cream and season with salt, pepper, and a pinch of nutmeg. Add the grated Gruyère cheese and 4 egg yolks, blending in the yolks one at a time. Whisk the egg whites until stiff and blend into the potato mixture. The mixture should be smooth and free of lumps.

Grease a soufflé dish and sprinkle it with about a tablespoon of fresh breadcrumbs. Pour in the mixture and cook in the preheated oven for 15 minutes. Increase the temperature to 400°F and cook for another 10-15 minutes or until the soufflé has risen and is golden brown on top. Serve immediately or the soufflé will fall.

Harlequin Soufflé

Soffiato Arlecchino

To serve 4

½ small red bell pepper

2 tbsp vegetable oil

6 tbsp butter

½ garlic clove

½ cup flour

2¼ cups milk

ground nutmeg

3 eggs, separated

½ cup canned or frozen, parboiled peas

1 cup grated Parmesan cheese

Preparation and cooking time: about 1¼ hours

Cut the pepper into ½-inch cubes and sauté for 5 minutes in the vegetable oil and 2 tablespoons of butter with half a clove of crushed garlic. Drain the pieces of pepper and place them on a plate covered with paper towels to absorb the excess oil.

Melt the remaining butter in a pan, stir in the flour and add the milk. Cook gently, stirring to produce a thick Béchamel sauce. Season with a pinch of salt, pepper and ground nutmeg. Away from the heat, stir in the 3 egg yolks, one at a time, the bell pepper cubes, the drained peas and the grated Parmesan cheese, mixing well after each addition. Preheat the oven to 375°F.

Beat the egg whites to a froth with a pinch of salt and fold them gently into the prepared mixture; pour it into a buttered soufflé dish (about 3½ pints in capacity) so that the mixture reaches just over halfway up the sides of the dish. Place in the oven for about 30 minutes; the soufflé should be well risen and brown. Serve immediately.

Ricotta Pie with Peas

Sfogliata di Ricotta ai Piselli

To serve 8

¾ lb puff pastry

a little flour

½ cup frozen peas

1-1¼ cups Ricotta cheese

3 eggs

¼ cup milk

½ cup grated Parmesan cheese

ground nutmeg

3 tbsp butter

Preparation and cooking time: about 1 hour plus any defrosting time

Defrost the pastry, if using frozen, and roll it out on a floured surface. Grease a 10-inch pie dish and line it with the pastry.

Preheat the oven to 375°F. Cook the peas in salted boiling water for 3-4 minutes. Sieve and mash the Ricotta. Blend in the eggs one at a time and then stir in the milk, the grated Parmesan cheese, a little salt and a pinch of ground nutmeg. Blend in 3 tablespoons of melted butter and the drained peas.

Pour the mixture into the pie shell and cook in the lower part of the oven for about 40 minutes. Turn the pie out on to a plate and serve hot.

Ricotta pie with peas

Crepe "Pie" with Sausage and Spinach Filling

Pasticcio di Crespelle al Verde

To serve 6-8

3 eggs

2 cups flour

3¾ cups milk

olive oil

¾lb spinach

8 tbsp butter

ground nutmeg

1 bouillon cube

1 cup grated Parmesan cheese

6oz sausages

½ garlic clove

2 tbsp dry white wine

Preparation and cooking time: about 2 hours

Place the eggs in a bowl, add a pinch of salt, 1½ cups of the sifted flour and 5 tablespoons of the milk. Stir until smooth, then dilute with 1¼ cups of the milk to a fluid batter. Use it to prepare 24 crepes using a lightly oiled crepe pan.

Mash the spinach and cook it for a few moments only; drain and squeeze out the remaining water then sauté in 2 tablespoons of the butter, seasoning with a little nutmeg. Purée it. Prepare a Béchamel sauce by melting 4 tablespoons of the butter, stirring in the remaining flour and pouring in the rest of the milk; season with the crumbled bouillon cube. Stir in the spinach purée and ½ cup of the Parmesan cheese. Preheat the oven to 400°F.

Skin the sausages, place them in a pan with a tablespoon of oil and half a garlic clove and fry lightly, mashing the sausage meat with a fork; moisten with the white wine and let it evaporate. Discard the garlic then add the sausage mixture to the Béchamel and spinach sauce. Place alternate layers of crepes and the spinach sauce in a round buttered pie dish 11 inches in diameter, sprinkling each layer with the remaining Parmesan cheese. On top of the pie put some curls of butter and bake in the preheated oven for 18-20 minutes. Serve from the pan cut into wedges.

This is a rather elaborate dish and may seem laborious. However, you can simplify its preparation by making the crepes the previous day: When they are all ready and cold pile them on a dish, cover with foil, and put them in the refrigerator. Next day, prepare the sauce and assemble the dish.

Artichoke pilaf

Artichoke Pilaf

Pilaf ai Carciofi

To serve 4

4 small artichokes

juice of ½ lemon

3 tbsp olive oil

2 tbsp dry white wine

3 cups stock (or use bouillon cube)

3 sprigs fresh parsley

¼ bouillon cube

1 small garlic clove

ground thyme

1 small onion

2 tbsp butter

¾ cup rice

1oz grated Parmesan cheese

Preparation and cooking time: about 50 minutes

Trim the artichokes, remove the tough outer leaves and put them in a bowl of water with the lemon juice. When they are all prepared, drain them and place them stalks upwards in a pan that will just hold them. Pour the oil, white wine and 6 tablespoons of the cold stock over them. Add the parsley, the crumbled quarter bouillon cube, the chopped garlic and a pinch of thyme. Cover and cook over a low heat, without lifting the lid, for about 30 minutes or until tender.

Meanwhile, heat the remaining stock. Preheat the oven to 400°F. Chop the onion finely and sauté it in 1 tablespoon of butter in a fireproof casserole. Add the rice, stir with a wooden spoon and let it brown for a few moments, then pour in the boiling stock and stir again. Return it to the boil. Cover the casserole with a sheet of buttered aluminum foil and put it in the oven for about 15 minutes, until the rice has absorbed all the liquid and is dry and fluffy. Take it out of the oven and fork in the remaining butter and the grated cheese. Turn it into a heated serving dish, place the quartered artichokes on top, garnish with fresh parsley and serve.

Artichoke and Quartirolo Cheese Pie

Teglia di Carciofi e Quartirolo

To serve 8

1 lb puff pastry

4 artichokes

juice of ½ lemon

1 small onion

1 large garlic clove

a handful of parsley

3 tbsp olive oil

3 tbsp butter

½ cup white wine

⅝ cup stock (or use bouillon cube)

a pinch of thyme

2 tbsp flour

¾ cup milk

½ cup grated Parmesan cheese

2 eggs

½lb Quartirolo cheese

1 tbsp breadcrumbs

Preparation and cooking time: about 1½ hours plus any defrosting time

Defrost the pastry if using frozen. Clean the artichokes, stalks as well and, as they are ready, put them in a bowl of cold water with the juice of half a lemon. Finely chop the onion with the garlic and parsley and fry in the olive oil and 5 teaspoons of the butter.

Drain the artichokes well, cut them in half and remove the chokes. Slice them thinly and add them to the skillet. Stir with a wooden spoon. Slice the stalks horizontally and add those too. After a few minutes pour in the wine and allow it to evaporate almost entirely. Bring the stock to the boil and pour it in. Stir well and turn the heat down to the minimum. Season with a pinch of thyme and cover the pan. Cook the artichokes until nearly all the liquid has been absorbed, then sprinkle with the sieved flour. Mix and pour in the boiling milk, stirring constantly. Simmer for a few minutes and add salt to taste. Preheat the oven to 350°F.

Now put everything through the food processor with the finest disk. Mix the Parmesan cheese and 2 eggs into the purée, stirring vigorously. Cut the Quartirolo cheese into thin slices. Roll out the pastry to a thickness of ⅛ inch then line a buttered 14 x 8 inch pie dish with low sides. Prick the pastry with a fork and sprinkle with a fine layer of breadcrumbs. Arrange the slices of Quartirolo cheese in the dish and then pour over the artichoke purée. Trim the pastry around the edges of the dish and roll out to make a cover for the pie, ensuring it adheres to the pastry beneath. Prick the surface with a fork and bake in the lower part of the oven for about 35 minutes until it is cooked and golden brown. Serve piping hot.

■ CHEESE, EGG & RICE DISHES ■

Rich Paella

Pella Ricca

To serve 4

¼lb lean pork

2oz Italian sausage

6oz cod fillets

2 garlic cloves

saffron threads

1 small piece red chili pepper

olive oil

1 medium onion

½lb peeled tomatoes

1 sprig fresh basil

¾lb white rice

2½ cups chicken stock

7 thin slices yellow pimiento

1 green leek leaf

7 French beans

Preparation and cooking time: about 1 hour

Cut the pork into small cubes; break up the sausage coarsely. Cube the cod fillets. Pound together in a mortar the garlic, a few saffron threads and the chili pepper. Heat a large skillet or fireproof paella dish with 5 tablespoons of olive oil, and gently fry the pork cubes, then the sausage and finally the cubes of cod. Remove each in turn and place them on a plate.

Preheat the oven to 400°F. Chop the onion and soften it in the oil in which you have cooked the meat and fish. Purée the peeled tomatoes and add them to the pan, with 2 or 3 chopped basil leaves and a little salt. Let the sauce simmer for 5 minutes, then add the rice and all the fried ingredients. Stir gently, mixing in the saffron, garlic and pepper mixture. After a few minutes, pour on the boiling stock, stir again and simmer for 5 minutes, uncovered.

Then cover the paella and cook it in the oven for about 10 minutes. Finally, let it rest for 5 minutes, then serve it garnished with the slices of pimiento, the blanched leek leaf and the boiled French beans.

Artichoke and quartirolo cheese pie
(center right)

DESSERTS

Italian desserts can be as substantial and elaborate as a festive panettone or as simple as seasonal fresh fruit. Real Italian ice cream, made from fresh fruit juices, eggs and cream, is a delight far different from manufactured ice cream. Simple to make at home, even without a freezer or ice cream machine, it is well worth the effort.

Bananas with Pistachios

Banane "Rosate" al Pistacchio

To serve 4

4 ripe bananas

2 tbsp sugar

4 tbsp rum

¼ cup pistachio nuts

5 tbsp red fruit jelly or rose hip jam

4-5 rose petals (optional)

Preparation time: about 20 minutes

Peel the bananas and halve them lengthwise. Lay them out on a large dish and sprinkle with the sugar and rum. Leave to stand in a cool place.

Meanwhile, parboil the pistachios in salted water for a couple of minutes. Peel them while they are still hot and chop them finely. Place the jelly in a bowl and stir until smooth. Place it in the center of a serving dish and arrange the bananas around it. Pour the rum marinade over the bananas and top with the pistachios. Garnish with 4-5 rose petals (if available) and serve immediately.

Netted Plums

Prugne nella Rete

To serve 4

For the sponge cake:

a little butter and flour

¼ cup butter

3 eggs plus 1 yolk

⅞ cup sugar

grated rind of 1 lemon

a little vanilla sugar

¾ cup all-purpose flour

½ cup cornstarch

For the caramel:

¾ cup sugar

For the topping:

10 large yellow plums

2 tbsp sugar

⅜ cup dry white wine

¾ cup plum jelly or jam

1 cup Amaretto

Preparation and cooking time: about 2 hours

To make the sponge: Preheat the oven to 350°F. Grease and flour a 9-inch dome-shaped cake pan. Melt 2 tablespoons of butter and leave it to cool while beating together 3 whole eggs and 1 yolk with the sugar, if possible using an electric whisk to make the mixture light and frothy. Stir in the grated lemon rind, the vanilla sugar, cornstarch and ⅝ cup of the sifted flour. Lastly, add the cool melted butter. Turn the mixture into a cake pan and bake it in the oven for 35 minutes. It is done when a tooth pick comes out clean. Turn the sponge out to cool on a wire rack.

While the sponge is cooking, wash and dry the plums, cut them in half, remove the pits and place them in a pan in a single layer. Sprinkle them with 2 tablespoons of sugar, add white wine and cook them over a moderate heat with the lid on for 5 minutes. Take them out of the pan and drain them on paper towels.

Add the plum jelly and ¼ cup of the liqueur to the juice left in the pan. Stir over a low heat until it becomes a thick syrup. When the sponge is cool, cut it into 3 layers, moisten them with the remaining liqueur, spread them with the jelly mixture (reserving 2 tablespoons) and reassemble the gateau on a serving plate. Spread the remaining jelly on top and cover it with the cooked plum halves. Leave it in a cool place (not the refrigerator) while you prepare the caramel.

To make the caramel: place the sugar with 3 tablespoons of water over a low heat, stirring gently at first until the sugar is completely dissolved. Cook until the sugar has completely caramelized. Dip a wooden spoon into the caramel and run it crisscross fashion over all the plums, like an irregular net. Serve immediately.

Amaretto Ice Cream

Gelato all'Amaretto

To serve 6

2¼ cups milk

1 vanilla pod

5 egg yolks

½ cup sugar

¼lb small macaroons

¼ cup Amaretto

Preparation and cooking time: 30 minutes plus freezing time.

Pour the milk into a saucepan; add the vanilla pod and slowly bring to the boil, then strain, discarding the pod, and leave to cool.

Meanwhile, beat the 5 egg yolks with a pinch of salt and the sugar until soft and frothy. Stir in the lukewarm milk, pouring it in a trickle, and whisk until well blended. Then pour the mixture back into the saucepan, place the saucepan on a very low heat and, stirring constantly, heat until it is about to boil.

Remove from the heat and strain the liquid through a fine sieve, then leave to cool at room temperature, stirring once in a while. Add the finely crumbled macaroons and Amaretto liqueur. Place in the refrigerator for about 1 hour, then pour the mixture into the ice cream machine and let it freeze.

■ DESSERTS ■ DESSERTS ■

Torrone Ice Cream

Gelato al Torroncino

To serve 6

5oz assorted candied fruit

¼ cup Maraschino liqueur

¼ lb *torrone* (Italian nougat)

2¼ cups fresh milk

1 vanilla pod

⅞ cup sugar

4 egg yolks

Preparation and cooking time: 30 minutes plus freezing time

Coarsely chop the candied fruit, of different colors and flavors, place it in a small bowl and moisten it with the Maraschino. Pound the *torrone* to a powder. In a saucepan heat 1¾ cups of the milk with the vanilla pod and the sugar. When the milk is hot and the sugar has dissolved, discard the vanilla pod.

Beat the 4 egg yolks in a bowl adding first the cold milk then the hot, pouring in a trickle and stirring constantly. When the ingredients are well mixed, pour back into the saucepan and heat for a couple of minutes, stirring, without bringing it to boil. Remove the saucepan from the heat and strain the mixture into a bowl. Let it cool, stirring occasionally, then leave it for at least 1 hour in the refrigerator. Just before placing it in the ice cream machine, mix in the candied fruit and the *torrone*.

■ DESSERTS ■ DESSERTS ■

Hazelnut Ice Cream

Gelato alla Nocciola

To serve 6

¾ cup shelled hazelnuts

2¼ cups milk

1 vanilla pod

½ cup sugar

5 egg yolks

Preparation and cooking time: 45 minutes plus freezing time

Spread the hazelnuts over the base of a baking pan and roast at 350°F for 7-8 minutes. Remove from the oven and, while still hot, place them in a metal sieve and rub them with the palm of your hand to remove their outer skins. Let them cool completely, then pound to a powder in a mortar or blender.

Heat 1¾ cups of the milk in a saucepan with the vanilla pod, a pinch of salt and the sugar. Beat the 5 egg yolks with a small whisk, adding first the cold milk then the hot, little by little and stirring constantly.

When the ingredients are well blended, pour the mixture back into the saucepan and place it on the heat for 2 minutes, stirring constantly and without letting the mixture boil. Immediately remove it from the heat and strain the liquid into a bowl. Leave to cool, stirring occasionally, then add the ground hazelnuts. Finally pour the mixture into the ice cream machine and freeze it.

■ DESSERTS ■ DESSERTS ■

Chocolate Ice Cream

Gelato al Cioccolato

To serve 6

2¼ cups milk

1 vanilla pod

5 egg yolks

½ cup sugar

1 tbsp unsweetened cocoa

¼ lb unsweetened cooking chocolate

1 egg white

Preparation and cooking time:

Pour 1¾ cups of the milk into a saucepan, add the vanilla pod and slowly bring it almost to the boil; remove from the heat and let it cool, then strain through a fine sieve, discarding the vanilla pod.

Beat the 5 egg yolks in a bowl with the sugar and the sieved cocoa until soft and smooth. Add first the cold milk, then the hot, pouring it in a trickle and whisking constantly. Pour the mixture back into the saucepan and place it over a low heat until it is about to boil, stirring constantly.

Remove it from the heat and add the finely crumbled chocolate, stirring well until it has melted and blended in. Strain the mixture through a fine sieve and let it cool completely before pouring it into the ice cream machine. Halfway through the process, add one egg white, whisked to a froth, to make the ice cream smoother and softer.

Vanilla Ice Cream

Gelato alla Vaniglia

To serve 6

2¼ cups milk

½ cup sugar

1 small vanilla pod

5 egg yolks

1 egg white

Preparation and cooking time: 30 minutes plus freezing time

Heat the milk in a saucepan with the sugar, a pinch of salt and the vanilla pod until about to boil.

Meanwhile beat the 5 egg yolks then add, little by little, first the cold milk, then the hot, stirring constantly. When the ingredients are well blended, pour the mixture back into the saucepan and heat for about 2 minutes, stirring.

Pour the mixture into a bowl and let it cool, stirring occasionally. Pour it into the ice cream machine, straining it through a fine sieve. Halfway through the process add 1 egg white whisked to a froth with a pinch of salt so that the ice cream will be very smooth and soft.

■ DESSERTS ■ DESSERTS ■

Rum and Coffee Ice Cream

Gelato di Caffè al Rum

To serve 6

2¼ cups fresh milk

rind of ½ lemon

5 egg yolks

½ cup sugar

½ cup strong black coffee

2 tbsp dark rum

Preparation and cooking time: 20 minutes plus freezing time

Bring the milk to the boil in a saucepan with the lemon rind, then let it cool. Beat the 5 egg yolks to a froth with the sugar, then add the warm milk, pouring it in a trickle through a sieve. Discard the lemon rind. Blend all the ingredients

thoroughly with a small whisk, then pour the mixture back into the saucepan. Add a pinch of salt and place the saucepan on a very low heat, stirring constantly, until the mixture is about to boil.

Remove the saucepan from the heat and strain the liquid through a fine sieve, then stir in the strong coffee and 2 tablespoons of rum. Leave the mixture to cool, first at room temperature, and then for at least 1 hour in the refrigerator. Then pour the mixture into the ice cream machine and freeze.

■ DESSERTS ■ DESSERTS ■

Pistachio Ice Cream

Gelato al Pistacchio

To serve

¾ cup pistachio nuts

1 cup sugar

2¼ cups milk

1 vanilla pod

5 egg yolks

Preparation and cooking time: 30 minutes plus freezing time

Plunge the pistachio nuts into salted boiling water for 1 minute, and shell them. Pound them in a mortar and, adding a tablespoon of sugar from time to time. Continue to pound them until they are reduced to powder.

Heat 1¾ cups of milk with the remaining sugar and the vanilla pod and bring slowly to the boil, stirring occasionally with a wooden spoon. Remove from the heat and discard the vanilla pod. Place the 5 egg yolks in a bowl together with the powdered pistachio nuts. Beat with a small whisk to obtain a smooth mixture. Add first the cold milk, then the hot, poured in a trickle through a fine sieve, and stirring constantly.

When the ingredients are well blended, pour the mixture back into the saucepan, place it on the heat and stir until it is about to boil. At this point remove the saucepan from the heat, pour the mixture into a bowl and leave to cool, stirring occasionally. When cold pour into ice cream machine and freeze.

Peach and Macaroon Pie

Crostata di Pesche all'Amaretto

To serve 6-8

a little butter and flour

¾ cup all-purpose flour

¼ cup sugar

grated rind of ½ lemon

1 egg yolk

¼ cup butter

1 tbsp dry vermouth

12 small macaroons

¾ cup peach jelly

1 tbsp apricot brandy

2 large yellow peaches, together weighing 1lb

1 tbsp Amaretto

redcurrants for garnish

Preparation and cooking time: about 1 hour plus cooling
Preheat the oven to 375°F. Butter and flour a round, smooth 10-inch pie dish. Place the flour on the pastry-board, add a pinch of salt, the sugar and the grated lemon rind. Make a well in the center and add the egg yolk, the softened butter, cut in small pieces, and the vermouth. Knead rapidly into a smooth dough, then roll out the pastry large enough to cover the bottom and sides of the prepared mold; prick the bottom of the pastry with a fork. Crumble over 7 macaroons. Set aside 2 tablespoons of peach jelly, place the rest in a bowl and, stirring, flavor it with the apricot brandy. Spread the jelly evenly over the macaroon crumbs.

Remove the stems of the peaches, peel, halve and pit them, then cut them into equal slices and arrange them in a circle, slightly overlapping, on the pastry; in the center put the remaining macaroons and sprinkle them with the Amaretto liqueur. Bake for about 40 minutes in the oven.

Remove the pie from the oven and let it cool in the mold; then place it on a large round plate. Melt the remaining jelly over a low heat, strain it through a fine sieve and brush the peach slices and the macaroons with it. As soon as the glaze has cooled and is firm, garnish the pie with sprigs of redcurrants and serve.

Peaches with Pine-nuts

Pesche ai Pinoli

To serve 4

4 equal-sized yellow peaches, perfectly ripe

butter

1 clove

2 inch piece lemon rind

2 tbsp sugar

6 tbsp brandy

½ cup pine-nuts

Preparation and cooking time: about 45 minutes

Remove the stems from the peaches, then wash and dry them; cut them in half with a small sharp knife and remove the stones. Melt a large knob of butter in a large skillet, then arrange the 8 half-peaches on the bottom of the pan, cut side down. Fry very gently for a few moments with the pan uncovered, then add a clove and the piece of lemon rind. Sprinkle the fruit with 2 tablespoons of sugar and moisten with 6 tablespoons of brandy. Move the pan slightly to make sure the peaches aren't stuck to the bottom, then lower the heat to the minimum, cover, and cook the half-peaches for about 20 minutes.

Place the half-peaches, with the cut side upwards, on a serving dish and in the hollow of each place a teaspoon of pine-nuts. Reduce the cooking liquid slightly, then strain it through a fine sieve directly on to the fruit. Serve immediately while still hot though peaches prepared in this way are also excellent lukewarm.

Fresh Apricot Compote

Composta di Albicocche, a crudo

To serve 6

1¼lb firm ripe apricots

4oz apricot jam

1 tbsp white rum

1 tbsp apricot liqueur

grated rind of 1 lemon

1 lime for garnish

7 Maraschino cherries

Preparation and cooking time: about 15 minutes plus 1½ hours' soaking

Remove the stalks from the apricots and wipe them with a damp cloth. Halve them, remove the stones, and slice them into a bowl. Strain the jam, dilute it with the rum and liqueur and add the grated lemon rind. Mix well and pour over the apricots, stirring carefully.

Cover the bowl with plastic wrap and leave in the least cold part of the refrigerator for at least 1½ hours giving it a gentle stir from time to time. Then distribute the apricots among 6 individual bowls. Garnish each one with 5 wafer-thin rings of lime and 5 slices of Maraschino cherry. Serve at once.

Fruit Cup

Coppa di Frutta

To serve 4

½ pomegranate

2 tbsp Cointreau

20 white grapes

2 tbsp sugar

juice of ½ lemon

4 ripe oranges

Preparation time: about 40 minutes

Peel the pomegranate and place the segments in a bowl. Sprinkle with the Cointreau and stir gently. Cover the bowl and place in a cool place. Allow the fruit to soak for about 15 minutes.

Wash and dry the grapes and cut each one lengthwise into 4 segments, taking care to remove the seeds. Place the segments in a bowl and dust with 2 heaping tablespoons of sugar. Sprinkle with the juice of half a lemon, stir and put aside in a cool place for a few minutes.

Peel the oranges, taking care to remove all the pith. Divide the oranges into segments and place in a bowl, squeezing any juice remaining in the peel over them. Add the pomegranate and grape segments, together with their juices, to the orange segments and stir well. Keep in the refrigerator until ready to serve.

Almond Puffs

Sgonfietti alle Mandorle

To serve 8

1 cup almonds, shelled but not peeled

¾ cup sugar

½ cup cornstarch

6 egg whites

a little butter

Preparation and cooking time: about 40 minutes

Preheat the oven to 350°F. Blanch the almonds in boiling water then peel them. Toast them lightly in the oven for a few minutes then leave them to cool. Turn the oven down to 300°F. Coarsely grind ⅞ cup of the almonds and cut the rest into slivers. Pour the sugar into a bowl together with the ground almonds and sift in the cornstarch. Whisk the egg whites until they are stiff and fold into the other ingredients using a gentle up-and-down movement so as not to deflate the egg whites.

Liberally butter 2 baking trays, then spoon dollops of the mixture a little larger than the size of a walnut on both trays and decorate with the almond slivers. Bake for about 20 minutes, until the meringues are slightly brown and firm to the touch. Remove them even if they are still a little sticky as they will harden on cooling. Lift the puffs off the trays with a metal spatula and cool them thoroughly before arranging them on a serving dish. They are best eaten as soon as they are cold.

Peach and macaroon pie (above left) and *peaches with pine-nuts; fruit cup* (right)

Panettone filled with Mandarin Orange Custard

Panettone Farcito al Mandarino

To serve 10-12

about 2 tbsp gelatin

4 eggs

⅜ cup sugar

1 mandarin orange

¼ cup flour

1¼ cups milk

⅜ cup mandarin orange juice

1 panettone, weighing about 2lb

¼ cup Cointreau

2 cups whipping cream

Preparation and cooking time: about 1 hour plus 6-8 hours' chilling

Dissolve the gelatin in cold water. Whisk together the egg yolks and the sugar in a saucepan until pale and frothy. Grate the mandarin orange rind and add this, then sift in the flour. Mix again, then dilute with the milk and the mandarin juice, adding them in in a trickle. Bring slowly to the boil, stirring constantly with a wooden spoon. Remove from the heat and dissolve the gelatin in the mixture. Leave it to cool, stirring from time to time to prevent a skin forming.

Meanwhile, turn the panettone upside down and, using a sharp-pointed knife, cut out a disk from the base, about ¾ inch from the edge. Set the disk aside. Hollow out the inside of the panettone, always keeping about ¾ inch from the edge. Make a large cavity and pour in the Cointreau. Whip the cream and fold it into the mandarin-flavored custard, which should be cold by now. Use an up-and-down movement, not a circular one, to prevent the cream from going flat. Pour the mixture into the panettone and replace the disk in the base to restore its original form. Place it upside-down in a bowl which is just the right size to hold the panettone and cover with plastic wrap.

Refrigerate for 6-8 hours or, better still, overnight. Turn out on to a serving dish and serve. Cut with a sharp, serrated knife to avoid crumbling it.

Panettone Charlotte

Charlotte di Panettone

To serve 8

about 1 lb apples

about 1½lb pears

about ½ cup butter

about ½ cup sugar

¾ cup dry white wine

1 panettone, weighing about 2lb

2 eggs

½ cup milk

⅜ cup cream

Preparation and cooking time: about 2½ hours plus cooling and chilling

Preheat the oven to 325-350°F. Peel, core and quarter the apples and pears. Heat 2 skillets with about 3 tablespoons of butter in each. As soon as the butter is hot, put the apples in one skillet and the pears in the other. Sprinkle each with 1 tablespoon of sugar and pour at least ⅜ cup wine into each skillet. Cook over a low heat until the fruit is cooked but still firm and the pieces intact.

Meanwhile, liberally butter a pudding mold with a capacity of 3½ pints then cut 2 aluminum foil strips, about 2 inches wide and long enough to place crosswise inside the mold with about ¾ inch at the ends to hang over the rim of the mold. Butter these too. Cut the panettone into thin slices. Place a layer of panettone on the bottom of the mold and press it down lightly to make it stick. Then place half the apples on top. Cover with another layer of panettone and then a layer of pears. Continue alternating the panettone, apples and pears in this way, finishing with a layer of panettone. Press down lightly so there are no spaces left.

Beat the eggs with the remaining sugar in a bowl and dilute with the milk and cream. Pour the mixture over the panettone and prick with a skewer to help the liquid penetrate. Leave the charlotte to rest for about 15 minutes then bake for about 1½ hours. Remove from the oven and leave to cool. Then turn it out on to a serving dish with the help of the strips of aluminum foil (which should then be discarded). Refrigerate the charlotte for a couple of hours before serving. This is a good recipe for using up leftover panettone and is especially suitable for children.

Panettone filled with mandarin orange custard (top) and *panettone charlotte*

Home-made Golden Raisin Cake

Dolce Casereccio all'Uvetta

To make 2 cakes

about 1½ sticks butter

3 cups flour

¼lb golden raisins

3 tbsp Strega liqueur

3 eggs

¾ cup sugar

1 lemon with an unblemished rind

1 tbsp pine-nuts

1 tsp vanilla-flavored baking powder

a little powdered sugar

Preparation and cooking time: about 1¼ hours

Preheat the oven to 350°F. The above ingredients will make 2 cakes, each to serve 5-6 people. Butter and flour a round fluted 3½-cup mold and a rectangular 9 x 5 inch one with about the same capacity. Soak the raisins in the Strega liqueur. Whip the egg yolks, setting the whites aside, with the sugar, a pinch of salt and the grated lemon rind.

When you have a light frothy mixture, incorporate 8 tablespoons of cooled melted butter, mixing constantly and vigorously. Continue beating for a few minutes, then drain the sultanas and add these too, floured and mixed with the pine-nuts. Sift in 2 cups of flour mixed with the baking powder. Add 2 tablespoons of the Strega in which the sultanas were soaked.

Whip the egg whites with a pinch of salt until they are firm and carefully fold into the batter which should be fairly stiff. Divide in half and pour into the molds, shaking them lightly to eliminate air bubbles. Bake the rectangular cake for 30 minutes and the round one for 40 minutes. Remove from the oven and leave to cool in the molds before turning out.

Before serving sprinkle one or both cakes with powdered sugar. Serve with cream, or with zabaglione or custard. The cakes can be kept for 3-4 days in their molds covered with foil. Leave in a cool place (not the refrigerator).

Little Doughnut Rings

Ciambelline "Golose"

To serve 4-6

1 cup all-purpose flour

grated rind of ½ lemon

¼ cup sugar

2 tbsp butter

½ tsp baking powder

a little milk

cooking oil

Preparation and cooking time: 1½ hours

Pour the flour on to a work surface and add a pinch of salt, the grated lemon rind, the sugar, the butter and a teaspoon of baking powder. Make a soft, but not too sticky, dough, adding a little warm milk.

Divide the dough into little pieces and roll them in your hands to form thin "cords" ¼ inch in diameter. Cut them into 5-inch lengths. Join the ends of each cord to form rings. Place on a baking tray on a sheet of lightly oiled aluminum foil and leave to stand for 10 minutes.

Heat plenty of oil in a deep-frying pan and fry the rings, a few at a time, until golden brown. Make sure that the oil is hot but not boiling throughout cooking. Drain the rings on paper towels, arrange on a plate and serve.

Little doughnut rings

St Valentine's Heart
"Cuore" di San Valentino

To serve 6-8

½lb puff pastry

8 macaroons

½ cup boiled, puréed chestnuts

½ cup powdered sugar

2 tbsp Amaretto

3 tbsp very fresh Mascarpone cheese (or cream cheese)

⅛ cup unsweetened cocoa

¼ cup pine-nuts

⅓ cup golden raisins

2 eggs

1 cup whipping cream

10 pink sugar almonds

1 tbsp colored sugar crystals

a little flour

Preparation and cooking time: 1½ hours plus any thawing time

Defrost the puff pastry, if using frozen, then roll it out to about ⅛ inch thick. Roll it round the rolling-pin, then unroll it on to a baking tray. Place on top of the pastry a mold or a piece of card cut into a heart shape that almost covers the pastry, and cut around it with a sharp knife. Discard the pastry trimmings. Prick the heart with a fork and leave to rest.

Preheat the oven to 375°F. Crumble 6 of the macaroons finely and put in a bowl with the puréed chestnuts, ¼ cup sieved sugar, the Amaretto liqueur, the Mascarpone cheese and the unsweetened cocoa. Stir well until smooth and creamy then mix in the pine-nuts and ¼ cup washed and dried golden raisins. Bind the mixture with the 2 whole eggs, beating vigorously, then spread over the puff pastry to about ½ inch from the edge. Bake on a low shelf for about 20 minutes.

Place the heart on a rack to cool. Meanwhile, crumble the rest of the macaroons very finely. Whip the cream until it is quite firm, then put into a pastry bag fitted with a round, fluted nozzle and pipe rosettes round the edge of the heart. Sieve the remaining powdered sugar over the top, then decorate the cake with the rest of the golden raisins, the crumbled macaroons, the pink sugar almonds and the colored sugar crystals. Serve immediately.

■ DESSERTS ■ DESSERTS ■

Chestnut Cup
Coppette di Castagne

To serve 4

1lb chestnuts, boiled and peeled

4oz sugar

4 tbsp Cointreau

a little vanilla sugar

6 tbsp whipping cream

6 pistachio nuts

Preparation and cooking time: about 30 minutes plus cooling

Place the chestnuts in a bowl that just holds them. Heat the sugar with 3 tablespoons of water, letting it dissolve gradually then come to the boil. Take it off the heat, add the Cointreau and vanilla sugar, stir it and pour it over the chestnuts. Cover the bowl with plastic wrap and leave it to cool completely, during which time the chestnuts will absorb much of the syrup.

Divide the chestnuts between 4 individual cups. Whip the cream until firm and, using a pastry bag, decorate each cup with a ring of cream rosettes. Blanch the pistachio nuts for a few seconds in slightly salted boiling water, remove the skins and dry them on paper towels. Chop them finely and sprinkle them on the cream. Serve immediately, since the chestnuts are at their best straight after cooling.

St Valentine's heart

Little Love Cookies
Biscottini d'Amore

To serve 6

1¼ cups all-purpose flour

ground cinnamon

ground cloves

grated rind of ½ lemon

5 tbsp sugar

1 tsp vanilla-flavored baking powder

1 egg

7 tbsp butter

1 tsp unsweetened cocoa

1 tsp brandy

Preparation and cooking time: about 1 hour

Mix the flour with a pinch of salt, a pinch of ground cinnamon and another of ground cloves, the lemon rind and the sugar on a pastry-board. Add the baking powder. Then make a well and add the whole egg and the softened butter cut into small pieces.

Knead all together quickly to give a smooth, even dough, then divide into 2 pieces, one twice as large as the other. Work 1 heaping teaspoon of sieved, unsweetened cocoa into the smaller piece of dough together with the brandy, kneading for a few minutes. Roll the larger piece out on the board sprinkled lightly with flour to a thickness of about ⅛ inch. Then cut into shapes using a heart-shaped cookie cutter and arrange them on 1 or 2 buttered and floured baking trays. Knead together the remaining dough, roll out and cut out more shapes. Continue until all the dough is used up. Preheat the oven to 350°F.

Now roll out the cocoa-flavored dough and cut smaller heart shapes out of that, placing them centrally on top of the first hearts and pressing them down lightly to keep in place. Lastly place the small cookies in the oven for about 12 minutes or until they are cooked and a light golden brown. Remove carefully from the tray using a pallet knife and allow to cool on a rack. If desired, sprinkle with a little powdered sugar before serving.

Chestnut "Macaroons"
"Amaretti" di Castagne

To make 36 "macaroons"

1 cup chestnuts, boiled and puréed

¾ cup very fresh Mascarpone cheese

½ cup powdered sugar

⅓ cup unsweetened cocoa

⅝ cup brandy

3 doz macaroons, plus 2 extra

Preparation time: about 30 minutes plus 1 hour's refrigeration

Combine the chestnut paste with the Mascarpone cheese in a bowl, then sift in the powdered sugar and the unsweetened cocoa and mix to a smooth paste with ⅜ cup of brandy. Put the mixture in a pastry bag.

Pour the remaining brandy into a dish and soak the 3 dozen macaroons, flat side down, for a few seconds. As you remove them from the brandy, arrange them on a serving dish. Pipe out a large swirl of the chestnut paste on to each macaroon and place them in the refrigerator for at least an hour.

Crumble the 2 extra macaroons and sprinkle them over the others before serving. These delicious cookies may also be presented in little paper cases arranged on a tray. They are delightful served with afternoon tea or with after-dinner liqueurs.

Little love cookies

Chestnut and Chocolate Roll

"Salame" di Castagne e Cioccolato

To serve 12

¾ cup butter

1 cup powdered sugar

⅞ cup unsweetened cocoa

¼ cup Amaretto

6-7 macaroons

1½ cup chestnuts, boiled and puréed

a little whipping cream (optional)

chocolate hundreds and thousands (optional)

Preparation and cooking time: about 40 minutes plus 3-4 hours' refrigeration

Soften the butter and cut into pieces in a bowl with a wooden spoon until light and frothy. Sift in the powdered sugar and the cocoa and mix in half the Amaretto. Grind the macaroons almost to a powder and add them, together with the chestnut paste and the remaining Amaretto, reserving 1 teaspoon. Blend all the ingredients together smoothly.

Pour the reserved teaspoon of Amaretto, diluted with 2 tablespoons of cold water, on to a sheet of aluminum foil. Spread the chestnut mixture on the foil and roll it up evenly and tightly. Seal the ends and refrigerate for 3-4 hours.

Just before serving, take it out of the refrigerator and remove the aluminum foil. Slice with a very sharp knife dipped in a bowl of hot water. Garnish, if you like, with a stripe of chocolate hundreds and thousands and serve with whipping cream.

Chestnut and chocolate roll (top right) *and* *chestnut macaroons*

Figs with Redcurrants and Ice Cream

Fichi Speziati con Ribes e Gelato

To serve 6

2lb fresh figs, not overripe

⅜ cup sugar

⅓ cup golden raisins

ground cinnamon

ground ginger

a few whole cloves

6 tbsp Alchermes liqueur

rind of 1 lemon

12 thin slices fruit bread

pint of redcurrants

6 tbsp vanilla ice cream

Preparation and cooking time: about 40 minutes plus 1 hour's marination

Using a small, sharp knife, peel the figs. Cut each one into 4 or 6 according to size and place in a stainless steel saucepan. Add the sugar, the raisins, a large pinch of cinnamon, a pinch of ginger and a few cloves. Pour over 2 tablespoons of Alchermes liqueur. Cut a 3-inch piece of lemon rind into needle-fine strips and add to the other ingredients. Cover and leave in a cool place for 1 hour.

Next, cook the figs over a low heat for about 15 minutes from the moment the liquid begins to simmer. Keep the pan uncovered and stir gently from time to time. Immerse the saucepan in cold water to cool.

Arrange the fruit bread in a glass salad bowl and pour over 4 tablespoons of Alchermes. Spread the fig mixture on top and cover. Keep in the refrigerator until it is time to serve. Then sprinkle the stemmed, washed redcurrants on top and decorate with slivers of ice-cream.

*Figs with redcurrants and ice cream (above) and **coronet cake***

Coronet Cake
Torta "Coroncina"

To serve 8-10

a little butter

a little flour

3 eggs

½ cup sugar

2 tbsp vanilla sugar

⅝ cup all-purpose flour

⅔ cup potato flour

3 large, very ripe figs

⅞ cup whipping cream

¾ cup Cointreau

powdered sugar

⅓ cup apricot jam

3 sprigs redcurrants

Preparation and cooking time: about 1¼ hours

Preheat the oven to 350°F. Butter and flour a round 12-inch cake ring (a Kugelhopf pan). Whisk the eggs with the sugar, the vanilla sugar and a pinch of salt until light and fluffy. Mix the flour and the potato starch and sift into the mixture. Fold in carefully using a wooden spoon and with an up and down motion. Pour into the cake pan and bake for about 30 minutes until a wooden skewer plunged into the cake comes out clean. Turn out on to a cooling rack and leave to cool.

Wipe the figs with a damp cloth, cut them in half and then into very thin slices using a small very sharp knife. Whip the cream until it is stiff. Cut the cake into 4 equal layers. Place the bottom round on a serving dish and pour over a third of the Cointreau. Then spread over a third of the whipped cream. Sprinkle with a teaspoon of powdered sugar. Repeat the procedure with the other two layers and lightly press on the fourth.

Decorate the top with the fig slices to form a coronet. Heat the apricot jelly over a low heat and when it is runny, sieve through a fine strainer and brush the figs with it. Leave until the jelly has cooled. Complete the decoration with the redcurrants and serve at once.

Zabaglione Dessert
Chiaroscuro allo Zabaione

To serve 4-6

3 eggs

3 tbsp sugar

8 tbsp dry Marsala wine

1 tbsp golden raisins

⅞ cup fresh whipping cream

12 chocolate-covered Savoy cookies

Preparation and cooking time: about 30 minutes

Separate the eggs, placing the yolks in a saucepan and adding 3 tablespoons of sugar. Stir with a wooden spoon until pale and frothy, then stir in, one at a time, 6 tablespoons of the Marsala wine. Heat the mixture in a double boiler, beating constantly with a small whisk until it thickens. Take care not to let it boil. Leave to cool.

Meanwhile, soak the golden raisins for 15 minutes in warm water. When the zabaglione is cold, whip the cream and carefully stir in 3 tablespoons. Refrigerate the rest of the cream until it is required for decoration. Drain the raisins thoroughly and stir in these too. Then spoon the mixture into a deepish square dish, distributing it evenly.

Pour 2 tablespoons of the Marsala into a soup bowl and add 2 tablespoons of water. Briefly dip the Savoy cookies in

the mixture, keeping the chocolate-coated side uppermost as you dip. Arrange the cookies diagonally on top of the zabaglione cream as you proceed, alternating the chocolate sides with the plain. Cut the cookies to fit the dish without leaving any gaps.

Put the remaining whipped cream into a pastry bag with a fluted round nozzle and make a decorative border of swirls around the Savoy cookies. Refrigerate until serving time.

Zabaglione dessert

Home-made Apple Cake

Torta di Mele, Casereccia

To serve 8

2 eggs

¾ cup sugar

grated rind of 1 lemon

ground cinnamon

ground cloves

1½ cups flour

¼ cup cornstarch

5 tbsp milk

1 tsp baking powder

2 tbsp butter

breadcrumbs

1lb apples, just ripe

⅓ cup apricot jam

Preparation and cooking time: about 1½ hours plus cooling

Preheat the oven to 350°F. Beat the eggs with ½ cup of the sugar, a pinch of salt and the grated lemon rind. Then add another pinch of salt, followed by a pinch of cinnamon and a pinch of cloves. Combine the flour and the cornstarch and sift these into the mixture. Gradually pour in the milk and sift in the baking powder. Mix all these ingredients together to form a smooth batter.

Butter a 10-inch cake tin and sprinkle it with breadcrumbs. Pour in the batter. Peel and halve the apples, core and slice them, not too thinly. Arrange the slices on top of the batter. Sprinkle with the rest of the sugar and intersperse with slivers of butter. Bake for about 45 minutes or until a toothpick comes out clean. Remove the cake from the oven and leave to cool. Heat the apricot jam over a low heat and, when it has melted, brush the surface of the cake with it and leave to cool. This cake is best eaten the same day.

Coffee Cream Puff

Sfogliata alla Crema di Caffe

To serve 10

1lb puff pastry

½ cup butter

8 almonds

1 egg

½ cup fresh Mascarpone cheese

1 cup powdered sugar

2 tbsp freeze-dried instant coffee

2 tbsp coffee liqueur

2 tbsp brandy

12 Savoy cookies

½ cup Amaretto

Preparation and cooking time: about 1 hour plus any thawing

Defrost the pastry, if using frozen. Preheat the oven to 375°F. Cut the butter into small pieces and leave to soften. Meanwhile, finely chop the almonds. Divide the pastry in half and roll out two rounds 10 inches in diameter. Place on two baking trays and prick with a fork all over. Separate the egg yolk from the white. brush the surface of the pastry with the white. Bake for about 20 minutes, or until the pastry is golden brown. Remove from the oven and place on a cooling rack.

Meanwhile, beat the butter with the Mascarpone cheese and ⅞ cup of powdered sugar, ideally with an electric mixer. Incorporate the egg yolk, the instant coffee, the coffee liqueur and the brandy. The cream should be light and fluffy by the time you have finished. Lay one pastry round on top of the other and trim until they are exactly the same size. (Keep the offcuts.) Place one round on a round cardboard cake base and spread a third of the coffee cream over it. Soak the Savoy cookies in the Amaretto and arrange these on top of the cream, breaking them up so that they do not jut out. Spread half the remaining cream over the cookies. Then sprinkle over the crumbled pastry offcuts and press down the second pastry round to ensure it adheres to the cream.

Cover the cake with the remaining cream and decorate with the chopped almonds. Place on a cake stand and refrigerate for at least 30 minutes before serving. Finally, sprinkle with a little powdered sugar or decorate as you please.

Imperial Cake

Torta Imperiale

To serve 12

4 tbsp butter

2 cups flour

7 eggs and 1 egg yolk

a little butter and flour

1 cup sugar

grated rind of ½ lemon

½ cup potato starch

¼lb almond cookies

2 tbsp vanilla sugar

1½ cups milk

2 tbsp Amaretto

1¾ cups whipping cream

½ cup powdered sugar

⅓ cup Cointreau

Preparation and cooking time: about 2 hours

Preheat the oven to 375°F. Put ½ cup of water in a small pan on the heat and add the butter and a pinch of salt. When the water comes to the boil and the butter melts, remove the pan from the heat for a moment and pour into it ¾ cup of sieved flour, all at once, stirring vigorously with a wooden spoon. Put the pan back on the heat and continue cooking, still stirring, until the batter begins to sizzle at the base. Then turn it out on to a plate, spread it out and leave to cool. Then put it back into the pan and add 2 whole eggs, one at a time, beating vigorously and adding the second only when the first is completely mixed in. Put the batter in a pastry bag fitted with a smooth, round nozzle and pipe 35 equal amounts on to a buttered, floured baking tray, keeping the buns well spaced.

Place the tray in the oven for about 15 minutes or until the buns are well risen and golden brown. Allow to cool on a rack. Turn the oven down to 350°F. Butter and flour a round cake pan 10 inches in diameter with a smooth base and sides. Beat together 3 whole eggs with ¾ cup of sugar, the grated rind of half a lemon and a small pinch of salt. When the mixture is smooth and fluffy, mix 1 cup of flour with the potato starch and sieve this into the batter, folding in gently with a wooden spoon. Pour the batter into the cake pan and place in the preheated oven for about 30 minutes, until a skewer or toothpick comes out clean. Turn out on to a tray and allow to cool.

Crush the cookies, using a pestle and mortar (or break into small pieces and pulverize in a blender). In a small pan, beat together 2 whole eggs, 1 egg yolk, ½ cup of sugar, ¼ cup of sieved flour, a pinch of salt and the vanilla sugar. Gradually add the cold milk, mixing with a small whisk. Stirring continuously, bring to the boil, then remove from the heat and stand the pan in cold water to cool. Add the crushed cookies and flavor with the Amaretto.

Whip the cream until very firm, add the sieved powdered sugar, then put in a piping bag, fitted with a small, round, smooth nozzle. Fill the buns with some of this and keep the rest for decoration. Cut the cake into three layers, pour 3 tablespoons of Cointreau over each, spread with the cookie mixture, then put the layers back together. Arrange the filled buns on the top, then fill the space between them with the rest of the whipped cream. Keep the cake in a refrigerator (for 3-4 hours maximum) until ready to serve.

Coffee cream puff (bottom)

May Evening Pie

Crostata "Sera di Maggio"

To serve 8

1½ cups flour

¾ cup sugar

grated rind of ½ lemon

6 tbsp butter

1 small egg

2 envelopes plain gelatin

1¼ lb ripe strawberries

½ cup Cointreau

⅔ cup fresh whipping cream

a few mint leaves for garnish

Preparation and cooking time: about 1 hour plus 3-4 hours' chilling

Mix the flour, ¼ cup of sugar, the grated rind of half a lemon and a pinch of salt together and make a well in the center. Cut the softened butter into small pieces and place in the well with the egg; mix quickly to a smooth dough. Roll it into a ball, wrap it in wax paper or plastic wrap and let it rest in the least cold part of the refrigerator for about 30 minutes.

Meanwhile preheat the oven to 350°F. Butter and flour a smooth round pie dish 9½ inches in diameter. Roll out enough dough to line the dish and prick it with a fork; cover it with a sheet of foil and place a few dried beans on top. Bake the pastry for about 30 minutes, in the lower part of the oven so that the dough cooks through. Remove the beans and the foil and let the pastry shell cool inside the dish.

Dissolve the gelatin in a little cold water. Remove the stems from 1lb of the strawberries, wash them in very cold water, drain them, then cut them into small pieces. Place them in a blender together with the remaining sugar and blend them first at low speed then at high speed for a couple of minutes. Heat the Cointreau in a saucepan; remove it from the heat and, while still hot, fold in the gelatin, stirring it until it is completely dissolved; add the strawberries and stir for a further 30 seconds.

Turn out the pastry shell on to a serving dish and pour over the strawberry mixture and distribute evenly. Keep the tart in the refrigerator for 3-4 hours or, even better, overnight, to firm the filling. A short time before serving, beat the whipping cream, put it in a pastry bag, and garnish to taste, finishing off with the remaining strawberries, washed but not stemmed, and a few mint leaves. Serve immediately.

■ DESSERTS ■ DESSERTS ■

Mother's Day Cake

Torta "Festa della Mamma"

To serve 10-12

butter

⅝ cup all-purpose flour

3 eggs plus 4 egg yolks

1⅛ cups sugar

4 tbsp vanilla sugar

2⅔ cup potato flour

1 tbsp gelatin

10 tbsp dry Marsala wine

¾ cup Amaretto liqueur

⅜ cup fresh whipping cream

5 large ripe strawberries

Preparation and cooking time: about 1¼ hours plus at least 2 hours' chilling

Preheat the oven to 350°F. Butter and flour a round, smooth, hinged mold about 10 inches in diameter. Beat 3 of the eggs with ¾ cup of the sugar, 1 envelope of vanilla sugar and a pinch of salt until you obtain a frothy mixture. Add the flour and the potato starch sieved together through a fine sieve. Fold them in very gently with a movement from top to bottom and vice versa, not round and round, using a wooden spoon. Pour the batter into the mold and place it in the oven for about 35 minutes or until a tooth pick comes out clean.

Unmold the cake on to a rack and let it cool. Meanwhile, dissolve the gelatin in a little cold water. In a copper bowl beat 4 egg yolks together with the remaining sugar and 1 envelope of vanilla sugar. When the mixture is frothy add 10 tablespoons of dry Marsala wine, making sure that each tablespoon is thoroughly absorbed before adding the next. Then add ¼ cup of Amaretto liqueur, pouring it in a trickle and stirring all the time. Place the copper bowl over a pan of barely simmering water and, still stirring, warm the zabaglione cream until it is almost boiling. At this point remove it from the heat and fold in the gelatin. Mix thoroughly until you are certain that the gelatin has been dissolved, then pour the zabaglione cream into a bowl and let it cool.

Cut the cake into 3 layers of equal thickness and place the lowest one back in the mold used to bake it, lined with waxed paper. Sprinkle the cake with a third of the remaining Amaretto liqueur and spread over it a third of the warm zabaglione cream. Repeat the same procedure with the second and third layer of cake. Refrigerate the cake for at least 2 hours, when the zabaglione cream will have firmed.

Beat the whipping cream until fluffy and put it in a pastry bag. Wipe the strawberries and remove the stems of 4 of them, then cut them in half lengthwise. Slide the blade of a small knife between the side of the mold and the cake, then open the hinge and detach the side of the mold. Slide the cake on to a serving dish by removing first the bottom of the mold and then the waxed paper, garnish the top with the whipped cream and the strawberries. Serve immediately.

Mother's day cake

Plum Crescents

Mezzelune alla Marmellata

To serve 6-8

2⅛ cups all-purpose flour

¼ tsp baking powder

½ cup sugar

1 tbsp vanilla sugar

grated rind of ½ lemon

2 eggs

6 tbsp butter

2 tbsp anise liqueur

a little flour

1 jar plum jelly

a little butter

a little powdered sugar

Preparation and cooking time: about 1½ hours

Sift the flour and baking powder on to a pastry-board or work surface. Add the sugar, the vanilla sugar and the grated lemon rind. Stir and then make a well in the center. Place in the well the eggs, the butter (cut into little pieces) and the anise liqueur. Combine with the flour to form a firm, smooth dough. Preheat the oven to 350°F.

Dust the board with a little flour and roll out the pastry to a thickness of ¼ inch. Cut into 3-inch circles with a serrated cookie cutter. Place a teaspoon of plum jelly on each piece of pastry and fold each circle in half, sealing the edges.

Place the crescents on a buttered baking tray which has been sprinkled with a little flour. Make sure that the crescents are not too close together as they will spread during cooking.

Bake in the oven for 20 minutes. Leave to cool and sprinkle with a little powdered sugar. Arrange on a dish and serve.

Strawberry Sauce for Lemon Ice Cream

Gelato Rosato

To serve 4

2¼ cups lemon ice cream

½lb fresh strawberries

3 tbsp Cointreau liqueur

1 tbsp sugar

8 wafers

Preparation time: about 15 minutes plus 2 hours' soaking

Keep the ice cream in the freezer for at least 2 hours before preparation. Rinse the strawberries in iced water, drain well and discard the stalks. Cut the strawberries into pieces and place them in a bowl. Pour on the Cointreau and sprinkle with the sugar. Cover the bowl and leave to soak for a couple of hours. hours.

Just before you are ready to serve, purée the strawberries with their syrup to form a smooth sauce. Remove the ice cream from the freezer and, using a scoop, place balls of the ice cream either in a large serving goblet or in individual glasses. Coat the ice-cream with the strawberry sauce and serve with the wafers.

Strawberry sauce for lemon ice cream (above); **plum crescents** (right)

Pudding with Almonds and Raisins

Crema Sformata con Mandorle e Uvetta

To serve 6

½ cup golden raisins

⅔ cup dry white wine

¾ cup almonds

2 eggs

¾ cup sugar

2 slices white bread, crumbled

1¼ cups cream

1¼ cups milk

ground nutmeg

1 tsp ground cinnamon

butter

Preparation and cooking time: about 1½ hours

Preheat the oven to 350°F. Soak the raisins in the white wine. Parboil the almonds in a little water for a few minutes, drain and peel them. Toast them in the oven for 3-4 minutes. Chop finely in a blender.

Reduce the oven temperature to 300°F. Beat the eggs, add the sugar and whisk to form soft peaks. Mix in the chopped almonds, the crumbled bread and the drained raisins. Add the cream and milk and flavor with a pinch of ground nutmeg and a teaspoon of ground cinnamon. Butter a 10-inch ovenproof pie dish and pour in the mixture. Bake in the preheated oven for at least 1 hour. The cake is ready when the center is firm and springy to the touch. Cool in the dish and then turn on to a plate.

Fried Ricotta Slices

Crema di Ricotta, Fritta

To serve 4-6

1 cup fresh Ricotta cheese

5 tbsp sugar

⅝ cup flour

5 eggs

1 cup cream

1¼ cups milk

oil

a little semolina

Preparation and cooking time: about 40 minutes

Sieve and mash the Ricotta and mix it with the sugar, a little salt and the sifted flour. Stir in the eggs one at a time to form a smooth paste. Whisk in the cream and milk.

Heat the mixture in a small saucepan, stirring constantly with a whisk, and allow it to thicken. Remove from the heat as soon as it starts to boil.

Grease a baking pan with plenty of oil and pour in the mixture, spreading it to a thickness of about ½ inch. Leave to cool and set and then cut it into diamonds. Coat the diamonds in the semolina.

Heat plenty of oil in a large skillet and fry the diamonds a few at a time, turning them carefully so that they brown on all sides. Drain on paper towels and arrange on a plate. Serve warm or cold.

Fried ricotta slices

Profiteroles in Spun Caramel
Piramide di Bigné

To make about 40 profiteroles

For the pastries:

5 tbsp butter, cut into pieces

1 cup flour

4 eggs

a little butter

For the custard:

2 eggs plus 2 egg yolks

½ cup sugar

¼ cup flour

2¼ cups milk

2 tbsp vanilla sugar

For the caramel:

½ cup sugar

Preparation and cooking time: about 2 hours

Bring to the boil a small saucepan containing 1 cup of water, the butter and a pinch of salt. As soon as it comes to the boil, remove it from the heat and pour in the sifted flour. Mix and return to the heat. Cook until the mixture no longer sticks to the edges of the pan and makes a slight crackling sound. Turn on to a working surface, spread out and leave to cool.

Preheat the oven to 375°F. Return the mixture to the pan and mix in the eggs one at a time. When the mixture is smooth, spoon it into a pastry bag. Pipe rosettes of the mixture on to a buttered baking pan, making sure that they are well separated – you should have enough mixture to make about 40 profiteroles. Bake in the oven for about 15 minutes. Before removing from the oven cut open 1 profiterole to check that it is cooked – it should be hollow and slightly crisp and golden in the center. Cool the profiteroles on a wire rack.

Meanwhile, prepare the custard filling: Beat 2 eggs, 2 extra yolks and the sugar until the mixture forms soft, white peaks. Sift in the flour and add the cold milk and the vanilla sugar. Heat gently and allow

to thicken, stirring constantly. As soon as the mixture comes to the boil, plunge the pan in cold water to cool. Pipe the mixture into the profiteroles and arrange them in a pyramid on a plate.

Prepare the caramel: Melt the sugar in the water over a moderate heat. Let it boil until it has turned light brown, remove from the heat and stir to cool and thicken. When the caramel begins to form threads, pour it over the profiteroles, holding the pan fairly high and moving it in circles so that the caramel falls in spun threads around the profiteroles. If the caramel thickens too much, melt it gently over a low heat. Do not keep the profiteroles too long before serving or the caramel will soften.

■ DESSERTS ■ DESSERTS ■

Chocolate Gateau
Torta "Gianfranco"

To serve 10

a little butter and flour

3 eggs plus 2 egg yolks

⅞ cup superfine sugar

2 tbsp vanilla sugar

¾lb unsweetened cooking chocolate

¾ cup flour

⅔ cup potato flour

3 tbsp unsweetened cocoa

½ tsp baking powder

⅝ cup milk

1¾ cups whipping cream

½ cup flaked almonds

Preparation and cooking time: about 1¾ hours

Grease with butter and sprinkle with flour a 10-inch round cake pan. Whisk 3 eggs with ½ cup of the sugar, a pinch of salt and the vanilla sugar until they form soft peaks.

Preheat the oven to 350°F. Melt 2½oz of the cooking chocolate on a low heat and leave to cool. Mix ⅝ cup of flour with the potato starch, the unsweetened

cocoa and a heaping teaspoon of baking powder and sift into the egg mixture, folding it in carefully with a wooden spoon. Bind in the melted chocolate and pour the mixture into the prepared pan. Bake in the oven for about 30 minutes.

Meanwhile, beat 2 egg yolks with the remaining flour, sugar and a pinch of salt. Gradually add the milk and bring to the boil, stirring constantly. Remove the pan from the heat and leave to cool, stirring from time to time.

Cut 4½oz of cooking chocolate into small pieces, melt it on a low heat and add it to the mixture, stirring vigorously. Leave to cool.

Turn the cake out on to a wire cooling rack. Whisk the cream until stiff and fold it into the chocolate mixture. Cut the cake into 3 equal layers and sandwich them together with two-thirds of the chocolate mixture. Coat the top and sides of the cake with chocolate mixture and sprinkle with the remainder of the cooking chocolate, grated.

Pipe rosettes of chocolate mixture on to the top of the cake and decorate with flaked almonds. Keep in the refrigerator and serve within 4-5 hours.

Profiteroles in spun caramel (top) and *chocolate gateau*

Chocolate and Amaretto Cup

Crema all'Amaretto

To serve 6-8

½ lb unsweetened cooking chocolate

¼ lb macaroons

4 egg yolks

½ cup sugar

⅜ cup flour

3½ cups milk

2 tbsp vanilla sugar

¼ cup butter, cut into small pieces

2-3 tbsp Amaretto

½ cup flaked almonds

Preparation and cooking time: about 50 minutes

Grate the chocolate and finely crush the macaroons. Whisk the egg yolks with the sugar until they form soft, whitish peaks. Fold in the sifted flour and 2 tablespoons of cold milk and stir until the mixture is smooth and free of lumps. Add the remaining milk and the vanilla sugar. Gently heat the mixture in a saucepan and bring it just to the boil, stirring constantly with a whisk. Cook for a few minutes, remove from the heat and stir in the butter, grated chocolate and crushed macaroons.

Pour the Amaretto liqueur into a serving bowl, making sure that the sides of the bowl are coated in the liqueur.

Pour in the prepared mixture and leave to cool. Top with the flaked almonds, cover with plastic wrap and keep in the refrigerator until ready to serve.

Apple Fritters

Fritelle di Mele

To serve 6

butter

¼ cake compressed yeast

2 tbsp milk

1½ cups flour

¼ cup cornstarch

1 egg

1 tbsp Calvados

⅛ cup sugar

about 6 tbsp light beer

1 lb apples, just ripe and not too large

oil for frying

powdered sugar

Preparation and cooking time: about 1 hour plus 2 hours' resting

Melt 2 tablespoons of butter in a *bain-marie* and dissolve the yeast in the warm milk. Sift the flour and the cornstarch together into a bowl. Make a well in the center and put in a pinch of salt and the egg yolk, setting aside the white. Pour in the warm melted butter, the Calvados, sugar, yeast and milk. Using a wooden spoon, combine the ingredients in the center of the well and when they are mixed together, start to incorporate the flour. Add the beer as the mixture becomes thicker. Finally, mix in 2 tablespoons of lukewarm water. Take care not to whisk vigorously, but stir continuously without lifting. Cover the dish and keep it in a slightly warm place for about 2 hours.

Whisk the reserved egg whites with a pinch of salt and carefully fold them into the batter, with an up-and-down rather than a circular movement. Heat a deep, heavy pan with plenty of oil. Peel and core the apples and cut them into rings about ¼ inch thick. Dry them thoroughly between layers of paper towels then dip them, one at a time, in the batter. When the oil is hot but not boiling, immerse the battered apple rings and fry until they are golden brown on both sides. Drain them on a plate covered with a double layer of paper towels. Serve very hot, sprinkled with powdered sugar.

Chocolate and Amaretto cup

Orange Profiteroles

Bignoline al Fior d'Arancio

To serve 8-10

1⅝ cups all-purpose flour

½ tsp baking powder

⅓ cup granulated sugar

2 tbsp olive oil

1 tbsp rum

grated rind of ½ lemon

2 eggs and 1 egg yolk

cooking oil

1 tbsp orange flower water

¼ cup liquid honey

2 tbsp glucose powder

2 oz candied orange rind

10 peeled almonds

Preparation and cooking time: about 2 hours

Sift the flour and baking powder on to a pastry-board or work surface. Make a well in the center and place in it the sugar, the olive oil, the rum, the grated lemon rind, a pinch of salt, the eggs and egg yolk. Fold the ingredients into the flour and combine to a firm, smooth paste. Divide into small balls about the size of a hazelnut, place on a lightly oiled sheet of aluminum foil and leave to stand for 30 minutes.

Heat plenty of oil in a large deep-frying pan and fry the balls a few at a time. When they are golden brown, drain them on paper towels.

Put the orange flower water, the honey and the glucose powder into a large pan. Heat gently and stir until the ingredients have melted. Leave to cool and then add the candied orange rind, the chopped almonds and the prepared profiteroles. Stir well and heap on to a dish. Serve.

Little orange profiteroles

Luscious Cherry Cake

Dolce Cremoso alle Ciliegie

To serve 8

½lb fresh cherries

1 cup sugar

1 stick cinnamon

1 clove

½ cup dry white wine

3 envelopes plain gelatin

2 eggs and 2 egg yolks

grated rind of ½ lemon

flour

2½ cups milk

½lb sponge cake, thinly sliced

½ cup Cointreau

Preparation and cooking time: about 1 hour plus chilling

Stem the cherries, wash them and drain them well. Remove the pits and place the cherries in a small saucepan. Add ¼ cup of the sugar, a small piece of cinnamon, 1 clove and the white wine. Cook the cherries over a moderate heat for about 15 minutes, until they are tender and the liquid has a syrupy consistency; remove from the heat and allow to cool.

Meanwhile dissolve the gelatin in cold water. In a small saucepan beat 2 of the eggs and 2 egg yolks together with the remaining sugar, the grated rind of half a lemon, a pinch of salt and the sifted flour. When creamy and smooth, dilute the mixture with the cold milk poured in a trickle. Place over the heat and, stirring continuously, bring the mixture to the boil. Remove from the heat and add the gelatin, mixing to make sure it has dissolved.

Line a rectangular cake pan measuring 10 x 5 inches with foil, pour some of the hot custard into it, and arrange on top some thin slices of sponge cake. Sprinkle lightly with Cointreau. Spread over the sponge cake a few cooked cherries drained of syrup (the syrup will be used at the end to moisten the cake), cover with some more of the custard, sponge cake and cherries. Continue with the layers until you have used up all the ingredients. Leave the cake to cool, then place in the refrigerator for at least 2 hours or in the freezer for about 30 minutes or until the cake is quite firm. Then turn out on to a serving plate, pour the cherry syrup over it and serve.

Melon Bavarian Cream
Bavarese di Melone

To serve 8-10

3 envelopes plain gelatin

1 perfectly ripe melon, weighing about 3½lb

½ cup sugar

2oz cleaned redcurrants

2 tbsp vanilla sugar

¾ cup whipping cream

¼ cup strawberry jam

Preparation and cooking time: about 1¼ hours plus at least 2 hours' chilling

Dissolve the gelatin in cold water. Wash and dry the melon, then halve it and remove the seeds. Remove the pulp with a spoon, without piercing the rind which will be used as a container. Place the pulp in a saucepan, add the sugar and the redcurrants. Place the saucepan on the heat and, stirring occasionally with a wooden spoon, simmer until the mixture has the consistency of jam, making sure that it does not stick to the bottom of the saucepan.

Remove from the heat, stir the mixture for a couple of minutes and pour it into a bowl; while it is still warm stir in the vanilla sugar and the gelatin. Mix well, then let it cool. Whip the cream and fold it into the melon cream when it is cold but not yet firm, mixing with a motion from top to bottom rather than round and round (to prevent the cream from going flat). Pour the strawberry jam into a small bowl and stir vigorously with a spoon to make it smooth.

Spread a layer of the melon Bavarian cream in each half shell of the melon and pour over each layer some of the strawberry jam. Refrigerate for at least 2 hours so that the Bavarian cream will firm, then cut each half into 4-5 slices, using a very sharp knife; place them on a serving plate and serve.

Sunshine Fruit Salad

Macedonia Solare

To serve 6

1 large slice ripe watermelon, weighing about 1¼lb

¼ cup white rum

a small bunch of black grapes

2 tbsp sugar

1 tbsp Cointreau

3 large yellow peaches (not too ripe)

juice of ½ lemon

fresh mint leaves for garnish

Preparation time: about 1¼ hours

Using a potato scoop or melon-baller, make small, equal-sized balls from the slice of watermelon. Discard the seeds, if any, place the melon balls in a bowl and sprinkle with the white rum; cover the bowl with plastic wrap and refrigerate for about 30 minutes.

Wash the bunch of grapes, dry it and remove the best grapes. Place them in a small bowl, sprinkle with a tablespoon of sugar and with 2 tablespoons of Cointreau, then set them aside to rest in a cool place or in the least cold part of the refrigerator, for about 15 minutes.

Wash the peaches and dry them, cut them into thin slices and drop them into a bowl; sprinkle with a tablespoon of sugar and the strained juice of half a lemon. Mix gently, cover the bowl and place it in the least cold part of the refrigerator for

about 15 minutes.

A short while before serving, arrange the fruit in circles on a large serving dish, garnish with leaves of fresh mint and serve.

Strawberry and Cointreau Cake

Cuore di Mamma

To serve 8-10

2 eggs plus 3 egg yolks

½ cup sugar

a little vanilla sugar

⅜ cup flour

½ cup potato starch

a little butter

1 tbsp gelatin

7 tbsp dry Marsala wine

1 tbsp brandy

⅞ cup whipping cream

1 cup fresh strawberries

½ cup Cointreau

Preparation and cooking time: about 1 hour plus at least 2 hours' chilling

Preheat the oven to 350°F. Beat 2 whole eggs with ⅓ cup of sugar, a little vanilla sugar and a pinch of salt until light and fluffy. Sift and fold in all but 2 tablespoons of the flour and the potato starch.

Butter a 3 pint heart-shaped cake pan, sprinkle in the remaining flour and pour in the mixture. Bake for about 20 minutes or until a wooden skewer plunged into the center of the cake comes out clean. Turn on to a wire rack and leave to cool. Clean the cake pan.

Soak the gelatin in cold water. Beat the 3 egg yolks with the remaining sugar until white and fluffy. Blend in the Marsala wine and then the brandy. Heat the mixture and bring it almost to the boil, stirring constantly. Pour the mixture into a bowl and blend in the gelatin immediately. Leave to cool, stirring from time to time. Finally, fold in the whipped cream.

Remove the stalks from the strawberries and slice them finely. Line the bottom of the cake pan with wax paper and brush it with a little Cointreau.

Return the heart-shaped cake to the pan and make holes in it with a fork. Sprinkle with the remaining Cointreau.

Pour half the prepared gelatin mixture on to the cake and sprinkle it with half the strawberries. Cover with the rest of the mixture and sprinkle with the remaining strawberries. Tap the cake pan gently and place it in the refrigerator for at least 2 hours.

Once the filling has set, run a knife around the edge of the cake and transfer it on to a plate. Keep in the refrigerator until ready to serve.

Mandarin Orange Trifle

Crema ai Mandarini

To serve 6-8

2 envelopes plain gelatin

4 egg yolks

½ cup sugar

a little vanilla sugar

1 tsp cornstarch

¾ cup milk

1¾ cups heavy cream

sponge cake

4 tbsp Strega

1 slice canned pineapple

1 brandied fig

1 small can mandarin oranges

4 tbsp orange marmalade

chocolate sprinkles

Preparation and cooking time: about 1 hour plus 2 hours' refrigeration

Dissolve the gelatin in a little water. Place the egg yolks, sugar, vanilla sugar, cornstarch and a pinch of salt in a saucepan and beat until smooth. Dilute with the cold milk and half the cream and bring to the boil, stirring with a small whisk. Remove from the heat, add the gelatin, and leave to cool but not set, stirring frequently.

Cut the sponge cake into enough ¾-inch cubes to cover the bottom of a large bowl or soufflé dish and soak them with the Strega. When the custard has cooled, whip the remaining cream until stiff and fold carefully into the custard. Spread the custard over the sponge pieces and refrigerate the bowl for at least 2 hours, or until the custard has set. Arrange the well-drained pineapple ring and the brandied fig in the center, and mandarin sections all round, slightly overlapping. Warm the marmalade with a little water, sieve it and use it to brush the fruit and the surface of the dessert; decorate with chocolate sprinkles and serve at once.

Crepes with Custard Filling

Crespelle alla Crema d'Uovo

Makes 14 crepes

4 very fresh eggs

¾ cup all-purpose flour

2⅜ cups milk

olive oil

⅝ cup sugar

1 tbsp vanilla sugar

¼ cup Cointreau

½ cup apricot or peach jelly

Preparation and cooking time: about 45 minutes

Beat 2 of the eggs in a bowl together with ⅝ cup of sieved flour and a pinch of salt. Gradually add 1 cup of cold milk, mixing continuously to prevent the formation of lumps. Heat a skillet brushed lightly with olive oil. When it is hot, pour in a ladlefull of the mixture and shake from side to side to ensure the entire surface of the pan is covered. Brown the crepe on one side and then toss and continue heating for a few seconds. Turn the crepe out on to a plate or marble surface and prepare a further 13 in the same way.

When the crepes are ready, prepare the custard filling: In a small saucepan, beat the remaining 2 eggs with the sugar and sift in the remaining flour. Add the vanilla sugar, then the rest of the cold milk, gradually, stirring constantly. When smooth, place the saucepan over the heat and bring to the boil, stirring continuously. Remove from the heat and stir in the Cointreau and then cool by plunging the saucepan into cold water. Do not stop stirring. Spread the mixture on the crepes and fold each one in four, then arrange on a serving dish. Heat the apricot jelly with 1 tablespoon of water and simmer for a few seconds. Then brush the surface of the crepes with this and serve.

Crepes with custard filling

Strawberry Mousse

Turbante Rosa Fragola

To serve 8-10

2 tbsp gelatin

a little almond oil

½lb just-ripe strawberries

½ cup sugar

1¾ cups whipping cream

4 tbsp Cointreau liqueur

2 tbsp grated coconut

10 equal-sized strawberries, with their stalks, for garnish

fresh mint leaves for garnish

Preparation and cooking time: about 1 hour plus overnight chilling

Soak the gelatin in cold water. Lightly oil a pudding mold with a capacity of about 3½ cups with the almond oil. Remove the stalks from the strawberries and wash them rapidly under cold running water. Lay them out to dry on a double layer of paper towels. When they are completely dry, process them in a blender with the sugar and pour the purée into a bowl.

Whip the cream until it is stiff and gently fold it into the strawberry purée, mixing with a wooden spoon with an up-and-down movement to prevent the cream from deflating. Heat 4 tablespoons of Cointreau in a small saucepan until the liqueur begins to simmer. Remove from the heat and stir in the gelatin until it has dissolved. Add the grated coconut to the strawberry mixture then slowly pour in the Cointreau and gelatin in a trickle. Mix constantly with an up-and-down movement.

Pour into the mold, bang it gently to eliminate any air bubbles, cover with plastic wrap and refrigerate overnight. Turn out the mousse on to a serving dish and garnish with the washed and dried strawberries and the mint leaves. Serve.

Festive dove (top) *and* **strawberry mousse**

Festive Dove

Colomba Augurale

To serve 8

a little butter and flour

3 eggs

1¼ cups sugar

¼ tsp honey

1 envelope vanilla sugar

⅝ cup all-purpose flour

⅔ cup potato starch

2¼ cups milk

1 tea bag

6 egg yolks

Preparation and cooking time: about 1½ hours

Preheat the oven to 350°F. Butter and flour a dove-shaped cake pan about 3½ pints in capacity. Whisk the 3 whole eggs with ½ cup of the sugar, ¼ teaspoon of honey, the vanilla sugar and a pinch of salt, until smooth and frothy. Mix the flour and potato starch and sift them into the sugar and egg mixture. Fold in with a wooden spoon using an up-and-down movement rather than a circular one so as not to deflate the mixture. Pour evenly into the mold and bake for about 30 minutes, until a skewer comes out clean. Remove the mold from the oven and, after a few minutes, turn the dove out on to a cooling rack.

While the cake is cooling, make the custard. Set aside ¼ cup of the milk and pour the rest into a saucepan. Bring gradually to the boil and remove from the heat. Put in the tea bag and leave to infuse for 5 minutes. Remove the tea bag, squeezing it thoroughly, and discard. Beat the egg yolks with the rest of the sugar until you obtain a frothy mixture. Then stir in first the reserved cold milk and then the tea-flavored milk, poured in gradually through a fine strainer. Mix in with a small whisk. Heat the saucepan gently and bring the custard to just below boiling point, taking care not to let it actually boil. Remove from the heat at once and immerse in cold water, stirring continuously until the custard has cooled.

Pour the custard into a jug or bowl and serve with the dove. Decorate the dove as you please.

Fruit Fantasy

Fantasia di Frutta

To serve 2

3 firm, ripe mandarin oranges or clementines

2 kiwi fruits

1 small banana

2 red and 2 green liqueur cherries

1 tbsp sugar

juice of ½ lemon

2 tbsp liqueur of your choice

Preparation time: about 30 minutes

Wash and dry the mandarins, then cut them in half crosswise, use a grapefruit knife to loosen the flesh from the skin, without actually removing it. Peel the two kiwi fruits and slice them thinly into 16-18 slices. Cut the same number of slices from the banana and finally cut both the red and green cherries in half.

Arrange the 6 half-mandarins in the center of 2 small oval-shaped dishes and decorate with the cherries. Put the slices of kiwi fruit round the outside, topped with the banana slices, and leave to rest for a few minutes (not in the refrigerator).

Meanwhile, put the sugar in a bowl, add the strained lemon juice and stir until the sugar is dissolved. Mix this cold "syrup" with the liqueur, stir again, pour over the fruit and serve immediately. This recipe is very simple, but very effective.

Fruit fantasy

Venetian Cake with Cream and Chestnuts

Veneziana con Panna e Castagne

To serve 10

2¼lb large round brioche, panettone or plain cake

1½ cups peeled, boiled chestnuts

¼lb semisweet chocolate

⅔ cup walnuts

1⅜ cups whipping cream

1 cup powdered sugar

⅝ cup rum

1 candied chestnut

Preparation time: about 1 hour

Cut the cake into 3 equal layers. Purée the peeled, boiled chestnuts in a food processor with the fine disk, or in a blender, and collect in a bowl. Finely crumble the chocolate and the walnuts. Whip the cream until stiff, sift in ⅞ cup of the powdered sugar, stirring with a top-to-bottom folding movement to avoid deflating the cream.

Place a layer of the cake on a serving plate, moisten it with half the rum, then spread it with half the whipped cream and half the chestnut purée, topped with half the chocolate and walnuts. Cover with the second layer of cake and fill in the same way. Cover with the top layer, place a small bowl in the center and sprinkle the remaining powdered sugar over the exposed surface of the cake. Remove the bowl and place the candied chestnut in the center of the cake. Serve as soon as possible without refrigerating. The undecorated cake can be cut at first into several more layers in which case the filling ingredients must be divided equally between all the layers.

Venetian cake with cream and chestnuts (top) and chestnut pagoda

Chestnut Pagoda
Pagoda di Castagne

To serve 8

1 cup chestnuts, boiled and reduced to a purée

⅞ cup fresh Mascarpone cheese or cream cheese

1 cup powdered sugar

3 tbsp unsweetened cocoa

2 tbsp brandy

3 tbsp Amaretto liqueur

⅝ cup whipping cream

1 sponge cake, about 9in in diameter, weighing ½lb

⅜ cup Cointreau liqueur

1 tbsp chocolate threads

1 tbsp white chocolate chips

6 small semi-sweet chocolate disks

Preparation time: about 1½ hours

Place the chestnut purée in a bowl and mix in the Mascarpone cheese, stirring with a wooden spoon until smooth. Sift over it ¾ cup of the powdered sugar and the unsweetened cocoa, mix well, then add the brandy and Amaretto liqueur, making sure that each tablespoon is thoroughly absorbed before adding the next.

Whip the cream until firm then fold in the rest of the sifted powdered sugar stirring with a wooden spoon from top to bottom rather than round and round. Spoon into a pastry bag with a small round nozzle, and keep in the refrigerator.

Place the sponge cake on a serving dish and moisten it with the Cointreau, then sieve on to it the mixture of chestnuts and Mascarpone cheese, arranging it in a small heap. Pipe the sweetened whipped cream around the edge, and sprinkle over the chocolate threads. Complete the decoration of the cake by placing the white chocolate chips on top of it and the chocolate disks evenly spread around it.

Keep the cake in the least cold part of the refrigerator until serving time. If you wish, instead of using sponge cake as a base, you can use any other risen cake.

Macaroon Grape Tart
Sfogliata Amarettata all'Uva

To serve 10

10oz puff pastry

butter

6 small macaroons

4 tbsp red vermouth

about 1lb white grapes

1 egg

½ cup sugar

3 tbsp flour

2 tbsp vanilla sugar

¾ cup milk

Preparation and cooking time: about 1¼ hours plus thawing

Defrost the pastry if necessary. Roll it out and use it to line a buttered round 10-inch pie dish. Prick the bottom with a fork, then sprinkle over 5 finely crumbled macaroons. Moisten with the red vermouth and leave in a cool place. Preheat the oven to 375°F.

Wipe the grapes with a damp cloth. Break the egg into a small saucepan, add ¼ cup of sugar, the sieved flour and the vanilla sugar. Whisk to prevent lumps forming, then dilute the mixture with the cold milk, poured in a thin stream.

Bring the mixture to the boil, stirring all the time, then immediately pour it over the macaroons. Arrange the grapes on top, pushing them down slightly, in 4 concentric circles. Crumble the remaining macaroons and sprinkle over the center of the pie. Place a single grape in the middle.

Put the remaining sugar into a small saucepan with a tablespoon of cold water, simmer for a few moments until you have a fairly thick syrup, then brush the grapes with it. Place the pie in the preheated oven for about 40 minutes, then remove and allow to cool in the mold before turning out and serving.

Oranges in Grand Marnier

Oranges in Grand Marnier
Arance al Grand Marnier

To serve 4

6 large ripe oranges, washed

6 cubes of sugar

¼ cup Grand Marnier

Preparation and cooking time: about 30 minutes plus 30 minutes' refrigeration

Pierce the oranges all over with a needle. Rub each orange with every side of a sugar cube to absorb the orange flavor. Place the sugar in a saucepan. Peel the oranges, remove all the pith and divide them into segments in a bowl. Squeeze any juice remaining in the peel over the sugar cubes.
remaining in the peel over the sugar cubes.

Heat the sugar gently until dissolved. When a light syrup has formed, remove the pan from the heat and pour in the Grand Marnier. Stir and allow to cool. Pour the liquid over the orange segments and refrigerate for 30 minutes before serving. If you like, you can place the oranges in individual goblets and garnish each one with a white grape.

September Fruit Salad

Capriccio Settembrino

To serve 4

2 apples

juice of 1 lemon

¼ cup sugar

1 peach

¾lb Victoria plums

½lb white grapes

¼ cup Cointreau

Preparation time: about 30 minutes plus 1 hour's refrigeration

Peel and core the 2 apples, cut into quarters and then dice. As they are ready, put them into a bowl containing the strained lemon juice. Add the sugar then mix carefully with a wooden spoon.

Remove the stalks from the peach and the plums and wipe with a damp cloth. Cut in half and remove the pits, then dice and add to the apples in the bowl. Wipe the grapes with a damp cloth and remove stalks and seeds. Cut the larger grapes in half. Add to the rest of the fruit. Mix well and pour over the Cointreau. Cover with plastic wrap and refrigerate for at least 1 hour. Mix carefully before serving.

Redcurrant and Lemon Cream Baskets

"Cestini" Con Crema e Ribes

To serve 4

5 large unblemished lemons

2 small macaroons

3 egg yolks

½ cup sugar

3 tbsp flour

1¼ cups milk

1 tbsp lemon liqueur

8 bunches redcurrants

8 fresh mint leaves

7 rolled wafers

Preparation and cooking time: about 1 hour

Wash and grate the rind of one lemon into a saucepan. Halve the other 4 lemons and squeeze them, reserving the juice for other uses. With a sharp knife, scrape out the flesh, leaving them smooth. Flatten the bases so that they will stand level.

Crumble the macaroons and divide them among the half-lemons. To the pan with the lemon rind add the 3 egg yolks, the sugar, the flour and 2 tablespoons of the milk, and beat to obtain a perfectly smooth mixture. Add the rest of the cold milk and, stirring all the time, bring the custard to boiling point. Remove from the heat and flavor with a tablespoon of lemon liqueur, then stand the pan in cold water and continue to stir until the custard is completely cooled.

Wash the redcurrants in ice-cold water and dry them on a cloth. Pick off the largest currants and arrange them over the macaroon crumbs in the lemon halves; fill up with the lemon cream, using a pastry bag with a plain round nozzle. Garnish each lemon half with a bunch of redcurrants and a mint leaf and arrange on a flat dish, interspersed with the wafers. Serve immediately, before the cream can absorb any bitterness from the lemon pith.

If you do not wish to use lemon halves as containers for this recipe, you could substitute individual puff pastry or shortcrust pie shells baked blind with dried beans to keep them in shape. The baskets will still need to be served quickly, before the pastry loses its crispness.

Stuffed Baked Apples
Mele Golose

To serve 10

¼ cup almonds, blanched

¼ cup hazelnuts, blanched

¼ cup groundnuts, blanched

¼ cup walnuts, blanched

1oz semi-sweet chocolate, broken into pieces

10 apples, equal in size and not too ripe

butter

1 small cinammon stick

3 cloves

spiral of lemon rind, 3 inches long

⅔ cup Muscat wine

¾ cup sugar

4 egg yolks

¼ cup cornstarch

a little vanilla sugar

2½ cups milk

4 tbsp Calvados

¼ cup pistachio nuts

⅝ cup whipping cream

Preparation and cooking time: about 1½ hours plus refrigeration

Preheat the oven to 375°F. Put the almonds, hazelnuts, groundnuts, walnuts and chocolate into a blender and process at maximum speed for a few seconds until the ingredients are all ground to a paste. Put the mixture in a bowl. Peel the apples, and, using an apple corer, cut into the base, stopping when you reach the stalk: You should hollow out the core just up to the stalk end, leaving it closed at the top. Remove the apple flesh from the cores, chop it and add to the ground nuts in the bowl, and mix well.

Stuff each apple with the mixture, pressing it in with a teaspoon. Butter an ovenproof dish which is just the right size to hold the apples and arrange them in it.

Break up the cinammon stick and put this in the dish, along with the cloves and the lemon rind. Pour in the Muscat wine and sprinkle over ¼ cup of sugar. Bake in the oven for about 45 minutes, basting from time to time with the juices.

Remove the cooked apples from the oven and set them aside while you prepare the custard. Beat the egg yolks in a saucepan with the remaining sugar and a pinch of salt. Then pour in the milk in a slow trickle, mixing constantly with a small whisk. Bring to the boil, remove from the heat and add the Calvados. Arrange the apples on a serving dish and pour over the custard at once.

Blanch the pistachio nuts in boiling salted water, chop them and sprinkle them over the custard-covered apples. Whip the cream until it is stiff and put in a pastry bag. Decorate the apples with swirls around the outside and one in the center. Keep in a very cool place or in the least cold part of the refrigerator until you are ready to serve.

■ DESSERTS ■ DESSERTS ■

Grape and Apple Cheesecake
Crostata di Mascarpone all'Uva e Mela

To serve 8

For the crust:

¼lb flour

¼ cup of sugar

½ cup butter

2 egg yolks

grated rind of 1 lemon

a little butter and flour

For the filling:

⅞ cup Mascarpone cheese

½ cup powdered sugar

2 egg yolks

2 tbsp brandy

For the topping:

20 small macaroons

a large bunch white grapes

1 apple

5 tbsp sugar

5 mint leaves

Preparation and cooking time: about 1½ hours

To make the crust: Put the sifted flour, sugar and a pinch of salt together in a bowl and add the butter, cut in small cubes. Rub it in with your fingers until the mixture resembles coarse breadcrumbs. Add the egg yolks and the lemon rind. Roll the pastry into a ball, wrap it in plastic wrap and leave it in the least cold part of the refrigerator for 30 minutes.

Meanwhile, preheat the oven to 375°F. Grease and flour a round 10-inch pie dish with a smooth bottom and fluted sides. Roll out the pastry and line the pan, pricking the bottom with a fork. Bake in the oven for about 20 minutes or until well cooked and golden. Leave to cool in the tin.

Meanwhile, prepare the filling: beat the cheese and sugar together, incorporating the egg yolks one at a time. Add the brandy.

Crumble the macaroons finely. When the pie shell is cold, take it out of the pan and set it on a plate. Sprinkle the macaroons over the bottom and pour in the filling. Wash and dry the grapes and arrange them on top together with thin slices of apple.

Dissolve 5 tablespoons of sugar in 1 tablespoon of water over a low heat. When it is a thick syrup, brush it, still hot, over the fruit. Decorate the center of the cake with the mint leaves and keep it in a cool place or the least cold part of the refrigerator. Serve within a couple of hours.

Grape and apple cheesecake

Coffee Ice Cream
Gelato al Caffè

4 tbsp ground coffee

2 tbsp vanilla sugar

1½ cups sugar

¾ cup cream

1 egg white

Preparation and cooking time: ½ hour plus cooling and freezing.

In a small saucepan bring 1½ cups of water to the boil, pour in the coffee and, stirring constantly, simmer over a very low heat until the foam has disappeared. Leave to infuse for about 15 minutes, so that the ground coffee sinks to the bottom of the saucepan, then strain the liquid coffee into a bowl.

Add the vanilla sugar and the sugar, stir until the sugar is dissolved then leave to cool. At this point mix in the cream and place in the refrigerator for at least 1 hour to cool completely.

Pour the mixture into an ice cream machine or container, add the egg white whisked to a froth, with a pinch of salt, so that the ice cream will be smooth and soft.

Ricotta Pie with Raisins
Torta di Ricotta alla Panna

To serve 8

¾lb pie crust

a little flour and butter

⅓ cup golden raisins

¼lb candied citron peel

1½ cups full-cream Ricotta

3 eggs

⅜ cup sugar

grated rind of 1 lemon

a little powdered sugar

Preparation and cooking time: about 1 hour plus thawing

Defrost the pastry if using frozen. Roll out the pastry on a lightly floured board and use it to line a buttered, floured pie dish with a diameter of 11 inches. Cut off the excess dough and shape into a ring with which to thicken the sides of the pie; then prick the base with a fork.

Preheat the oven to 350°F. Wash and dry the raisins; cut the candied citron peel into small cubes. Put the Ricotta through a sieve, collecting it in a bowl and mix in, one at a time, the yolks of the three eggs, then the sugar, the grated rind of the lemon, the diced citron peel and the raisins, stirring vigorously. Finally, fold in gently the three whites, beaten until they are quite firm with a pinch of salt.

Pour the mixture into the pastry shell and bang the mold on the table over a folded towel, so that there are no air bubbles in the mixture. Bake for about 45 minutes. Finally, turn out the dessert and leave it to cool. Before serving sprinkle with powdered sugar.

Ricotta pie with raisins

Meringue Gateau

Torta Meringata

To serve 10

For the meringue:

a little almond oil

⅜ cup egg whites

2 cups powdered sugar

a little vanilla sugar

For the éclairs:

2 tbsp butter

2½ tbsp flour

1 egg

For the custard:

3 eggs

½ cup sugar

a little vanilla sugar

⅜ cup flour

2¼ cups milk

1 tbsp cocoa powder

1 tbsp Grand Marnier liqueur

1 tbsp Maraschino liqueur

⅜ cup whipping cream

Preparation and cooking time: about 4 hours

To prepare the meringue: Lightly grease an 11-inch disk of wax paper with a little almond oil and place it on a small baking pan. Preheat the oven to 225°F. Whisk the egg whites with a pinch of salt and sieve in 1¾ cups of the powdered sugar and the vanilla sugar, a little at a time, beating briskly until the mixture is well risen and firm. Using a pastry bag with a round nozzle, cover the disk of wax paper by piping two overlapping spirals. Sprinkle the remaining powdered sugar on top and bake for a couple of hours; then turn off the oven and leave it another hour before taking it out to cool.

To prepare the éclairs: Butter and flour a small baking pan. Bring ¼ cup of water to the boil in a saucepan with the diced butter and a pinch of salt. As soon as the butter is completely melted, remove from the heat and sieve in the flour, beating briskly with a wooden spoon. Return the pan to the heat and

continue to cook, stirring continuously, until the mixture begins to sizzle on the base. Turn it on to a plate and spread it out to cool.

Return it to the pan and beat in the egg, making sure the mixture is completely smooth. Using a pastry bag with a round nozzle, make at least 30 walnut-sized blobs on the prepared baking pan. Bake at 375°F for 15 minutes then turn out to cool on a wire rack.

To prepare the custard: Beat the 3 eggs, the sugar, the vanilla sugar, the flour and a pinch of salt together in a saucepan. When smooth, gradually add the milk. Bring to the boil, stirring all the time. Remove from the heat and divide into two, adding the unsweetened cocoa and Grand Marnier to one half and the Maraschino to the other. Let them cool, giving them a frequent stir, then put them into 2 separate pastry bags with round nozzles.

To assemble the gateau: Whip the cream and pipe it into the eclairs, then sprinkle them with a little powdered sugar. Just before serving, set the meringue base on a large plate, make a ring round the edge with the yellow custard and set the eclairs on it. Cover the rest of the meringue with alternate stripes of the two custards and serve immediately.

Baskets of Grapes

Cestini all'uva

6 baskets

1 lb vanilla ice cream

½ pint whipping cream

⅓ cup butter

⅓ cup all-purpose flour

⅓ cup powdered sugar

2 egg whites

a large bunch of black grapes

Preparation and cooking time: 45 minutes

Preheat the oven to 420°F.

1) Beat the egg whites in a bowl until stiff, then gradually whisk in the sugar and keep beating for 2-3 minutes. Stir in 2 tablespoons of flour and 4 tablespoons of melted butter and stir to form a smooth batter.

2) Grease and flour a baking tray. Pour 3 tablespoons of the mixture on to it, keeping them well apart.

3) Spread the mixture on the tray with the back of a spoon into 3 thin omelets about 5 inches in diameter.

4) Bake for 6-7 minutes until golden at the edges. Remove them quickly, transferring each on to an upturned glass.

5) While soft press them against the glass bottom to shape into baskets.

Repeat with the remaining mixture.

6) When cool put in a scoop of ice cream in the center of each basket. Garnish all around with the washed and dried grapes. Decorate with whipped cream.

1

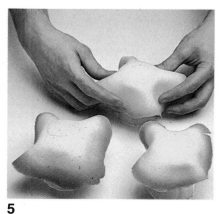

2

3

4

5

6

GLOSSARY OF PASTA NAMES

Anelli
Small ring-shaped pasta used in soup.

Angolotti
Crescent-shaped dumplings usually stuffed with meat.

Bucatini
Hollow, thicker version of spaghetti.

Cannelloni
Tube-shaped pasta for stuffing.

Cappelletti ("little hats")
Pasta stuffed in the shape of little peaked hats.

Cavatappi
Tube pasta in a corkscrew shape.

Conchiglie ("conch shells")
Ridged or smooth shell shaped pasta.

Conchigliette
Smaller version of conchiglie.

Elicoidali
Smaller, twisted type of cannelloni.

Farfalle ("butterflies")
Also known as "bows" which they resemble, found in various sizes.

Fettuce
Egg noodle, wider than tagliatelle.

Fettuccine
The Roman version of the egg noodle, narrower and thicker than tagliatelle.

Funghini
Small, mushroom-shaped pasta.

Fusilli
Long, corkscrew-shaped spaghetti.

Gemelli ("twins")
Two short pieces of spaghetti twisted together.

Lasagne
About 2 inches (5 cm) wide, the broadest of the noodles, made with egg pasta and used in baked dishes.

Lasagne verdi
Green lasagne, made with spinach.

Linguine
Flat type of spaghetti of which tagliolini are a thinner version.

Lumache
Short, broad tubes of pasta resembling small shells.

Maccheroncini
Smaller version of macaroni.

Maccheroni (macaroni)
Term used for all commercially made dried pasta, but also for the "elbow", slightly curved tubular pasta.

Maruzze ("seashells")
Very similar to conchiglie, also comes in varying sizes.

Orecchiette ("little ears")
Small shell-shaped pasta.

Pappardelle
Tuscan version of fettuccine, usually over $\frac{1}{2}$ inch (1 cm) wide, it can have a straight edge, often cut with a fluted pastry wheel to give a crimped edge.

Penne ("pens")
Also known as quills, due to the diagonal cut at both ends.

Quadrucci ("little squares")
Small squares of tagliatelle.

Ravioli
Stuffed pasta squares.

Riccie ("curly")
Applied to noodles of various sizes when one or both sides are wavy.

Rigatoni
Large ridged pasta tubes which, like lasagne, are often used in baked dishes.

Rotelline
Smaller version of ruote di carro.

Ruote di carro ("cartwheels")
Most popular in the south of Italy.

Spaghetti
Long, thin strands of pasta.

Spaghettini
Thinner version of spaghetti.

Stellette ("little stars")
Small pasta used in soup.

Tagliatelle
The classic egg noodle about $\frac{3}{4}$ inch (2 cm) wide.

Tortellini
A speciality of Bologna, small ring-shaped dumplings.

Tortelloni
Egg pasta, stuffed and square-shaped.

Tortiglioni
Spiral-shaped pasta, referred to as "twists".

Trenette
Narrow, almost square noodles traditionally served with pesto.

Vermicelli
The name given to spaghetti in southern Italy, it's very thin and often sold in clusters.

Ziti
Long macaroni, often used in baked dishes.

GLOSSARY OF CHEESE NAMES

A brief description of some of the cheeses used in the recipes.

Appenzell
A hard Swiss cheese, with a fruity flavor. During ripening it is steeped in wine, cider, herbs and spices.

Bel Paese
Soft, creamy, slightly sweet cheese.

Dolcelatte
A creamy moist cheese, off-white in color with blue-green veins running through it. A milder, creamier version of Gorgonzola.

Emmental
A dull yellow cheese, with evenly distributed, small walnut-sized holes and a sweet, nutty flavor. Originally a Swiss cheese, there are now also Italian and French versions.

Fontina
A delicate nutty flavored cheese. It has a light brown, slightly oiled rind and a straw colored paste with a few small round holes.

Gorgonzola
A soft cheese, straw colored with blue-green veining. It can be one of the most pungent and strong flavored of the blues. It is at its best when firm and fairly dry.

Gruyère
A hard, pale yellow Swiss cheese with a full, fruity flavor and small holes.

Mascarpone
A creamy and mild cheese that is often served with a fresh fruit or flavored with powdered chocolate or coffee, or liqueurs.

Mozzarella
A delicately flavored cheese which should, ideally, be eaten as soon as possible after buying. A lightly smoked version is also available. Traditionally made from water buffalos' milk, today those that are exported are made from cows' milk.

Parmesan
A hard-grating cheese. Available by the piece or ready-grated and can be rather expensive.

Pecorino
A slightly sharp cheese made from sheep's milk.

Provola
A firm cheese with a glossy golden yellow skin and a delicate nutty flavor.

Provolone
A smooth, creamy, dense cheese which is made from cows' milk coagulated either with calves' rennet (sweeter types), or kids' rennet (sharper types). It is delicate and mild when young and piquant when matured.

Quartirolo
A pressed cheese with a slightly pronounced fruity flavor.

Robiola
A quick-ripening, soft cheese.

Ricotta
A fresh, white soft cheese with a fine granular consistency. It is mild, verging on sweet.

Sbrinz
An aromatic and full flavored cheese made from unpasteurized milk.

Stracchino
A soft light yellow cheese with a pinkish surface and rind and a pronounced fruity flavor.

INDEX